Multinationals from Developing Countries

Multinationals from Developing Countries

Edited by
Krishna Kumar
Maxwell G. McLeod
East-West Center

LexingtonBooks
D.C. Heath and Company
Lexington, Massachusetts
Toronto

338.88
M961

Library of Congress Cataloging in Publication Data

Main entry under title:
   Multinationals from developing countries.

   Includes index.
   1. Underdeveloped areas—International business enterprises—Case
studies. I. Kumar, Krishna. II. McLeod, Maxwell G.
HD2755.5.M8445   338.8'891724   80-8531
ISBN 0-669-04113-0

Published simultaneously in Canada

Printed in the United States of America

International Standard Book Number: 0-669-04113-0

Library of Congress Catalog Card Number: 80-8531

To Sonia

Contents

List of Figures
and Tables

Preface and Acknowledgments

In 1977, the East-West Culture Learning Institute of the East-West Center initiated a program of research on multinational corporations. The thrust of this program is multidisciplinary. It is primarily, though not exclusively, concerned with exploring the social and cultural implications of the operations of multinational corporations at national and international levels. Initially, the program was confined to the study of skills transfer in export-processing zones and with regard to women employees in electronics multinationals, but later it was broadened to include multinationals from developing countries.

As a part of this program, the Institute organized an international conference in 1979 on multinationals from developing nations. This conference was attended by nineteen scholars from various parts of the world. The participants presented scholarly papers on different aspects of the subject and identified a set of research priorities that could be investigated in a cross-cultural setting. Several papers presented at this conference form the nucleus of this book, to which we have added some new contributions.

We hardly need stress that the purpose here is not to present conclusive findings. The phenomenon of developing-country multinationals is too recent to permit such an attempt. We do not have sufficient information or data about their emergence, structure, functioning, and implications. Our goal has been to identify what we consider an "interesting field of inquiry" by presenting conceptual and substantive contributions on the subject. We hope that this book will stimulate the interest of scholars from different countries and will promote further studies.

Several friends have helped us in this endeavor. Dr. Verner C. Bickley, director of the Institute, has been most gracious in his support of this project. We have profited from the advice of Professor Louis T. Wells, Jr., of the Harvard Business School and Professor David A. Heenan of the University of Hawaii. The contributors were kind enough to abide by the time schedules we imposed on them. Ms. Caroline McCarley and Ms. Elizabeth M. Bollier of Lexington Books have been most helpful. Mrs. Charlene Fujishige and Ms. Jenny Ichinotsubo typed the draft of this book with considerable speed and accuracy. We wish to record our gratitude to all of these friends.

Finally, we are grateful to Parizad, the wife of the senior editor, and to their daughter Sonia for their patience, as we spent many evenings working on this manuscript. As a token of our feelings, we have dedicated this book to Sonia.

Introduction

Krishna Kumar

The typical reaction to the title *Multinationals from Developing Countries* is genuine skepticism if not utter disbelief. We are so accustomed to associating multinationals with the nations of North America and Western Europe that we react negatively to the possibility suggested by the title of this book. And yet, as the eleven contributions to this book demonstrate, both private- and public-sector firms from many developing nations are rapidly internationalizing their operations.

By all accounts, the number of developing countries whose firms now qualify for the label *multinational* has been steadily increasing over the past 10 years. What is still more significant, the total number of overseas projects undertaken by the firms of these countries has been growing at a rapid rate. The data presented in the following chapters about the foreign direct investment made by the enterprises from countries such as Argentina, Brazil, Hong Kong, India, Korea, Mexico, and Taiwan unmistakably reveal this trend. This is in spite of the fact that foreign investment by the multinationals from developing nations is generally underestimated, since these firms often find it prudent to keep their investments well-guarded secrets wherever possible.

Some conceptual clarification about the meaning of developing nations' multinationals is necessary in order to avoid unnecessary confusion. By *developing nations* we mean all nonsocialist nations of Africa, Asia, and Latin America that are not the members of the Organization for Economic Cooperation and Development (OECD). We therefore use the term as a synonym for *third-world nations*. Although these nations display marked differences among themselves, they do share a set of common structural properties that justify the use of a single category for them. Following the United Nations, we define a *multinational firm* as an enterprise that owns production or service facilities in one or more countries other than the one in which it is based. This definition is undoubtedly less restrictive than those that are generally used in studies of American and European corporations. Thus the expression *developing-country (DC) multinational* refers to a firm that is located in one of the developing nations and owns production or service facilities outside its national boundaries. Such enterprises can operate in extractive, agricultural, industrial, or service sectors.

The main focus of this book is on Asian and Pacific nations, as both homes and hosts of DC multinationals. It also includes one contribution dealing with Latin America and one about Nigeria. The only developing region that is not covered here is the resource-rich Middle East. The foreign investments by these countries, because of their distinctive economic and political conditions, constitute a class by themselves. They therefore require a different kind of theoretical and empirical analysis, one that is hardly possible within the limits of a single chapter.

Several questions can be raised about DC multinationals at both micro and macro levels. Some of these are as follows: What kinds of firms are internationalizing their operations? What are the sectors in which they are operating? What are the competitive assets of these enterprises that enable them to compete effectively with other firms in host nations? What is the relationship between the parent firm and its subsidiaries or joint ventures? What kinds of developing nations are the homes and hosts of the direct foreign investment by DC firms? What are the policies of the host and home nations toward DC multinationals? The contributors to this book grapple with these questions in light of the available empirical data. They provide us both theoretical and analytical studies of the subject.

In chapter 1, John H. Dunning explains the emergence of DC multinationals with reference to his eclectic theory of international production. His theory postulates that the propensity of a country's enterprises for engaging in foreign direct investment is determined by ownership, internalization, and locational advantages that are available to them as compared with enterprises from other nations. Dunning also contends that a nation's investment position as measured by its *net foreign investment* (foreign investment in the country minus its overseas investment) is also related to its level of economic development. For this purpose, he presents a four-stage developmental model that stipulates that as a country passes from a lower stage to a higher stage of development, its net outward investment tends to grow. Dunning therefore suggests that the foreign direct investment of a developing nation is a function of its stage of economic development and its particular characteristics of those of its firms that "make for a unique combination of ownership, location, and internalization advantages." He presents time-series data for two developing nations, Brazil and Korea, that indicate that the net outward investment from these countries has increased over time. He attributes this trend to the rising ownership rather than falling locational advantages of these countries, which are related to the structure of industry and the strategy of their firms.

Dunning suggests that the future of foreign direct investment from developing nations will depend on the extent to which the specific endowment, market, and environmental characteristics of these nations generate ownership advantages that are best exploited by foreign investments by their firms.

In chapter 2, Louis T. Wells, Jr., further discusses some of the issues mentioned by John Dunning. He specifically focuses on two important but interrelated questions: What are the special assets of the firms from DC that enable them to compete with local entrepreneurs and the multinationals from industrialized nations? and Why do these firms, in the first instance, prefer to exploit their special assets through direct foreign investment rather than through the sale of skills and machinery?

In his answer to the first question, Wells suggests that the special assets of these firms follow from the peculiar nature of their home markets, which is conducive to innovations markedly dissimilar to those that take place in the industrialized world. According to him, the markets in DCs induce entrepreneurs to develop "small-scale, labor-intensive processes and products" and to find ways to "substitute available local inputs for imported ones." As a result, many firms in the developing nations have come to possess technologies that are multipurpose, labor-intensive, and do not require huge capital outlays. Moreover, they are capable of using locally available raw materials and other inputs. This, Wells contends, gives the firms from many developing nations a competitive edge over other multinationals in host nations where these technologies are more appropriate to their needs and socioeconomic environments.

In answering the qustion of why firms from developing nations tend to internalize their skills and innovations, Wells suggests that their reasons are similar to those of the enterprises of industrialized countries. However, there are some unique considerations that should not be ignored. Since most of the DC firms are generally unknown, potential buyers do not have information about their manufacturing technologies. Moreover, the machinery and equipment developed by these firms is often not patented, and therefore these firms are reluctant to share their technologies without collaborative arrangements. In addition, sometimes technological skills developed by these firms are embedded in the knowledge of managers and technicians and are not codified in manuals or easily transferable procedures. Factors such as these lead DC manufacturing firms to directly establish overseas subsidiaries. Wells also discusses other considerations that are applicable in the case of foreign direct investment by such non-manufacturing firms as banks and financial institutions, consulting firms and construction companies.

In chapter 3, Donald J. Lecraw presents the findings of a study he conducted in the ASEAN region. In this study, Lecraw collected data about twenty-three subsidiaries of DC multinationals and compared their structural and behavioral characteristics with those from the industrialized nations. His findings indicated that as compared with the subsidiaries of multinationals from industrialized nations, the DC firms were smaller in size, used more labor-intensive technologies, imported fewer inputs, exported less to foreign countries, had greater local equity participation, and were perhaps more profitable. Moreover, these firms produced unbranded, low-quality products and competed on the basis of price. While Lecraw rightly advises great caution in making generalizations from his limited sample, it should be noted that these findings are essentially in accord with previous research. Lecraw suggests a modified version of the product-cycle theory as a partial explanation for the internationalization of DC firms.

Lecraw also examines the possible effects of competition on the profitability attained by multinationals. His data suggest that while rivalry among the multinationals reduced profitability, DC-based firms did not actively compete with their counterparts from the industrialized nations. They generally operated in different fields. Thus Lecraw concludes that these firms have limited countervailing power against firms from industrialized countries.

In chapter 4, Sung-Hwan Jo analyzes the growth, patterns, and prospects of foreign direct investment by Korean firms. He contends that Korean foreign direct investment (FDI) should be examined in the context of Korea's changing factor endowments, national policy packages, and the rapidly changing international economic environment. Three features of the contemporary Korean situation become obvious from Jo's discussions. First, Korea is a natural-resource-scarce nation that requires a stable supply of raw materials for its industrial expansion and growth. Second, since 1965 the country's economic development has been characterized by what Jo calls "export-substitution" growth, which involves the substitution of traditional and simple labor-intensive products by sophisticated labor-intensive consumer and industrial goods for export. And finally, Korean businessmen and government policy planners have become apprehensive about the current sources of raw materials as well as the existing markets for their products. Because of the surging nationalism, Korea is not certain that it can procure vital raw materials from resource-rich nations without making special arrangements with them. Moreover, its exports are facing growing protectionism from the industrialized countries and increasing competition from developing nations. Korean direct investment, Jo suggests, should be seen as a response to the preceding conditions.

The main objective of Korean firms in establishing overseas subsidiaries is not to replace home-based industrial production but to expand it. To Jo, Korean FDI can be properly considered as an "extended form of export marketing activities." An additional objective of the Korean investors is to secure a stable supply of raw materials through the promotion of subsidiaries and joint ventures in resource-rich nations.

Jo classifies FDI by Korean firms in five categories: (1) investment in resource-rich countries to gain raw materials; (2) investments in civil construction and engineering-related industries; (3) investment in on-site trading, warehousing, and distribution channels to secure overseas markets for exports; (4) manufacturing in developing nations to serve local markets; and (5) investments in research and development in industrialized nations to gain access to sophisticated technology. These categories support his contention that the primary motivation behind Korean investments is to expand and diversify exports for maintaining the dynamic industrial growth at home. Jo is cautious about the future prospects of Korean FDI despite its impressive growth during the last 5 years.

In chapter 5, Edward K.Y. Chen provides a glimpse of the increasing FDI by Hong Kong-based firms in the manufacturing sector. He specifically focuses on their operations in Indonesia, Malaysia, Singapore, Taiwan, and China. One is mildly surprised to learn that Hong Kong is the largest investor in manufacturing in China. About 500 Hong Kong firms are presently operating in China under various functional but flexible arrangements. His data also indicate that Hong Kong's investment in the remaining four countries is no less significant. These firms often have used the ethnic networks to establish their overseas subsidiaries. Chen also presents the findings of a small survey conducted by him to identify the motivations and competitive advantages of Hong Kong multinationals.

Chen's analysis shows that most of the Hong Kong firms have established their overseas subsidiaries or joint ventures not to cater to the home markets of the host nations but to maintain and, wherever possible, increase their present level of exports to industrialized nations. This makes them attractive to the other developing nations, which are anxious to earn foreign exchange. In this respect, their objective is identical with that of the multinationals from the industrialized nations, which have established their subsidiaries in export-processing zones to take the advantage of lower wages and managerial costs. Some other motivations identified by Chen are evasion of quota restrictions imposed by several industrialized nations by locating their bases of production in countries not under such restrictions, seeking the economies of scale in the use of machinery and capital goods, and the minimization of risks through diversification. Chen suggests that the competitive edge of Hong Kong firms over multinationals from industrialized nations is "mainly accounted for by the high quality and relatively low cost of their management personnel."

In chapter 6, Wen-Lee Ting and Chi Schive focus on Taiwan, which, following the path of Hong Kong and Korea, is emerging as an important source of direct investment and technology transfer. The data presented by Ting and Schive clearly demonstrate that the volume of FDI from Taiwan has been increasing over the past 8 years, although political uncertainties have undoubtedly affected its growth process. Ting and Schive identify three major motivations behind Taiwanese investment drive: procurement of raw materials, pursuit of profits by supplying host-country markets and the sale of technology, and expansion of exports. Thus the case of Taiwan seems quite similar to that of Korea.

Ting and Schive also present case studies of two Taiwanese multinationals, "Gamma Corporation," a leading electrical and electronics manufacturer, and Tuntex Fiber Company, a synthetic-fiber producer. One common feature of the two enterprises has been that they both received their original technologies from the industrialized nations. However, with little investment in research and development, these firms succeeded in making suitable adaptations in the imported technologies. The possession of the adapted technologies gave them a competitive advantage in foreign markets, which they capitalized on. The case of these firms goes to confirm the formulation of Louis T. Wells, Jr., that the main strength of DC multinationals lies in their technologies, which are more suitable to the needs of developing nations. Another common feature of the two enterprises is what Ting and Schive call "an ethnocentric orientation" with regard to the management of subsidiaries. Not only are most of the planning and control decisions centralized in the Taipei headquarters of Gamma Corporation, but virtually all management and technical personnel in its subsidiaries are home-country nationals. This also seems to be the case with Tuntex, which has sent, according to Ting and Schive, a team of sixty persons from its headquarters to oversee construction of its overseas plant. On the whole, it seems that the internationalization process of the two firms has followed the familiar pattern of the prior success in the home country followed by outward investment as a defensive/aggressive strategy for continued growth.

In chapter 7, Ram Gopal Agrawal points out that the foreign investments by Indian firms are different from those of others in that the firms have formed joint ventures, not fully or partially owned subsidiaries. In fact, the government of India insists that its entrepreneurs establish, as far as possible, joint ventures, preferably as minority equity holders. This policy is obviously dictated both by the need to prevent outflow of the Indian capital and ideological considerations. The data put forward by Agrawal indeed show that this policy has been faithfully implemented; barring a few exceptions, all 200 Indian foreign projects are joint ventures. Most of the them are located in Asian and African countries and cover a wide range of manufacturing and service industries. Agrawal suggests that because of similar socioeconomic conditions, developing nations prefer the labor-intensive technologies of the Indian firms—and that explains their rapid expansion in foreign countries.

Agrawal also attempts to answer two criticisms which are generally leveled against foreign direct investment by India. First, is it prudent for a capital-poor nation to permit the export of its capital? His answer is that the Indian participation in the joint ventures has been primarily in the form of the supply of capital goods, machinery, basic materials, technical know-how, and management services. Only in a few cases has the government allowed cash remittances or financial participation. Thus in practice there is little export of capital, if at all. Therefore the criticism is unfounded. Second, and related to the first, is the question of whether Indian joint ventures do not adversely affect domestic production and consumption. Agrawal suggests that this apprehension is also unjustified, since Indian joint ventures operate in the industries in which India has underutilized or unutilized capacity. Therefore, instead of curbing industrial production, the foreign investment by Indian firms helps it while at the same time "strengthening the industrial structure." Moreover, it contributes to the growth and diversification of the nation's exports.

Indian joint ventures are viewed from the perspective of a host nation, Indonesia, in chapter 8 by Kian-Wie Thee. The host developing nations usually prefer joint ventures over subsidiaries because they are supposed to provide greater indigenous participation and control. Thee suspects that this might not be true of the Indian joint ventures. Because of the paucity of suitable collaborators, many Indian firms, following in the footsteps of Japanese enterprises, have resorted to the practice of using nominal Indonesian shareholders.

Most of the Indian joint ventures, according to Thee, are manufacturing light consumer and engineering goods for local consumption. Unlike the Japanese firms, they are located throughout Java rather than being concentrated in Jakarta, which perhaps implies that they are contributing to more balanced regional growth. There is the possibility that the average total investment of an Indian textile joint venture is slightly higher as compared with those from Japan and Hong Kong. Thee cautions, however, against any sweeping generalization in view of the lack of empirical data on the production levels of these operations. Thee also refers to the unenthusiastic attitude of Indonesian businessmen and officials toward Indian investors, which is hardly atypical. DC firms often complain that they encounter a lack of enthusiasm that poses an obstacle to their successful functioning.

In chapter 9, Nambudiri, Iyanda, and Akinnusi focus on the subsidiaries of DC multinationals that are operating in Nigeria. Their investigations cover eight firms that invested in the country for both defensive and aggressive reasons. Some of the firms were earlier involved in the import business and later established manufacturing subsidiaries in pursuance of the government's policy of promoting "indigenization." Others started local manufacturing to exploit the local markets. One of the most interesting findings in this chapter is that seven out of eight firms imported their machinery from industrialized and not from home developing nations. This finding questions the hypothesis, propounded by some contributors to this book, that DC firms generally take advantage of their adopted technologies in their drive for foreign expansion.

What then are the competitive advantages of DC multinationals in Nigeria? The authors contend that they have cost advantages. Their cost of managerial and technical manpower is lower as compared with the subsidiaries of the multinationals from industrialized nations. They are able to effectively function with smaller staffs and usually pay lower salaries. Moreover, their overhead costs are also low for a variety of reasons. Nambundiri, Iyanda, and Akinnusi also point out that these firms have some marketing advantages that pertain to "product selection, distribution, and catering to the special requirements of the local market." Often their products are cheaper and more functional. They are not advertised, but are sold largely through local networks. The authors suggest that these firms have "specialized knowledge of markets" that enable them to identify market segments they can satisfy.

In chapter 10, Eduardo White views the internationalization of Latin American firms as a natural consequence of the process of industrialization in the relatively small markets of the region. According to him, three factors have facilitated the growth of intraregional investments in Latin America: the impressive economic growth registered by several countries, the general improvement in the balance-of-payment situation, and the implementation of the various intraregional integration programs that provide preferential treatment to the movements of goods and services. While for the whole region, the FDI by Latin American firms looks marginal, White stresses the fact that there are various countries, sectors, and firms for which overseas direct investment plays a significant role. For example, the performance of Argentina, Brazil, and Mexico as the home countries of multinationals has been quite impressive. The smaller and less-developed nations, such as Ecuador, Paraguay, and Uruguay, have been the recipients of these investments. White's findings indicate that various motivations, such as access to raw materials, preservation of the existing markets or the search for the new ones, and the better utilization of capital and manpower through the economies of scale, explain the internationalization of Latin American firms. There are, however, two additional motives that are important in Latin American context: diversification of risks in unstable political systems, and circumvention of domestic tax burdens, labor laws, and foreign-exchange restrictions. White also discusses some of the competitive advantages the Latin American multinationals enjoy over those of industrialized nations. His findings generally confirm the hypotheses put foward by other contributors.

White predicts that more and more Latin American firms will embark on a program of overseas expansion in the future. However, he does not see them as alternatives to the multinationals from industrialized nations because the former "operate in markets with relatively low levels of concentration and technological intensity." Moreover, they remain dependent on the multinationals from industrialized nations for the procurement of original technologies which they imitate, adapt, and modify. He concludes that DC firms will continue to offer better terms to recipient countries with regard to local participation and restrictive practices as long as "they remain small, less diversified internationally, and do not become dependent on patented and sophisticated technologies.''

In chapter 11, Krishna Kumar deals with the subject of FDI by the public-sector enterprises of developing nations. Kumar suggests that over the past several years, the number of public enterprises from developing countries that have internationalized their operations has rapidly increased. Like the private-sector firms, they have established overseas subsidiaries and joint ventures in order to have access to raw materials, sell manufacturing technologies, and market their products and services. Since they are highly susceptible to the political influences of the home governments, Kumar suggests that we should not overlook the political considerations that affect their overseas direct investments. Kumar also mentions some exclusive competitive advantages that public-sector multinationals can enjoy over private-sector firms. They undoubtedly receive direct and indirect subsidies from their governments. They also are able to use the various organs of the government in scanning investment opportunities, negotiating with foreign enterprises, and solving various bottlenecks at the implementation stage. Moreover, they are generally regarded as "safe" partners by their foreign collaborators. There are, however, some disabilities which, according to Kumar, are imposed on them by virtue of their being state enterprises, such as rampant bureaucracy, political impediments to foreign expansion, and the lack of adequate incentives to the managers. Kumar suggests that the public-sector multinationals cannot be regarded as an unmixed blessing to both home and host nations. They have both costs and benefits which deserve to be considered case by case by the concerned nations.

Thus the broad picture of the phenomenon of DC multinationals that emerges from the various contributions can be briefly stated as follows: Most DC multinationals come from nations that are relatively more industrialized. These countries have come to possess a sizable indigenous industrial sector and a growing entrepreneurial class. Their investments have usually gone to the less industrialized of developing nations. Although some of their firms have established subsidiaries in industrialized countries, their overall investments in these nations can, at best, be described as marginal. They are more designed to provide service and support facilities for exports from the home rather to directly engage in manufacturing in the industrialized nations.

There are many motivations that explain the overseas investments drives of DC multinationals. Some manufacturing firms establish subsidiaries to protect their existing foreign markets or in search for new ones in the context of a growing trend toward protectionism in both the developing and the developed world. Others, especially from natural-resource-scarce countries, make foreign investments in extractive industries, agriculture, or fishing to secure a continual supply of the needed raw materials or other products. Still others try to take the advantage of lower costs of production in the host nations, especially for export purposes. Some also try to circumvent quota restrictions imposed by industrialized nations by partially locating manufacturing in other developing nations. In some cases, especially when the domestic markets are small, DC firms internationalize their operations to take the advantage of the economy of scale or to minimize their risks. In a few instances, the national government's policies designed to prevent monopolistic or oligopolistic conditions at home contribute to the migration of capital to other countries. In short, practically all the major explanatory variables that have been used to explain overseas drives of the multinationals from industrialized nations have predictive value about DC multinationals. Their relative importance is likely to differ, however. The majority of the firms from Asia, as the various studies indicate, invest abroad to promote their exports and to secure vital raw materials.

What are the competitive assets of DC multinationals? Here again, no single explanatory variable can be identified. However, most of the observers seem to agree that these firms compete in international markets on the basis of their labor-intensive, multipurpose manufacturing technologies that can be used on a small scale to cater to relatively limited markets. These technologies are usually less expensive and do not require large capital investments. Moreover, DC firms have the advantage of low management and technical costs as compared with those of Western multinational corporations. Often their products are less expensive and more suitable to the needs of the consumers.

Several studies included in this book also suggest that most manufacturing DC multinationals do not operate in industries in which they can encounter stiff competition from their counterparts from the affluent nations. Often they go to industries in which technologies have become mature and are not regarded as profitable by other enterprises. Thus there seems to be a kind of division of labor between the firms from industrialized and developing nations. However, there are some gray areas even in the manufacturing sector in which the two categories of firms compete. DC multinationals in the service sector are more prone to offer competition to firms of industrialized countries.

DC multinationals are generally medium- and large-sized enterprises. The majority of them operate in the manufacturing sector. Their organizational structure is often simple. While the larger DC firms maintain strict control over their subsidiaries, others exercise minimal control and supervision. Most of these firms have established joint ventures in host nations.

The policies of governments, both in home and host nations, have been marked by a certain degree of ambivalence. The home governments do not relish the idea of the export of the domestic capital unless it promotes exports or facilitates imports of needed raw materials. Only recently have some home governments formulated policy guidelines for outward investments. The host nations are usually not convinced of the capability of these DC firms. Despite the widespread rhetoric, most of the host nations in Asia or Africa do not favor the multinationals from developing countries over those from the industrialized world when evaluating a proposal.

These ideas can only be treated as working hypotheses. They should not be elevated to the status of valid generalizations. The existing data base on DC multinationals is extremely limited. The task of the contributors to the book was to raise critical issues, identify important hypotheses, and suggest some profitable paths for empirical and theoretical analysis. That most of them have gone beyond their assigned task is indeed a tribute to their knowledge and insights, but the reader must be forewarned about the possible limitation of this book. Our hope is that these hypotheses will be tested, refuted, refined, and reformulated on the basis of ongoing investigations.

Fortunately, several research enterprises are presently underway to study the phenomenon of DC multinationals. The Harvard Business School Project on this subject under the leadership of Louis T. Wells, Jr., has been doing interesting work in this area. In fact, his researchers have affected current thinking on DC multinationals. Eduardo White also has been directing an investigation focused on Latin America at the Instituto para la Integracion de America Latina. His findings are now reaching the English-speaking audience. A project dealing with Asian countries also has been started at the East-West Center. This project, coordinated by myself, especially focuses on the social, cultural, and political implications of the rise of DC multinationals. Besides these cross-national projects, individual scholars in many developing nations have been conducting interesting research. The output of all these endeavors will certainly illuminate the phenomenon of DC multinationals and also will contribute to the theoretical advancement of our knowledge and the formulation of appropriate policies by the home and host nations. At least, this is our hope, and this is the most social scientists can aspire to.

1

Explaining Outward Direct Investment of Developing Countries: In Support of the Eclectic Theory of International Production

John H. Dunning

The main thesis of this chapter is that the emerging phenomenon of outward direct investment by developing countries can be usefully explained by the eclectic theory of international production, as can differences in the level and composition of that investment between developing countries. In support of this contention, this chapter pays especial attention to the dynamics of both inward and outward direct investment and makes use of an investment-development model that suggests that the propensity of a country to engage in foreign direct investment by foreign firms is a function of its stage of economic development—both absolutely and relative to that of other countries.

First, let me briefly summarize the eclectic theory of international production, that is, production financed by foreign direct investment.[1] The theory suggests that the propensity for a country's enterprises to engage in foreign direct investment is determined by three conditions. The first condition is the extent to which the enterprises possess or can gain access to assets or rights to assets which its (foreign) competitors do not possess or possess in the same degree or on the same terms. The second condition is whether it pays these enterprises to exploit these proprietary advantages themselves, that is, internalize their use or sell them, or the right to use them, to foreign firms to use (that is, externalize their sale). The third condition is whether or not the enterprises choose to locate at least part of the production of the output generated by the advantages outside their home countries. The more a country's enterprises possess ownership-specific advantages, the greater the incentive is to internalize them; and the more these enterprises find it profitable to exploit the advantages outside their national boundaries, the more likely they are to engage in foreign direct investment. By the same token, a country is likely to attract inward investment when the reverse conditions apply. A country's involvement in international direct investment

I am indebted to Mr. R.D. Pearce for statistical assistance in the preparation of this chapter.

then becomes a function of the ownership and internalization advantages of its enterprises relative to those of other nationalities and its location-specific endowments relative to those of other countries.

A good deal of work has been done on identifying the nature of these advantages and the conditions under which they are most likely to exist. Some of these are illustrated in table 1-1. As can be seen, the presence of (permanent) ownership advantages may be explained by reference to the theory of industrial organization and the extent to which market imperfections create barriers to competition; internalization advantages depend on the extent to which the market mechanism is capable of capturing the full economic rent of these advantages; and location advantages depend on relative input (including transport) costs, productivity, market characteristics, and government policies of alternative locations.

This approach to explaining international production has been called eclectic for the following reasons. It embraces the three main forms of foreign involvement by enterprises, namely, direct investment, exports, and contractual resource transfers[2] (for example, licensing, management contracts, technical service agreements, and so forth), and offers an explanation of which route of exploitation is preferred. In all three vehicles, the possession of ownership advantages is a necessary prerequisite for involvement. However, the possession of internalization advantages suggests that firms will exploit these advantages by way of exports or foreign direct investment rather than by a contractual resource exchange; whereas the equity-investment route, rather than exports, will be chosen where locational advantages favor a foreign rather than a domestic production base. The matrix in figure 1-1 summarizes the conditions determining these choices.

In identifying the forces influencing these advantages, economists have found it useful to distinguish three structural characteristics, namely, those which are specific to particular countries, particular types of activities (or industries), and particular enterprises—that is to say, the propensity of a particular enterprise to invest overseas will vary according to its home country, the country(ies) in which it is proposing to make an investment, the range and type of products (including intermediate products) it is intending to produce, and its underlying management and organizational strategy (which *inter alia* may be affected by its size and its attitude toward risk diversification). Again, as is illustrated in table 1-2, these characteristics can be readily identified. It is worth observing that they are not always independent of each other. For example, in explaining why different countries' enterprises may have different propensities to invest, one may turn to the industrial composition of such investment, but this is, in part, a reflection of the specific endowments of the countries in question.

Combining the data in tables 1-1 and 1-2, one has the kernel of the eclectic theory of international production. Up to now, most empirical tests

Table 1-1
The Eclectic Theory of International Production

1. *Ownership-Specific Advantages* (of enterprises of one nationality, or affiliates of same, over those of another).

    a. *Which need not arise owing to multinationality.* Those owing mainly to size and established position, product or process diversification, ability to take advantage of division of labor and specialization, monopoly power, better resource capacity and usage.

    Proprietary technology, trade marks (protected by patent and other legislation)

    Production, management, organizational, and marketing systems; R&D capacity; "bank" of human capital and experience

    Exclusive or favored access to inputs, for example, labor, natural resources, finance, and information

    Ability to obtain inputs on favored terms (owing, for example, to size or monopsonistic influence)

    Exclusive or favored access to product markets

    Government protection (for example, control on market entry)

    b. *Which those branch plants of establishment enterprises may enjoy over de novo firms.*

    Access to capacity (administrative, managerial, R&D, marketing, and so forth) of parent company at favored prices

    Economies of joint supply (not only in production, but purchasing, marketing, and financing arrangements)

    c. *Which specifically arise because of multinationality.* Multinationality enhances preceding advantages by offering wider opportunities.

    More favored access to and/or better knowledge about information, inputs, and markets

    Ability to take advantage of international differences in factor endowments, markets, and government intervention

    Ability to diversify risks, for example, in different currency areas

2. *Internalization Incentive Advantages* (that is, to protect against or exploit market failure).

    Avoidance of transaction and negotiating costs

    To avoid costs of enforcing property rights

    Buyer uncertainly (about nature and value of inputs, for example, technology, being sold)

    Where market does not permit price discrimination

    Need of seller to protect quality of products

    To capture economics of interdependent activities (see 1b above)

    To compensate for absence of futures markets

    To avoid or exploit government intervention (for example, quotas, tariffs, price controls, tax differences, and so forth)

    To control supplies and conditions of sale of inputs (including supplies to competitors

Table 1-1 *(continued)*

To control market outlets (including those which might be used by competitors)

Where permitted, to be able to engage in practices, for example, cross-subsidization, predatory pricing, and so forth, as a competitive (or anticompetitive) strategy

3. *Location-Specific Variables* (may favor home or host countries).

Spatial distribution of inputs and markets

Input prices, quality, and productivity, for example, labor, energy, materials, components, and semifinished goods

Transport, communication availability, and costs

Government intervention

Control on imports, including new tariff barriers, tax rates, incentives, climate for investment, political stability, and so forth

Infrastructure (commercial, legal, transportation)

Psychic distance (language, cultural, business, and customs differences

Economics of R&D production and marketing (for example, extent to which scale economies make for centralization of production)

of this approach have been directed to that part of the theory concerned with explaining the industrial composition of a particular country's outward or inward direct investment (or capital stake). Little work has so far been done on explaining the geographical origin of outward or inward direct investment or why the industrial spread of such investment differs

		Advantages		
		Ownership	Internalization	(Foreign) Location
Route of Servicing Market	Foreign direct investment	Yes	Yes	Yes
	Exports	Yes	Yes	No
	Portfolio resource transfers	Yes	No	No

Figure 1-1. Conditions Determining the Forms of Foreign Involvement by Enterprises

Table 1-2
Some Illustrations of How the Conditions for Foreign Direct Investment May Vary According to Country-, Industry-, and Firm-Specific Considerations

Conditions	Country (Home-Host)	Industry	Firm
Ownership	Factor endowments (e.g., resources and skilled labor) and market size and character. Government policy toward innovation, protection of proprietary rights, competition, and industrial structure. Government controls on inward direct investment.	Degree of product or process technological intensity. Nature of innovations. Extent of product differentiation. Production economics (e.g., if there are economies of scale). Importance of favored access to inputs/markets.	Size, extent of production, process, or market diversification. Extent to which enterprise is innovatory or marketing-oriented or values security and/or stability, e.g., in sources of inputs, markets, etc.
Internalization	Government intervention and extent to which policies encourage MNEs to internalize transactions, e.g., transfer pricing. Government policy toward mergers. Differences in market structures between countries, e.g., with respect to transaction costs, enforcement of contracts, buyer uncertainty, etc. Adequacy of technological, etc. infrastructure in host countries and ability to absorb portfolio resource transfers.	Extent to which vertical or horizontal integration is possible/desirable, e.g., need to control sourcing of inputs or markets. Extent to which internalizing advantages can be captured in contractual agreements (see the early and later stages of product cycle). Use made of ownership advantages. See the IBM with Unilever type operation.	Organizational and control procedures of enterprise. Attitudes toward growth and diversification (e.g., the boundaries of a firm's activities. Attitudes toward subcontracting contractual ventures, e.g., licensing, franchising, technical-assistance agreements, etc.
Location	Physical and psychic distance between countries. Government intervention (tariffs, quotas, taxes, etc.). The exchange rate.	Origin and distribution of immobile resources. Transport costs of intermediate and final good products. Industry-specific tariff and nontariff barriers. Nature of competition between firms in industry. Can functions of activities of industry be split? Significance of "sensitive" locational variables, e.g., tax incentives, percentage of labor in total costs.	Management stategy toward foreign involvement. Age and experience of foreign involvement. (Position of enterprise in product cycle, etc.) Psychic-distance variables (culture, language, legal and commercial framework). Attitudes toward centralization of certain functions, e.g., R&D, office and market allocation, etc. Geographic structure of asset portfolio and attitude toward risk diversification.

between countries. Some work by behavioral or organizational theorists has been done on firm-specific factors influencing the structure and timing of foreign direct investment (Brooke and Remmers, 1970; Stopford and Wells, 1972; Aharoni, 1973), but by their nature, it is difficult to incorporate these into any general body of theory.[3]

The focus of this book is mainly on the country-specific determinants of foreign direct investment and, in particular, on those which are applicable to such investment by developing countries. This chapter next explores the proposition that the propensity of a developing country to engage in foreign direct investment is partly a function of its stage of economic development and partly a function of its particular characteristics or those of its firms which make for a unique combination of ownership, location, and internalization advantages whatever its stage of development.

Let us first look at the relationship between the net outward direct investment (NOI) of a country and its gross national product (GNP), both variables being normalized by size of population. The data[4] in table 1-3 set out a frequency distribution of outward, inward, and net outward investment flows and flows averaged for the period 1967-1975 and the GNP per capita for 1971 of fifty-six countries.[5] Depicted as a diagram, these data would suggest a U-shaped or inverted-L-shaped investment-development pattern with countries falling into four main groups that correspond to four stages of development. The first group of countries consist of those in which there is little inward and no outward direct investment and a zero or a small negative NOI; this group comprises the twenty-two countries with a GNP per capita of $400 or less.

The second group of countries comprises those in which inward direct investment is rising but outward direct investment remains near zero, that is, where NOI is negative and becoming larger; there are eighteen countries in this stage of development with a GNP per capita of between $400 and $1,500. The third stage of development is where NOI is still negative but is becoming smaller; this may occur either because, with a constant and small outward investment, inward investment is falling, or because outward investment is rising faster than inward investment. Some ten countries with GNP per capita from $2,000 to $4,750 fall into this category. The fourth stage is where NOI per capita is positive and rising; this suggests that either the level of inward investment has fallen below that of outward investment or that outward investment is rising faster than inward investment. Only six countries with GNPs per capita ranging from $2,600 to $5,600 come within this category.[6] They are all developed countries and are dominated by the United States, which, in money terms, is by far and away the largest net outward investor per capita.

This kind of investment-development pattern can be explained by use of the eclectic theory just described and is summarized in table 1-4. In stage 1,

Table 1-3
Outward and Inward Direct-Investment Flows per Capita, by Income of Country, 1967-1975

Countries Grouped by 1971 per Capita Income	Investment (Annual Average) per Capita ($)					
	Weighted Average[a]			Unweighted Average[b]		
	Outward	Inward	Net Outward	Outward	Inward	Net Outward
Over $4,000 (6 countries)	33.0	16.3	16.7	24.8	30.3	− 5.5
$2,500 to $4,000 (8 countries)	20.1	15.4	4.7	22.9	30.4	− 7.5
$1,000 to $2,500 (5 countries)	4.6	15.8	−11.2	1.8	50.5	−48.7
$500 to $1,000 (8 countries)	0.3	9.3	− 9.0	0.3	20.4	−20.1
$400 to $500 (7 countries)	0.1	7.3	− 7.2	0.1	8.0	− 7.9
$300 to $400 (7 countries)	0.2	4.0	− 3.8	0.1	4.1	− 4.0
$125 to $300 (7 countries)	0	3.1	− 3.1	0	2.1	− 2.1
Less than $125 (8 countries)	0	1.4	− 1.4	0	1.6	− 1.6

Source: IMF, with adjustments, in some cases, by author to allow for reinvested profits.

[a]Weighted average, obtained by summing outward/inward/net outward investment flows for the x countries in the group and dividing by the population of the x countries. This gives a country with a large population a dominating influence on the result for an income group, for example, the United States in the over $4,000 group.

[b]Unweighted average, obtained by (1) calculating outward/inward/net outward flow per capita separately for each of the x countries in an income group; (2) summing these separate results; and (3) dividing by x.

Table 1-4
Inward and Outward Direct Investment and Stages of
Economic Development

		Inward Investment		*Outward Investment*
Stage 1	Of	Substantial	Od	None
	I	Substantial	I	Not applicable
	Ld	Few	Lf	Not applicable
Stage 2	Of	Substantial	Od	Few
	I	Substantial	I	Few
	Ld	Improving	Lf	Few
Stage 3	Of	Declining/ more specialized	Od	Growing
	I	Declining	I	Growing
	Ld	Declining	Lf	Growing
Stage 4	Of	Declining/ more specialized	Od	Increasing
	I	Declining	I	Substantial
	Ld	Declining	Lf	Increasing

Key to symbols: O = ownership advantages; L = locational advantages; I = internalization advantages; f = foreign; and d = domestic.

there is no outward investment because the country's own enterprises are generating no ownership-specific advantages to make this possible or because what advantages there are, are best exploited through other routes, namely, portfolio resource flows and/or exports. However, neither is there any inward direct investment, simply because there are insufficient location-specific advantages to warrant the setting up of affiliates by foreign firms. This may be so because domestic markets are not large enough, or because of a lack of an adequate or appropriate industrial, commercial, legal, transport, and communication infrastructure and the backup resources (for example, skilled labor) required to make the exploitation of such resources as are available profitable. There may be some arms-length import of capital and/or technology in this stage, but this is more likely to take the market or intergovernment route (aid and portfolio investment); goods also will be imported from foreign firms rather than being produced locally by them.

In stage 2, inward direct investment begins to become profitable as domestic markets enlarge and/or local infrastructure is improved. Import-substituting investment replaces or supplements exports (often stimulated by host governments imposing barriers to imports); resource investment to supply goods for foreign markets becomes worthwhile, as local labor is better educated, an acceptable legal and commercial framework is established, transport and communications are improved, and the economy is better managed. At the same time, since there still remain insufficient backup indigenous resources, most capital inflows are likely to be internalized, except where government policies restrict inward direct investment. As in stage 1, outward direct investment remains negligible (except, perhaps, that of a portfolio kind, for example, by resource-rich countries), simply because the country's enterprises have not yet established ownership advantages sufficient for them to overcome the disadvantages of international production, although some exporting of the kind that may eventually lead to outward investment may occur.

Stage 3 is a particularly interesting one. Net inward investment per capita now starts to fall. This could be so because the ownership advantages of foreign affiliates fall as the indigenous firms, stimulated either by the presence of such affiliates or by government aid, become more competitive; but it also could be that outward investment is starting to rise as the indigenous firms develop their own particular ownership advantages, which they find it best to exploit through foreign direct investment.[7] This may mark the beginning of a country's international investment specialization, in which it seeks to attract inward direct investment in those sectors in which its comparative location advantages are strongest but the comparative ownership advantages of its enterprises are weakest, while its own enterprises invest abroad in those sectors in which their comparative ownership advantages are strongest but their comparative location advantages are weakest.

In stage 4, a country is a net outward investor; that is, its investment flow abroad exceeds that of foreign-owned firms in its own country. This reflects the strong ownership advantages of its firms and/or an increasing propensity to exploit these advantges from a foreign rather than a domestic location. This may be so because of high (real) labor costs (normally associated with high levels of economic development) or the need to export resources (including some types of labor) to help sustain its international competitive position in world markets, or it may be due to increasing barriers to trade to the kinds of goods exported by these countries. Again, depending on the amount of specialization, outward investment may be associated with substantial or little inward investment. For example, the point of zero NOI could mean that the country engages in no inward or outward investment, that is, is self-sufficient in its investment, or that it has a sizable outward investment that is balanced by an equally sizable inward investment.

The interpretation of the investment development cycle just outlined is based on cross-sectional country data. It suggests that a country's international investment position is related to its level of development as measured by GNP per capita.[8] However, to properly test the proposition that countries pass through identifiable development stages, it is necessary to look at time-series data for individual countries over quite a long period. Unfortunately, except in the case of a few developed countries, data are not available for us to do this, but the overall picture does lend some support to the idea of an investment-developmental cycle. Certainly the United States fits nearly into this pattern, as do most continental European countries and Japan; of the developing countries, there are some, for example, Nigeria and Indonesia, that over the last 15 years have emerged from the first to second stage, while others, including some of the newly industrialized developing countries (NICs), for example, Hong Kong, South Korea, Brazil, and Mexico, appear to be moving quickly from the second to the third stage.

Since it is these latter countries in which this book is especially interested, let us look in more detail at the developing countries that had any outward direct investment stake in 1976. While, in general, as table 1-4 shows, there is a positive correlation between outward investment and GNP per capita, deviations from any "best-fit" line are sufficient to suggest that ownership, internalization, and location factors making for such investment are themselves influenced by characteristics *specific to the individual countries*.[9] Indeed, this conclusion may be generalized for both developed and developing countries. Figure 1-2 plots the relationship between NOI per capita and GNP per capita. It can be seen that although the U-shaped (or inverted-L-shaped) relationship exists, the variations around the best-fit line at any particular GNP (or range of GNPs) per capita (we have depicted the four stages in the figure) are as great or are greater than the variations among levels of GNP. Any attempt, then, to formulate a generalized explanatory model of the outward direct investment of developing countries must take account of these variations. Why is it, for example, that with the same level of GNP per head, Brazil is a quite significant outward investor while Malaysia is not?

To suggest some answers to these questions—but not to subject these to any formal statistical testing[10]—let us examine more closely the pattern revealed by figure 1-2. In table 1-5 we can easily distinguish examples of countries in each of the four development stages that are substantially above or below the best-fit line. The question is, Can one identify any common characteristics of these countries that might explain these deviations? It is precisely here where the eclectic theory of international production seems to offer a useful set of hypotheses, for the theory suggests that the location-specific characteristics of countries above the line are such as to produce either above average ownership-specific advantages of that country's firms in foreign markets, coupled with the desire to internalize these advantages, and/or below average location-specific advantages, which

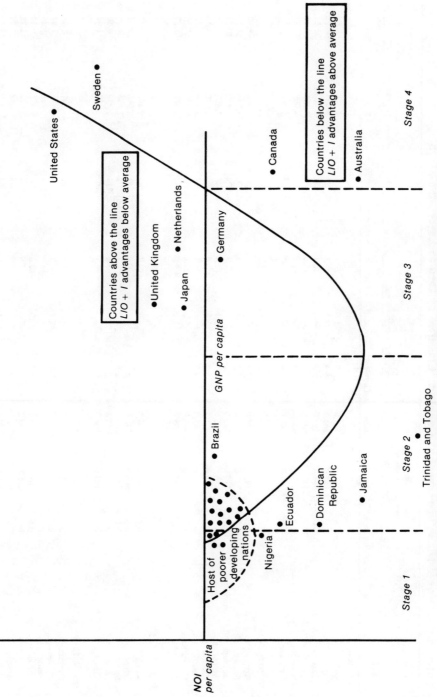

Figure 1-2. Illustration of Investment-Development Cycle of Countries

Table 1-5
Outward and Inward Direct Investment by Countries, Classified by Income Levels, 1967-1975

	Value of Investment (Annual Average), (millions of dollars)			Investment per Capita			GNP (millions of dollars)	Annual Average GNP/Population (dollars)	Population (millions)
	Outward	Inward	Net Outward	Outward	Inward	Net Outward			
Over $4,000									
Sweden	304.0	121.0	+183.0	37.7	15.0	+22.7	44,956	5,578	8.06
United States	8,145.0	1,881.0	+6,264.0	39.4	9.1	+30.3	1,116,270	5,405	206.52
Canada	579.0	969.0	−390.0	26.7	44.8	−18.1	103,132	4,772	21.61
Denmark	77.0	169.0	−92.0	15.5	34.1	−18.6	20,467	4,126	4.96
Australia	133.0	747.0	−614.0	10.3	58.2	−47.9	52,588	4,099	12.83
Germany	1,172.0	1,253.0	−81.0	19.2	20.5	−1.3	248,168	4,061	61.11
$2,500 to $4,000									
Norway	68.0	193.0	−125.0	17.4	49.5	−32.1	15,234	3,906	3.90
France	552.0	747.0	−195.0	10.8	14.6	−3.8	191,490	3,736	51.25
Belgium and Luxembourg	203.0	718.0	−515.0	20.2	71.6	−51.4	36,324	3,622	10.03
Netherlands	1,006.0	856.0	+150.0	76.5	65.1	+11.4	44,845	3,407	13.16
Finland	31.2	27.0	+4.2	6.7	5.8	+0.9	13,999	3,010	4.65
Austria	30.0	116.0	−86.0	4.1	15.6	−11.5	20,577	2,726	7.45
United Kingdom	2,011.0	1,057.0	+954.0	36.2	19.0	+17.2	146,647	2,639	55.56
Japan	1,171.0	166.0	+1,005.0	11.1	1.6	+9.5	278,547	2,632	105.87
$1,000 to $2,500									
Israel	0.9	61.4	−60.5	0.3	20.0	−19.7	7,663	2,496	3.07
Italy	359.0	901.0	−542.0	6.7	16.7	−10.0	111,781	2,068	54.05
Spain	63.0	347.0	−284.0	1.9	10.2	−8.3	51,072	1,496	34.15
Gabon	0	53.8	−53.8	0	107.6	−107.6	714	1,428	0.50
Trinidad and Tobago	0	102.0	−102.0	0	98.1	−98.1	1,167	1,122	1.04
$500 to $1,000									
Surinam	0	1.7	−1.7	0	4.5	−4.5	341	897	0.38
Jamaica	0	94.6	−93.7	0	49.3	−48.8	1,709	890	1.92
Panama	0	20.8	−20.8	0	14.0	−14.0	1,261	846	1.49
Barbados	0.4	10.8	−10.4	1.7	45.0	−43.3	198	825	0.24
Costa Rica	0	30.2	−30.2	0	17.0	−17.0	1,197	672	1.78
Brazil	29.0	679.0	−650.0	0.3	7.1	−6.8	61,318	642	95.54
Malaysia	0	206.0	−206.0	0	19.1	−19.1	5,564	516	10.79
Nicaragua	0	13.3	−13.3	0	6.9	−6.9	988	515	1.92

$400 to $500									
Dominican Republic	0	70.6	−70.6	0	16.8	−16.8	1,952	465	4.20
Ivory Coast	0.2	29.2	−29.0	0	6.6	−6.6	2,012	454	4.43
Algeria	5.0	108.0	−103.0	0.4	7.3	−6.9	6,557	442	14.85
Tunisia	0	44.4	−44.4	0	8.5	−8.5	2,203	421	5.23
Guyana	0	4.4	−4.4	0	6.0	−6.0	306	419	0.73
Peru	0	64.0	−64.0	0	4.6	−4.6	5,789	416	13.92
Guatamala	0	34.8	−34.8	0	6.4	−6.4	2,239	415	5.40
$300 to $400									
Columbia	3.1	59.4	−56.3	0.1	2.8	−2.7	8,407	397	21.20
Ecuador	0	71.0	−71.0	0	11.4	−11.4	2,297	370	6.21
Paraguay	0	11.0	−11.0	0	4.6	−4.6	826	347	2.38
El Salvador	0	9.0	−9.0	0	2.5	−2.5	1,197	333	3.60
Honduras	0	7.4	−7.4	0	2.9	−2.9	801	315	2.54
Jordan	0	1.3	−1.3	0	0.6	−0.6	716	302	2.37
South Korea	11.0	122.0	−111.0	0.3	3.7	−3.4	9,869	301	32.77
$125 to $300									
Ghana	0	29.5	−29.5	0	3.3	−3.3	2,590	290	8.92
Morocco	0	5.8	−5.8	0.1	0.4	−0.4	4,258	272	15.67
Senegal	0.5	10.1	−9.7	0.1	2.6	−2.5	1,006	260	3.87
Bolivia	0	1.8	−1.8	0	0.4	−0.4	1,212	239	5.07
Nigeria	0	259.0	−259.0	0	4.6	−4.6	11,652	205	56.74
Sierra Leone	0	7.9	−7.9	0	3.1	−3.1	468	181	2.59
Uganda	0	1.0	−1.0	0	0.1	−0.1	1,477	145	10.20
Less than $125									
Haiti	0	3.6	−3.6	0	0.8	−0.8	520	121	4.31
Indonesia	0	152.0	−152.0	0	1.2	−1.2	13,542	110	122.87
Zaire	0	78.0	−78.0	0	3.5	−3.5	2,414	108	22.27
Niger	1.2	6.2	−5.0	0.3	1.5	−1.2	443	108	4.12
Benin	0	3.1	−3.1	0	1.1	−1.1	293	105	2.79
Malawi	−1.0	10.3	−11.3	−0.2	2.3	−2.5	406	89	4.57
Chad	0	6.9	−6.9	0	1.9	−1.9	329	88	3.72
Ethiopia	0	12.4	−12.4	0	0.5	−0.5	1,989	79	25.26

encourage outward investment and discourage inward direct investment. However, the characteristics of countries below the line are such as to produce either below average ownership-specific advantages of that country's firms and/or above average location-specific advantages, which might discourage outward and encourage inward investment.

Of course, it is not quite as simple as this. The NOI line represents the difference between outward and inward investment. Therefore, it follows that deviations above or below the line may be due to deviations in either outward or inward investment or a combination of the two.[11] Such deviations, in their turn, may reflect the industrial structure of the country and the extent to which it engages in international specialization. As has already been said, a zero NOI in stage 3 could mean that a country neither imports nor exports direct capital, or that it fully participates in international investment and there is an exact balance between outward and inward flows. In the latter, countries would tend to exploit their firms' ownership advantages in lines of activity in which their resources (including markets) were comparatively the better suited and import those (through direct investment) in those areas for which their endowments were comparatively less suited.

In table 1-1 we identified the main components of the three conditions necessary for outward direct investment. The absence of these conditions would suggest not only that outward investment would not occur, but also that such countries would be invested in by foreigners. This, however, will be the case only if markets, the availability and price of domestic resources, and the economic and political environment are attractive to the inward investor.

Which of the ingredients listed in table 1-1 and in the previous paragraph are most likely to (1) be significant, and (2) vary in their value according to country-specific characteristics? Partly this depends on the type of foreign direct investment being considered. The literature generally distinguishes between two main types: the first is that designed to supply goods mainly for local consumption (in place of imports and in competition with local producers and other foreign affiliates), and the second is to supply goods for export mainly, although not exclusively, to developed countries.[12] While the first kind of investment is dominated by the size and structure of the local market, government policy toward imports, and transport costs, the second is largely determined by the availability and cost of natural resources and certain kinds of labor and tax levels. In both cases, the investing firm is assumed to have some kind of ownership advantage over local producers or other foreign companies. Usually this takes the form of technology, management and organization skills, capital, access to markets, and a (differentiated) product protected by a trade mark. As an inducement to exploit this advantage through direct investment, not only must there be an adequate local infrastructure and legal and commercial framework, but there must also be, in the case of the second kind of investment, available resources of the kind in question and, in the first case, adequate markets and/or a policy by the host government of import substitution.

Using this kind of approach, it is possible to suggest a series of hypotheses about the causes of deviation of countries above or below the best-fit line. From the viewpoint, first, of inward investment, one might expect that countries which are (1) rich in natural and/or human resources, (2) have a sizable population, (3) offer a congenial environment to inward investment, (4) have a well-developed infrastructure, and (5) possess an acceptable legal or commercial framework and yet (6) whose indigenous firms have not generated sufficient ownership advantages for them to successfully compete with foreign enterprises will be those which will be above the line; those with the absence of these things, or those in which competition from indigenous firms is strong, or those in which the government does not encourage inward direct investment will be below the line.

From the viewpoint of outward investment, countries will be above the line (that is, they will engage in more than the average outward investment) when they are able to generate strong ownership advantages for their firms (for example, technology, management, and marketing skills), but when it is profitable (or less risky) to utilize these advantages outside their home countries, for example, because of high labor costs, lack of resource availability, the need to diversify risks (Lecraw, 1977), or the need to circumvent transport costs or barriers to trade imposed by host countries. On this basis, one might predict that countries which, at a given stage of development, were recording above average (real) wage rates and whose populations were small (and thus not able to generate firm economies of scale from a domestic market) and technologically advanced would generate above average outward investment, while contries whose prosperity rested more on immobile resources (for example, minerals and agriculture) would generate less than average outward investment.

From the viewpoint of the developing countries, one would expect that those most likely to become international investors would be those whose resource endowments generated ownership-specific advantages that needed to be internalized and exploited from a foreign location. In some instances, this may take the form of vertical forward integration, for example, date-processing plants by Tunisian firms in Southern France or shrimp canning by Indian enterprises in Sri Lanka; in others, vertical backward integration, for example, Brazilian oil-refining companies in the Middle East. In the cases of horizontal integration, the comparative ownership advantage of multinational enterprises (MNEs) from industrialized developing countries tends to be concentrated in sectors requiring intermediate or mature technology and plentiful semiskilled labor and where economies of scale are an unimportant production advantage.

Thus Indian firms specializing in mature, intermediate, and small-scale engineering technology invest in other parts of Southeast Asia (Lall, 1979), while South Korean firms export technology, labor, and management to assist in construction projects in the Middle East.[13] There is also a general preference for the joint-venture involvement, particularly when breaking into established markets requires the marketing or sourcing expertise of indigenous companies; in other instances, the contractual form of business arrangement is considered adequate, for example, Indian and Spanish hotel chains. In general, MNEs from developing countries appear to be more flexible in arrangements than those from the developed countries, especially from the United States, and there is some suggestion, at least, that their size threshold for international production is smaller.[14]

Later chapters in this book will focus in some detail on the form, content, and geographic distribution of the investment by developing countries. The present analysis has attempted to suggest a framework for explaining this investment that could be incorporated into any general explanation of the operations of MNEs. In so doing, it has suggested the necessary and sufficient conditions for international production. It has argued that these need to be related to country-, industry-, and enterprise-specific characteristics. And from these two sets of data, it has asserted that it is possible to suggest *which* countries are most likely to generate outward investment, and why the level and structure of investment varies among countries.

So far our attempt to explain the outward investment of developing countries has used cross-sectional data, the implication being that as countries advance in their development, they will take on at least some of the characteristics of those at a higher stage of development. It is also possible to use the eclectic approach to explain why a particular country may change its international investment position over time. Thus, if the ratio between its outward and inward investment (or capital stake) is increasing, this suggests that either the (net) ownership advantages of its enterprises have increased (thus enabling it to reduce its dependence on inward investment and its own enterprises to penetrate foreign markets more effectively), or it has become a less-attractive locational base (which encourages its own firms to exploit foreign markets by foreign rather than domestic production and foreign firms to exploit its own markets by exports rather than local production). Without an examination of these ownership- and location-specific factors separately, there is no a priori way to identify the reasons for a rise in outward/inward investment ratios. Moreover, without knowledge of the value of the components of the ratio, one cannot tell whether a country is becoming less or more dependent or international direct investment flows.

Up to now there have been few attempts to explain changes in a country's international investment position using the eclectic theory as a basis, although I have tried to do this for the United Kingdom for the period 1962-1977 (Dunning, 1979*b*). Earlier in this chapter, I hinted at reasons for the investment-development cycle of countries. As far as the newly emerging foreign investors from developing countries are concerned, we have to rely on IMF data for the last 16 years. To take just two examples, Brazil and South Korea, table 1-6 portrays the changing outward/inward investment ratio for the period 1960-1977, taking six periods.[16] In both cases, the ratio has risen over the period. Separate data on inward and outward investment suggest that this is primarily because outward investment has risen rather than because inward investment has fallen. *Inter alia*, this is shown by the fact that outward *plus* inward investment per capita has been rising. This, in turn, suggests that it has been the rising ownership-specific advantages rather than the falling location-specific advantages of these countries that have been responsible for the changing ratio. The identification and evaluation of these advantages, which are linked to the structure of industry and the strategy of firms, both of which (particularly the former) are affected by the resource endowments of the country, government policy, and market size, are a matter for separate research.

Summary

Let me now summarize the main thesis of this chapter.
   1. A country's propensity to engage in foreign direct investment and/or be invested in by foreign enterprises rests on (a) the extent to which its enterprises (relative to enterprises of other nationalities) possess net ownership advantages, (b) whether it pays these enterprises to internalize these advantages or sell them (through the market) to other enterprises,[17] and (c) whether it is profitable for enterprises to locate their production units, to exploit these advantages, in the home country or a foreign country.
   2. It is possible to identify the nature of these advantages by reference to (a) industrial organization theory, (b) location theory, and (c) the theory of the firm.
   3. The extent to which one country's enterprises possess the capacity and willingness to produce abroad will *inter alia* depend on (a) country-, (b) industry-, and (c) enterprise-specific factors. These factors (particularly a and b) are clearly interlinked, but given a and b, the advantages just described will differ among enterprises; given a and c, they will differ among industries; and given b and c, they will differ among countries.
   4. Countries vary in their propensity to engage in foreign direct investment or be invested in because of their different (a) levels and structures of resource endowments, (b) sizes and characteristics of markets, and (c) government policies (for example, toward foreign direct investment,

Table 1-6
Inward and Outward Direct-Investment Flows for Brazil and South Korea, 1960-1977
(Annual Average, Millions of Dollars)

	(a) Inward[a]	(b) Outward[a]	(b)/(a)
Brazil			
1975-1977	1,555	135	8.7%
1972-1974	1,100	45	4.1
1969-1971	403	10	2.5
1966-1969	161	0	0
1963-1965	109	0	0
1960-1962	139	0	0
South Korea			
1975-1977	150	13	8.7
1972-1974	198	7	3.5
1969-1971	64	2	3.1
1966-1968	11	0	0
1963-1965	2	0	0
1960-1962	0	0	0

[a]Includes author's estimates of reinvested profits for some years.

innovation, industrial concentration, and so forth). These differences will reflect themselves in the extent and kind of ownership, location, and internalization advantages that different countries possess and, *inter alia*, the industrial spread of their outward and inward direct investment and capital stake.

5. There is some evidence to suggest that the forces determining the level of inward and outward direct investment and the balance between the two are linked to a country's stage of development and that it is reasonable to think of a four-stage investment-development process or cycle, in which, after the first stage of little inward and outward investment, inward investment rises markedly, then outward investment begins to rise and/or inward investment falls but NOI is still negative, and finally NOI becomes positive. The developing countries now emerging as outward investors are approaching the third stage.

6. At any particular stage of development, countries may differ from each other in their international investment involvement and structures. The deviations from the average NOI can be explained by different country-specific characteristics, which are reflected in the possession of ownership, location, and internalization advantages set out earlier.

7. The eclectic theory also may be used to explain changes in the outward/inward investment (or capital stake) ratio of a particular country over

time—either in the short or medium period or in the long run. In the case of the one industrialized country—the United Kingdom—a rising outward/inward direct capital stake in manufacturing industry between 1960 and 1976 reflected both rising ownership advantages on the part of U.K. firms and falling location advantages on the part of the United Kingdom as a site for production. One suspects that in the more recent past, for example, since around 1973, the falling outward/inward investment stake of the United States has reflected the opposite combination of forces. In the case of the two developing countries—Brazil and South Korea—chosen for illustration, the rising outward/inward investment primarily reflects the rising ownership advantages of their own enterprises vis-à-vis those of other countries. Here, it should be noted that ownership-specific advantages, for example, size of firm, also may account for part of these advantages, as may the geographic distribution of the investment.[18]

8. Any attempt to forecast the future of outward direct investment by developing countries must rest, therefore, on the answer to the following question: To what extent do the specific endowment, market, and environmental characteristics of developing countries, either taken as a group or individually, generate ownership advantages for their enterprises relative to those generated by developing countries, which are best exploited by foreign direct investment rather than by exports or portfolio resource transfers? Anything that generates such advantages by favoring the particular characterization of developing countries will aid their foreign investment; anything that does not favor these characteristics will work in the opposite direction.

9. The empirical data of this chapter have been couched exclusively in terms of inward and outward investment flows. A complete explanatory model of the kind described would need data on exports and imports and on portfolio resource flows, for investment flows reflect both the ownership advantages of firms *and* the way in which these are exploited. A change in either or both may affect the timing and nature of both the investment-development cycle described in this chapter and the position of a particular country at a point in the cycle.

Notes

1. For a more detailed discussion of this theory, see Dunning (1977, 1979*a*, and 1980).

2. Defined as arms-length sale or leasing of factors of production, including technology.

3. Although there is an increasing overlap between the explanation of behaviorists and economists, for example, with respect to size, age, market structure, and diversification policy.

4. International Monetary Fund (IMF) data, but for some countries, also incorporating author's estimates for reinvested profits. Investment then embraces capital flows and reinvested profits, but because of differences in interpretation of the threshold of direct investment, the valuation of profits and the significance of intracompany debts, the data should be regarded as approximate and not directly comparable between countries.

5. I have chosen to express my data in terms of average investment flows; it would have been possible (and it would have produced exactly the same intercountry patterns) to have taken the aggregate investment flows over the period in question, which is long enough for the flow to be a reasonably good proxy of the stock of investment at the end of the period.

6. Note that the income ranges covered by countries whose investment behavior is classified in groups 3 and 4 overlap. This suggests that especially in these later stages, investment behavior cannot be fully explained by GNP per capita. As we shall see, the eclectic theory aspires to explain these exceptional cases as well as the more normal cases.

7. Especially if they perceive that supplying foreign markets from a foreign location is likely to involve them in less risk than supplying them from a domestic location. It does not seem unreasonable to assume that the more risk a particular country is thought to be as a location for inward investment, the more likely its own firms will be prompted to exploit foreign markets from a foreign production base.

8. It has been suggested that a more appropriate measure, particularly in the later stages of development, would be the relative level of development, that is, the outward investment ratio of the United States may decrease as its GNP per capita increases, if the GNP of its major competitors was increasing at a faster rate.

9. The rank correlation for the twenty-six countries with a positive outward investment was 0.86.

10. Since this chapter was completed, some statistical testing has been attempted on an extended coverage of countries. See Dunning 1981.

11. By the same token, a country on the line could be deviating from the norm in both its outward and inward investment, but the two deviations cancel themselves out.

12. This might include (natural) resource-based, export-platform, and rationalized-product-specialization investment (for example, as in the European Economic Community).

13. For further illustrations of foreign direct investment by developing countries, see Lecraw (1977), Heenan and Keegan (1979), Wells (1977 and 1978), and Diaz-Alejandro (1977), and Lall (1979).

14. Partly, of course, this is a function of industry- and country-specific characteristics of the firms.

15. Even the preceding paragraph ignores that part of a country's changing position in terms of the changing propensity to internalize the inputs and export of resources.

16. To help even out fluctuations on a year-by-year investment flow, for example, owing to takeovers and so forth.

17. Foreign firms in the case of outward resource flows; domestic firms in the case of inward resource flows.

18. For example, owing to such factors as geographic and/or psychic distance or proximity; cultural, political, and economic ties, and so forth. Note that the geographic distribution of foreign investment of less-developed countries (LDCs) is very different from that of most developed countries. This reflects, *inter alia*, that the ownership/internalization advantage of one country's enterprises over those of another may vary considerably according to the destination of the investment. See also Stopford's explanation of the geographic composition of U.K. direct investment (Stopford, 1976).

References

Aharoni, Y. 1973. *The Foreign Investment Decision Process*. Cambridge, Mass.: Harvard Univ. Press.

Brooke, M.Z., and Remmers, H.L., 1970. *The Strategy of Multinational Enterprise*. London: Longman.

Bornschier, V. 1978. *Multinational Corporations in the World Economy and National Development*. Sociologisches Institut der Universität, Zurich.

Diaz-Alejandro, C.F. 1977. Foreign direct investment by Latin Americans. In T. Agmon and C.P. Kindleberger (Eds.), *Multinationals from Small Countries*. Cambridge, Mass.: M.I.T. Press.

Dunning, J.H. 1977. Trade, location of economic activity and the multinational enterprise. A search for an eclectic approach. In B. Ohlin, P.O. Hesselborn, and P.J. Wiskman (Eds.), *The International Allocation of Economic Activity*. London: Macmillan.

_____ . 1979*a*. Explaining changing patterns of international production: in defence of the eclectic theory. *Oxford Bulletin of Economics and Statistics* 41 (November).

_____ . 1979*b*. The UK's international investment position in the mid 1970s. *Lloyds Bank Review* (July).

_____ . 1980. Trade, location of economic activity and the multinational enterprise. Some empirical issues. *Journal of International Business Studies* 10 (Spring/Summer).

_____ . 1981. Explaining the international direct investment position of countries; towards a dynamic approach. *Weltwirtschaftliches Archiv* 117, Heft 1.

Heenan, D.A., and Keegan, W.J. 1979. The rise of third world multinationals. *Harvard Business Review* (January-February).

Lall, S. 1979. Developing countries as exporters of industrial technology. In H. Giersch (Ed.), *International Economic Development and Resource Transfer*. Tubingen: Mohr.

Lecraw, F. 1977. Direct investment by firms from less developed countries. *Oxford Economic Papers* 29.

Prasad, A.J. 1978. Export of technology from India. Unpublished Ph.D. thesis, Columbia University.

Stopford, J.M. 1976. Changing perspectives on investment by British manufacturing multinationals. *Journal of International Business Studies* 7.

Stopford, J.M., and Wells, L.T. 1972. *Managing the Multinational Enterprise*. London: Longman.

Wells, L.T. 1977. The internationalization of firms from developing countries. In T. Agmon and C.P. Kindleberger (Eds.), *Multinationals from Small Countries*. Cambridge, Mass.: M.I.T. Press.

_____ . 1978. Foreign investment from the third world. The experience of Chinese firms from Hong Kong. *Columbia Journal of World Business* (Spring).

2

Foreign Investors from the Third World

Louis T. Wells, Jr.

In the calls for cooperation among the third-world countries, little has been said about the role of foreign private direct investment.[1] While grand schemes are being debated in international organizations, business managers from developing countries have been quietly adapting know-how and transferring appropriate technology to neighboring nations. With little attention and almost no help from governments, small-scale, labor-intensive processes are being spread among developing countries.

Until recently, there had been few data available to estimate the importance of direct-investment flows moving from developing country to developing country, and there had been no studies that examined the kinds of transfers of technology that have accompanied the investments. This chapter reports recently available evidence on both these matters. Further, it speculates on the reasons why certain third-world firms have been able to survive abroad against the competition of both multinationals and local firms in the markets where they invest.

Some Facts

In connection with my study of foreign investment from the developing countries, approximately 1,100 foreign-owned projects in less-developed countries (LDCs) have thus far been identified as having parents in other developing countries. The projects recorded apparently represent only a fraction of the total number of foreign investments undertaken by developing-country firms. Data from other sources also indicate that such investments are numerous and that they are rapidly growing. The U.N. Center on Transnational Corporations reports a little more than $180 million direct investments from other Latin American Free Trade Association (LAFTA) countries in the mid-1970s in Argentina, Brazil, Chile, Colombia, Ecuador, Mexico, and Venezuela. Perhaps more significant, the growth rates have been spectacular. In Brazil, the total moved from $22.6 million in 1971 to $42.2 million in 1976. In Colombia, the total more than doubled from 1971 to 1975. In Ecuador and Venezuela, the totals more than

This material is based upon work supported by the National Science Foundation under Grant No. PRA78-10238. Any opinions, findings, conclusions, or recommendations expressed in this publication are those of the author and do not necessarily reflect the views of the National Science Foundation.

23

tripled from 1971 to 1976 and 1970 to 1974, respectively. (No growth figures were available for the other countries.) In 1976, Thailand, Indonesia, the Philippines, and Hong Kong reported direct-investment stock from other developing Asian countries of over $1.5 billion, according to the U.N. Center.

There can be little doubt that the statistics reported by developing countries considerably underestimate the flows of direct investments within the third world. Much of such investment is either outright illegal or at the edge of legality under the laws of the country in which the parent enterprise is located. I have encountered Peruvian managers, for example, who are unwilling to talk to researchers about their firms' foreign investments because of their possible violations of Peruvian exchange controls. Indian firms have used their registered foreign subsidiaries to establish further subsidiaries, avoiding the watchful eye of Indian bureaucracy and the published data. Moreover, some of the firms from the developing countries are particularly adept at evading registration as foreign investors in their host countries. One of their objectives is to invest in sectors that are officially closed to foreign investment. For example, Hong Kong firms operate in Indonesia as domestic investors through unregistered joint ventures.

The vast majority of the manufacturing investments originate in the developing countries that have large industrial sectors. In Latin America, Argentina, Brazil, and Mexico are the principal sources, it seems. In Asia, the largest fraction of investment comes from Hong Kong, Korea, India, Malaysia, and Singapore. Only a very occasional firm undertakes direct investment from Bolivia, Bangladesh, or a West African country.

The greatest fraction of the investment is to countries at a lower or, occasionally, the same level of industrialization as the parent. The flows would typically be from, say, Argentina to Bolivia or from India to Indonesia rather than the reverse. There are few manufacturing subsidiaries of developing-country firms in the industrialized countries. Those which do exist are almost all support facilities for exports from the parent enterprise. Typical would be a final assembly plant for components produced at home, such as a Hong Kong-owned furniture assembly plant in the United States.

Moreover, most subsidiaries of developing-country firms are located within the region of the home firm. Indian firms rarely venture beyond the Indian Ocean; Hong Kong firms usually establish their subsidiaries within Southeast Asia; the horizons of Latin American firms rarely extend outside South or Central America. Indeed, there are exceptions; a few Hong Kong firms have spread their investments as far as West Africa, for example, and a number have established export operations in Mauritius. However, such far-flung operations account for only a small fraction of the total investments.

In spite of some well-publicized foreign projects undertaken by state-owned firms from the developing countries, the vast majority of the investments emanate from privately owned companies. Given the importance of state-owned firms in many of the developing countries, the infrequency of state-owned foreign projects may be a bit surprising. From the evidence at hand, it seems that state-owned firms are more likely to sell their know-how outright; the private firm is prone to supply its technology through direct investment. Given the reluctance of governments to see capital flow abroad, it is hardly surprising that state enterprises find it difficult to obtain home support for overseas investment.[2]

**Theory of Foreign Direct Investment and LDC
Manufacturing Firms**

Much of the theory of foreign direct investment starts from the assumption that certain firms have some sort of special assets that give them a competitive edge abroad.[3] Various theories take different approaches to determine which firms are likely to have exploitable assets and whether they are likely to exploit those assets abroad through direct investment or by selling them to an enterprise in a foreign country.

For a decade or so, attention has focused on the nature of the assets that might make a firm competitive abroad. The product life-cycle theory proposes one model. According to its premises, firms innovate for their home market, generating skills and knowlege that, in some cases, are then exploitable abroad. Since managers are responsive to their home markets, the nature of a particular firm's advantage is influenced by the characteristics of that firm's national market. Given the nature of the U.S. market, U.S. firms are particularly likely to generate high-income and labor-saving products or processes. As incomes and labor costs increase outside the United States, the skills acquired at home by U.S. firms turn into assets that can be exploited elsewhere. The peculiar nature of the U.S. market, as a bellwether of other markets, has led to the particular vitality of U.S.-based multinationals, according to the theory.

Innovation is not a U.S. monopoly, of course; firms of other countries also have innovated, but in response to their own home-market characteristics. European and Japanese firms, for example, might (and have, according to the data available) develop raw-material- or capital-saving products or processes. Through such innovations, these firms would acquire a competitive edge in these kinds of manufacture. To the extent that markets foreign to the innovating enterprises provide outlets for similar products or processes, firms are likely to be able to exploit their skills abroad.

As incomes in Europe and Japan have caught up with U.S. incomes, and as the European Economic Community (EEC) has become a reality, the argument that differences in home markets might explain differences among multinational firms from the industrialized countries has become less persuasive.[4] Although the markets of the industrialized countries are tending to converge, the differences between the markets in the industrialized countries and those in the developing countries still remain very substantial. The power of the product life-cycle model may be waning for explaining differences among investors from the industrialized nations, but it still provides a powerful framework for examining investment from the developing nations.

More recently, the attention of researchers has been focused on why firms choose to exploit their skills through direct investment abroad rather than by selling their skills to overseas firms. Licensing arrangements and other forms of transfer, it would seem, could provide a return for the innovators equal to that accruing from direct investment. However, where the transfer of knowledge is involved, there are often significant advantages in "internalizing" the transfer.[5] It seems that firms from the developing countries choose to internalize the use of their skills abroad for reasons similar to those which influence firms from industrialized nations. Direct investment reflects market imperfections that can be overcome by transferring the skills inside the enterprise.

If certain firms from the developing countries have skills that enable them to earn profits abroad, what are they? Remember that developing-country investors must survive abroad against local firms, which are likely to know the market for products and factors of production more intimately than any foreign enterprise. Moreover, local firms are likely to be preferred by the host government. In addition, investors from the developing countries must survive against multinational enterprises from the advanced countries. Thus the firms from another developing country must have signficant skills that compare favorably with those of both groups of potential competitors.

The special assets of the developing-country investors appear, like those of the multinationals, to derive from the peculiar nature of their home markets. Those markets are, in certain aspects, sufficiently different from those of the industrialized countries that they generate quite different innovations and thus skills to exploit.

Data for foreign investment in Indonesia, the Philippines, Mauritius, and Taiwan underline the difference between the firms from other developing countries and investors from the industrialized nations. Previous research had pointed out that multinationals from the industrialized countries are concentrated in industries that are characterized by large expenditures on research and development (R&D) and on efforts to differentiate products. The distribution of firms from developing countries is markedly different, as the tables 2-1 and 2-2 show. Findings for Mauritius, the Philippines, and Taiwan seem to be similar.[6] The different skills of the

Table 2-1
Product Differentiation and Origin of Investors (Indonesia)

Percent of Sales of Industry Spent on Advertising[a] (U.S.)	Number of Industries (3-Digit SIC)	
	In Which LDC Firms Are Proportionally More Important	In Which Developed-Country Firms Are Proportionally More Important
Low advertising (less than 1 percent)	7	9
Medium advertising (1 percent or more, but less than 2 percent)	1[b]	3
High advertising (2 percent or more)	1[b]	7

Source: Louis T. Wells, Jr., and V'Ella Warren, "Developing Country Investors in Indonesia," *Bulletin of Indonesian Economic Studies* (March 1979).
[a]Data available only for a limited number of industries.
[b]Industries with only one investor from a developing country.

developing-country firms appear to lead them, in many cases, into different industries from those that attract enterprises from the industrialized nations.

One characteristic of the developing-country markets that seems important in creating special skills is size. Another is the shortage of many inputs for the production process. For a wide range of manufacturing products, the markets in the less industrialized countries are relatively small. Moreover, in most such countries labor is relatively abundant and inexpensive. However, imported components and materials are expensive and difficult for local manufacturers to lay their hands on. High tariffs, licensing, and foreign-exchange controls limit the availability of imported inputs. Thus there are incentives for the entrepreneur to develop small-scale, labor-intensive processes and products and to find ways to substitute available local inputs for imported ones.

It is from innovations that reflect these peculiarities that a number of firms in the more advanced developing countries have generated special skills. They have then discovered that those skills are exploitable in other countries. Almost inevitably they can be applied in countries further down the ladder of development. There, markets later provide opportunities and challenges of the kind to which the firm has already responded at home.

The small size of the market in most developing countries has led a number of firms to develop technology for manufacturing in small volumes. In some cases, the technology used is similar to what was once used by firms in the industrialized countries. The old techniques have,

Table 2-2
R&D and Origin of Investors (Indonesia)

Percent of Sales of Industry Spent on R&D[a] (U.S.)	Number of Industries (3-Digit SIC)	
	In Which LDC Firms Are Proportionally More Important	In Which Developed-Country Firms Are Proportionally More Important
Low R&D (less than 1 percent)	9	49
Medium R&D (1 percent or more, but less than 2.5 percent)	2	9
High R&D (2.5 percent or more)	3[b]	13

Source: Louis T. Wells, Jr., and V'Ella Warren, "Developing Country Investors in Indonesia," *Bulletin of Indonesian Economic Studies* (March 1979).

[a]Data available for only a limited number of industries.

[b]281 (industrial inorganic chemicals), 282 (plastic materials and synthetic resins, synthetic rubber, synthetics and other man-made fibers), and 371 (motor vehicles), which contains only one LDC firm.

however, usually been abandoned and forgotten by enterprises accustomed to mass markets. Nevertheless, the adaptations required to turn large-scale processes into small-scale ones may, in some cases, seem rather trivial. Equipment may simply be scaled down or some hand operations may be substituted for automated processes that involve large-scale equipment. In other cases, however, the technology is more original.

Regardless of the type of adaptation that must be made, an important aspect of the design of most small-volume plants is flexibility. Many firms in developing countries have found ways of using multipurpose equipment. This equipment can be used to make various parts of a product, or it can be adapted to manufacture alternative models of an item or even different products. Extra pieces of certain equipment might be on hand in the factory so that production can be shifted to variants of a particular product, and so on. An illustration of this aspect of plant design in projects owned by developing-country investors is provided by an Indian firm operating in Indonesia. The original plant was built and owned by a U.S. parent. It was designed to manufacture long runs of a single grade of textile. When the plant soon ran into financial trouble, it was sold to an Indian firm, which quickly modified and replaced machinery so that the factory could be used to manufacture a broad and shifting line of textiles. Within a couple of years, the losses had virtually disappeared and profits seemed just around the corner. A large part of the turnaround seemed to result from the ability of the redesigned plant to operate closer to capacity by producing for the many small market segments in the developing country.

The fact that developing-country investors exploit skills based on flexibility in product line has another consequence. It seems to be one of the reasons why such firms concentrate in the principal cities of their host countries. In Indonesia, for example, two-thirds of the LDC investors have located their plants in Jakarta, while less than half of the multinationals from the industrialized countries have chosen that site for manufacturing. A likely explanation for the different locations is as follows. The multinational that produces long runs of standardized products expects to influence demand considerably through its own marketing programs. Since forecasting and responding quickly to changes in demand are less critical for such a firm, it can locate production facilities far from the market without penalty. However, the firm whose life depends on quick response to fleeting market signals is likely to locate its facilities close to those markets. Only so can it be immediately sensitive to the signals and cut the lead time in getting the right products to market. The developing-country investors seem more frequently to fall into this latter category.

Small-scale manufacture is often inherently more labor-intensive than large-scale production. The empirical evidence is now rather convincing that the technologies employed by foreign investors from developing countries are indeed more labor-intensive than the technologies of the multinationals from the industrialized countries. In Indonesia, the average developing-country investor used $2,500 of capital per worker; the average advance-country firm in Indonesia, $16,500.[8] One study has even demonstrated that foreign investors from the developing countries use more labor-intensive technologies than those used by local competitors in the markets in which they invest.[9]

The expense and scarcity of imported materials and components have led firms in developing countries to find ways of using standard, locally available inputs. In fact, a study of R&D in Indian firms reported that the principal aim of R&D in Indian firms was to find ways to avoid the need to import.[10] Once a firm has found ways of using local materials, that skill can be useful in other countries that have similar scarcities and similarly available local substitutes. It has been said that the success of Indian firms in vegetable oil processing abroad is a result of the technologies they developed in response to government restrictions at home on the import of vegetable oils and the use of edible oils for soap production.

There are other innovations by firms in developing countries that can lead to foreign investment. An Indian firm, for example, has developed dyes that are less sensitive to intensive sunlight than the dyes generally available from the temperate industrialized countries. It has been able to exploit the formulations abroad.

Innovations in response to small markets, scarce foreign inputs, and other special characteristics of developing-country markets fit well into the product life-cycle theory. However, one must still explain why firms choose direct investment rather than sale of the skills through license agreements or machinery exports to exploit their know-how. Developing-country firms choose to exploit their skills through direct investment for reasons that appear to be rather similar to those governing the decisions of the multinationals from the advanced countries, but there are some peculiarities as well.

Very similar are the problems of evaluating an asset about which the buyer knows few details and the seller cannot reveal more without losing control over the asset. In the case of equipment, the problem is further complicated. In many cases of developing-country skills, much of the skill is embodied in the machinery itself. In a world of perfect markets, the machinery could be sold to a would-be user abroad for a price that reflected the competitive edge its ownership would convey. Like the buyer of such assets from a firm from the industrialized country, a potential purchaser would need some assurance that the value of the asset would not be eroded by further sales to local competitors. More important, however, buyer and seller are simply not likely to come together. Although the machinery markets are well developed for equipment from the industrialized countries, marketing networks are not generally in place for equipment from the developing nations. Moreover, it would be a rare local entrepreneur to whom it would seem a sensible proposition to seek out his plant in countries outside Japan, Europe, or North America.

Even though technology is sometimes embodied in machinery, in many cases it is captured in the knowledge of managers, evolving out of their experience. This appears to be especially the case for the special skills of developing-country firms in small-scale manufacture. While the multinational enterprises can, in many cases, capture in machinery and manuals much of their production know-how for the more mature products they make in developing countries, the task is a much more formidable one for a plant based on flexible use of equipment for constantly changing short runs of various lines. The complex task of managing such a process is not easily reduced to a manual—or conveyed quickly to a local manager.

Indeed, the difficulty of transferring the managerial know-how is probably one of the important factors in leading developing-country investors to use more expatriate personnel than do multinationals from the industrialized countries.[11] (Of course, the lower cost of managers from other developing countries, compared with the cost of managers from the advanced countries must play a significant role as well.)

The problem of transferring skills to another country is compounded when the firm has not faced the need at home to codify its knowledge. Since the parent from the developing country is generally much smaller than the parent of a multinational, and since the parent is not likely to have branch plants in the home country, the developing-country firm has usually not faced the need to transfer skills from individual to individual or from one plant to another. Moreover, with close physical proximity among managers and, in many cases, close family relationships, the developing-country firms have rarely developed formal control systems.[12]

Note that the state enterprises from the developing countries are somewhat more likely to have encountered the need to develop formal systems at home than have their private counterparts. More rapid turnover of management, a larger management cadre, and larger operations mean that some systemization has been required at home. As an explanation of why such firms apparently prefer licensing or other forms of sale when they transfer technology to other countries, the existence of formal systems that are more easily transferred to other enterprises probably supplement the easily understood bureaucratic difficulties faced by a government-owned enterprise in investing abroad.

Nonmanufacturing Firms

The product life-cycle framework provides a fairly powerful tool for understanding the foreign direct investments of manufacturing firms based in the developing countries (for the export-oriented firms, see my "Foreign Investment from the Third World"). However, a significant number of overseas direct investments from the developing countries are not for manufacturing. In the case of service and raw-material investments it seems that foreign investment is induced by factors quite similar to those which led to the internationalization of nonmanufacturing firms from the industrialized countries.

Consider the banks. Without any systematic effort to that end, I have identified 325 overseas branches and subsidiaries of 72 banks headquartered in the developing countries. The geographic spread of the banks is quite different from the spread of manufacturing investments. In fact, some 100 of the overseas operations are in the industrialized countries.

Interviews with managers of a small number of banks from developing countries suggest reasons for their international spread that have close parallels to the reasons for the spread of banks based in the industrialized countries. The principal reasons fall into three categories: to serve their home firms, to serve foreign firms, and to serve their own needs.

The initial establishment of overseas operations appears to stem primarily from the need on the part of the bank to serve customers at home who have businesses abroad. Serving exporters appears to be the main drive. If the banks do not establish a presence in export markets to handle credit evaluations, export documentation, and so on, domestic customers selling in those markets will, the bank fears, turn to established international banks for their needs. The result is likely to be a loss even of some business at home to the local branches of those international banks. Thus it is not surprising to find that developing-country banks have established branches of subsidiaries in principal markets for their exports. Thai banks, for example, have branches where Thai exporters sell rice.

In developing countries that host significant investments from multinational enterprises, local banks would like to capture the business of those firms. However, without a presence in the multinationals' home countries, the local banks will, they fear, lose that business to the established international banks. Thus major banks from countries open to foreign investment have in many cases established branches or subsidiaries in New York, Houston, London, and elsewhere to serve those multinational customers. Brazil's Banco Real, for example, is establishing a network of U.S. facilities to serve U.S. firms with Brazilian subsidiaries.

Finally, the banks from developing countries have established certain operations abroad to assist in placing their funds in foreign markets. Banks with dollar and sterling assets have found it convenient to manage those assets out of their own branches in New York and London rather than handling the funds from a distance or relying on correspondent relationships.

Of course, once established, the overseas subsidiaries and branches conduct business other than that which was primarily responsible for their establishment. Local loans, local deposits, and international remittances, especially involving expatriates from the banks' countries of origin, provide additional business.

Although a few consulting and accountancy firms provide stories similar to those of the banks, engineering consultancies and construction firms fall into a rather different category, it seems. To a large extent, the construction and engineering firms from the developing countries are involved in the export of factors of production: technical and manual work forces. In both cases, they provide labor to countries short of manpower—particularly in the oil-rich Middle East—from countries with abundant manpower: India and Brazil, particularly, for engineers; the Philippines, Korea, and elsewhere for construction labor.

Similar services have long been provided by firms from the advanced countries, but they face much more expensive labor costs and, for typical projects, no longer have a technological edge. Indeed, the developing-country firms may, in some cases, have technical advantages, with their experience in the design of small-scale facilities, the use of locally available materials, or in construction to a lower standard of finish, but the principal advantage of such firms appears not to be in technology, but rather in their ability to offer adequate human factors of production at a low cost to other developing countries where those factors happen to be expensive.

The relatively few raw-material investments by firms from developing countries evidence motivations rather similar to those which led firms into foreign raw materials from the industrialized countries. In most cases, there was an advantage to be gained from vertical integration. Hong Kong furniture manufacturers have, for example, integrated into timber operations in Borneo when faced with concentrated suppliers, erratic prices and quantity, and an inability to establish reliable long-term sales contracts.[13] Perhaps unique has been the motivation of timber firms in the Philippines. Faced with exhausted concession areas at home, some of these firms have simply moved their trained crews and their equipment across to nearby Indonesian and Malaysian Borneo to continue logging. In these special cases, the firms seem to be more like the construction firms: they provide skilled manpower to skill-scarce Borneo.

In a few cases, state enterprises have sought raw materials abroad for reasons reminiscent of the behavior of state firms from Europe. In attempts to control sources of raw materials independent of the multinationals, they have attempted to exploit foreign sources in the national interest. An Indian enterprise, for example, has taken part in efforts to explore for oil in the Middle East. The Brazilian national oil company has joined in drilling efforts in other countries.

Government Policies

Few host governments have explicit policies either to discourage or to encourage foreign investment from other developing countries. A very small number of countries have sought investors from other developing countries. Mauritius has courted Hong Kong firms with access to export markets, for example, but the only explicit differentiation in treatment of developing-country and other investors that I have encountered is that of Egypt, which distinguishes between foreign and Arab investors, allowing the latter to invest in certain industries closed to other foreign investors. In spite of the lack of explicit policies, in practice the policies of many developing countries discriminate against investors from neighboring lands.

In a number of countries, the discrimination is a result of ethnic bias. In some Southeast Asian countries, where resident Chinese minorities are only tolerated, Chinese investors from Taiwan and Hong Kong are not the preferred choice of foreign-investment authorities. Similarly, there may be feelings against Indian investors in countries that have unpopular Indian minorities.

In many countries there is bias against investors from developing countries that arises out of the behavior of bureaucrats. The civil servant who fears that he must justify his decision at some later date is more likely to prefer a well-known firm from an industrialized country to an unknown company from another poor country. After all, who can blame him if a Sherwin-Williams, CPC, or Colgate does not do what it promised or fails in the future. However, the risks seem much higher for a Teck Chiang Manufacturing, CIPCA, or Acme Electrical Industries.

Other aspects of government policy serve to discourage investment from developing countries. Perhaps primary among these is the long approval process required by some host countries. The large investor is usually better equipped to spend the management time required to shepherd a proposal through a costly approval process than is the small investor.

Moreover, the developing-country investor's advantage in small scale, labor-intensive technologies is eroded by the many policies that favor large-scale, capital-intensive manufacture in the third world. These include tax incentives based on size of investment, financial instititutions that prefer to lend against fixed assets, restrictions on imports of second-hand equipment, prices of labor and machinery tilted against the use of labor, and labor laws that turn labor into a fixed cost. Correction of some of the policies discouraging investors from other developing countries might well lead to an increased inflow of small-scale, labor-intensive technology. Although developing-country investors bring their own special kinds of problems, an increase in such investment can make some contribution to reducing unemployment and to spreading more appropriate skills in host countries. This is a complex issue, however, and it involves estimates of the access of the firms to export markets and their impact on local suppliers, for example.

Less surprisingly, home governments also have not been very helpful to the international spread of their firms. Some countries, such as India and Taiwan, have instituted a formal approval process for outgoing investment. Some countries, such as Hong Kong, have done nothing to discourage overseas ventures. There are a very few countries, such as Korea, that provide incentives in the form of insurance and fiscal benefits to investors that can demonstrate substantial net benefits for the home country. For the home country, certain potential gross benefits can be identified easily, but only with extreme difficulty can they be weighed against the costs. The receipts for technology, through royalties and dividends, represent income from technology that may have been purchased elsewhere and for development already undertaken at home. Associated exports, in the form of materials, complementary products, and most important, machinery, would probably not have been made without the investment. On the cost side, the investment may entail a foreign-exchange outflow and the utilization abroad of entrepreneurial, management, and technical persons who might have been active at home. Their opportunity costs must be estimated for any complete calculation of the costs and benefits to the home country.

Whatever the costs and benefits as perceived by the governments involved, it appears that the ingenuity of managers in developing countries will ensure the continued spread of such projects. Large numbers of firms have found ways to work around the restrictions imposed on them.

Notes

1. On the subject of foreign direct investment from the developing countries, see Carlos Diaz-Alejandro, "Foreign Investment by Latin Americans," and Louis T. Wells, Jr., "The Internationalization of Firms from the Developing Countries," in T. Agmon and C.P Kindleberger (eds.), *Multinationals from Small Countries* (Cambridge, Mass: M.I.T. Press, 1977); K. Balakrishnan, "Indian Joint Ventures Abroad: Geographic and Industry Patterns," *Economic and Political Weekly* 11(22); David A. Heenan and Warren J. Keegan, "The Rise of Third World Multinationals," *Harvard Business Review* (January-February 1979):101-109; Peter O'Brien, Syed Asif Hasnain, Eduardo Luchuga Jimenez, "Direct Foreign Investment and Technology Exports among Developing Countries: An Empirical Analysis of the Prospects for Third World Cooperation" (Vienna, January 1979, mimeographed); Eduardo White et al., *Las Empresas Conjuntas Latinoamericanas* (Buenos Aires: IN- TAL, 1977); Donald Lecraw, "Direct Investment by Firms from Less Developed Countries," *Oxford Economic Papers* 29 (3):442-457; Louis T. Wells, Jr., and V'Ella Warren, "Developing Country Investors in In- donesia," *Bulletin of Indonesian Economic Studies* (March 1979):70-84; Louis T. Wells, Jr., "Foreign Investment from the Third World: The Ex- perience of Chinese Firms from Hong Kong," *Columbia Journal of World Business* (Spring 1978); "The New Multinationals," *Business India*, August 20 to September 2, 1979; and the UNCTAD series: "Joint Ventures among Asian countries," by Ram Gopal Agrawal; "Joint Ventures among Arab Countries," by Ibrahim F.I. Shihata; "Joint Ventures among African Countries," by Pius N.C. Okigho; and "Joint Ventures among Latin American Countries," by Antonio Casas-Gonzalez.

2. U.N. Commission on Transnational Corporations, *Transnational Corporations in World Development: A Re-examination* (New York: U.N. ECOSOC, 1978), pp. 246-247.

3. This chapter does not discuss the firms from developing countries that have set up manufacturing plants in other developing countries to sup- ply export markets. For a discussion of these firms, see Wells, "Foreign In- vestment from the Third World."

4. See Raymond Vernon, "The Product Cycle Hypothesis in a New In- ternational Environment," *Oxford Bulletin of Economics and Statistics* (forthcoming).

5. See Peter J. Buckley and Mark Casson, *The Future of the Multina- tional Enterprise* (New York: Holmes and Meier, 1976).

6. Vinod Busjeet, doctoral dissertation in progress at Harvard Business School; and Wen-Lee Ting, "Transfers of Intermediate Technology by

Third World Multinationals'' (Tatung Institute of Technology, Taiwan, 1979, mimeographed).

7. Wells and Warren, "Developing Country Investors in Indonesia."

8. Ibid.

9. Lecraw, "Direct Investment by Firms from Less Developed Countries."

10. Ashok V. Desai, "Research and Development in India," Margin (January 1975):54-55

11. Wells and Warren, "Developing Country Investors in Indonesia."

12. Data collected by Vinod Busjeet in the Philippines and Mauritius confirm the lack of formal systems in LDC-based international firms.

13. See Wells, "Foreign Investment from the Third World."

3 Internationalization of Firms from LDCs: Evidence from the ASEAN Region

Donald J. Lecraw

Recently firms in less-developed countries (LDCs) have begun to make foreign direct investments (FDI) in other LDCs and, in a few instances, in developed countries. FDI by private firms from LDCs has been small compared with that of other transnational corporations (TNCs) and hence it has gone largely unnoticed.[1] Not surprisingly, little research has been carried out on these firms. Their impact on the economies of home and host countries, however, may be substantial and may differ from that of firms based in developed countries.

This chapter suggests a theory to explain the internationalization of firms in LDCs, tests some of the implications of that theory using data collected from a sample of firms in the ASEAN region, and analyzes the ability of firms from LDCs to compete with TNCs from developed countries and the effect of this competition on the economy of the host country.

The Sample

The data used in the analysis were collected from a sample of twenty-three firms based in LDCs that had invested in the five countries of the ASEAN region: Thailand, Malaysia, Singapore, Indonesia, and the Philippines.[2] The characteristics and activities of these firms were compared with those of 130 TNCs from developed countries that operated in the same six industries in the ASEAN countries. The ASEAN region was used for this study for two specific reasons. First, in general, the countries in ASEAN have been open to FDI from all countries and of almost all types.[3] Barriers to FDI historically have been low or nonexistent; that is, firms that have desired to invest were able to do so largely unhampered by host-country legislation or practice, except in a few strategic industries. Consequently, the patterns of FDI have not been distorted by host-government policies to the extent that they have been in many other less-developed countries.

Second, the ASEAN countries have all had a high level of FDI from all the major groups of home countries: the United States, Europe, Japan, and other LDCs. This allowed an analysis of the impact of FDI from each of the

The research and writing of this chapter were partially funded by the United Nations Center on Transnational Corporations and the Center for International Business Studies, School of Business Administration, University of Western Ontario.

groups as well as an analysis of how firms from the different home countries compete with each other and with locally-owned firms.

A drawback of using the ASEAN region for the study was that the private foreign direct investment by firms from LDCs (hereafter FL) had been carried out largely by firms whose owners came from two ethnic groups of regions: the Chinese, and those from the Indian subcontinent. Hence the analysis based on this sample may lead to some conclusions that cannot be generalized to firms from other LDCs that have made investments in other regions. This characteristic of the sample can be seen in table 3-1. Although the FL was undertaken by firms from seven countries, the owners of all but one of the firms were either Chinese or Indian.

The sample used in the analysis of this study comprised 153 firms that had made FDI in the ASEAN region. It was *not* a random sample of the FDI in the region. Six 4-digit industries were selected in which there had been substantial FDI in each of the five countries in the region and in which there was at least one firm operating from each of the four home-country groups—the United States, Europe, Japan, and LDCs. Within the constraints of the overall population of foreign firms, an attempt was made to have an equal representation of foreign firms based in the four home-country groups.

Since much of the information needed for the study concerned the financial characteristics of the firms and their competitive and structural practices, the firms contacted were reluctant to provide the information unless absolute confidentiality could be guaranteed. The number of foreign firms in some of the four-digit industries in some of the countries was so small as to make identification possible even if the name of the firm was not reported. Consequently, to satisfy the needs for confidentiality of the firms that participated in the study, the results of the analysis are given only as industries 1 through 6 and countries A through E. When specific industries or

Table 3-1
Country of Origin and Nationality of LDC Firms

Country	Number of Firms	Ethnic Groups
Taiwan	6	Chinese
Singapore	5	Chinese
Philippines	1	Chinese
India	5	Indian
Pakistan-Bangladesh	1	Pakistani
Hong Kong	4	Chinese
Korea	1	Korean

countries are mentioned, either the industry or the country has been changed so that the industry and country cannot be identified. This procedure limits the usefulness of this study for both academics and those who formulate policy toward FDI in LDCs. The detail and scope of the data, however, could not have been obtained in another way. Hopefully, the benefits of this rich data more than offset the costs of nonidentification of the industries. Even with these confidentiality provisions, the participation rate by firms that were contacted was only slightly over 75 percent. No sample bias between participants and nonparticipants was found along the dimensions of size, industry, or host or home country of the firms.

Methodology

The analysis of this chapter falls into two parts. The first part tests for differences and similarities between LDC firms and other firms that made FDIs in the ASEAN region: size, ownership, structure, choice of technology, financial variables, imports, exports, and so forth. Discriminant analysis is then used to find a discriminant function that uses these variables to identify a firm as based in an LDC or in a developed country. The second part uses multiple regression techniques to analyze the impact of the LDC firms on the competitive environment of the host country and the potential for foreign-owned firms to earn excess profits.

A Theory of FDI by Firms from LDCs

The motivations for FDI by firms from developed countries—the United States, Japan, and Europe—have been described and analyzed at length.[4] The driving forces behind FDI by firms based in LDCs are yet not well understood.[5] The product life-cycle theory of FDI, as formulated by Vernon (1966) and developed by a host of researchers since, cannot be used without major modifications. Until recently, this theory has served as a powerful tool to analyze FDI by TNCs in the manufacturing sector from developed countries.[6] This theory rests on the possession by TNCs of proprietary product and process R&D and marketing and management skills that cannot be efficiently exploited via the market, a high income elasticity of demand for their products, and barriers to trade.[7] These firms usually produce in oligopolistic industries at home. If they reinvest their profit at home and expand output, the structure of their industries would be altered and fierce competition might ensue, thereby lowering profits. Instead, they invest abroad and preserve the oligopolistic structure and competitive environment of their industry at home.[8]

The characteristics of private, locally owned firms in LDCs are completely different from those firms in developed countries that have invested abroad. At first glance, locally owned firms in LDCs do not possess proprietary skills or knowledge in management, technology, or marketing to give them either the motivation or expertise to invest abroad.[9] Their products and production technology are old and freely available on the competitive world market. Their products compete largely on the basis of price both at home and abroad and hence require little marketing skill. These firms operate at home in industries that have low barriers to entry in the form of R&D, product differentiation, large absolute capital costs, and so forth. Standard industrial organization theory would predict that profits for firms in such industries would approach the normal profits of pure competition rather than the oligopolistic profits of the TNCs. If this description is correct, locally owned firms in LDCs would have neither the necessary capital generated from excess profits nor the necessary motivations to preserve the oligopoly structure of their industries at home that have led to FDI from TNCs from developed countries. Yet LDC firms have made direct investments in the ASEAN region in many of the same industries as other TNCs: consumer electronics, drugs, soap, household cleaners, machine tools, paper, textiles and clothing, food processing, and so forth.[10]

This seeming paradox raises two interrelated questions: (1) Why do locally owned firms in LDCs invest in other LDCs? and (2) How can the foreign subsidiaries of these LDC firms compete with the subsidiaries of TNCs from developed countries and with locally owned firms in the host-country market?

One explanation of foreign direct investment by firms from less-developed countries parallels the product life-cycle theory that has been used to explain FDI by TNCs from developed countries. Initially locally owned firms in LDCs produce for their domestic market. Owing to the low level of income and small market size of their home country, their products are of low quality and produced by small-scale, labor-intensive techniques. These firms are protected by generally high tariffs and often quotas or an outright ban on imports. Despite low barriers to entry in the form of large capital costs, low R&D, or advertising, the manufacturing industries in these countries are often highly concentrated. Managerial and entreprenuerial skills are scarce and often concentrated within a small group of families. Moreover, these families often control the channels of distribution. This concentration leads to a generally noncompetitive environment within the modern manufacturing sector.[11] Hence, despite the absence of the barriers to entry that are typical of concentrated industries in developed countries, locally owned firms in LDCs can earn high profits. In addition, they may be reluctant to reinvest in their domestic industry for fear of over-supplying their small domestic market and reducing their profits. One alternative to investment within the "base industry" of the firm is conglomerate diversification within the home country. This route has been taken by some firms in LDCs. A second alternative is to export products to other, usually smaller and less industrially developed, LDCs or to developed countries.

As the economies of the smaller "downstream" LDCs develop in size and level, however, local entrepreneurs may acquire the expertise and capital necessary to begin manufacturing products that had previously been imported from other larger or more developed LDCs, such as Hong Kong, India, Taiwan, Singapore, and Korea. The generally high tariff levels in most LDCs may make production profitable for local firms even if they are not as experienced or efficient as the firms in the other LDCs that had previously supplied the market through their exports. In response to this threat to their export markets, LDC firms may decide to make a direct investment, even though products they had previously exported would then be replaced by local production by their own subsidiary. This scenario is a modified version of the product life-cycle theory of trade and investment, but applied to downstream FDI from more advanced to less advanced LDCs. This chain of hypotheses received some support from the data gathered from the LDC firms in the sample. Of the twenty-three LDC firms, nineteen had supplied their host country with exports prior to making their direct investment.[12]

If firms from LDCs have indeed been motivated to make direct investments to preserve their market share in the host country (as the preceding theory presentation suggests), they could use the same appropriate small-scale technology to produce the same old non-R&D or non-marketing-intensive products that they produce at home. In their home market, the LDC firms may have gained experience in using and adapting labor-intensive, small-scale production techniques to produce undifferentiated products of low to medium quality at low cost. Both the production technology and the products themselves that these firms have produced for their home markets may be well-suited for the factor markets and demand conditions that exist in other LDCs. LDC firms also might tend to use a higher level of local inputs than other foreign firms since the technological sophistication of their products and processes may be lower and the demands for quality output not as great as that for other TNCs. However, since they may use more labor-intensive technology, their need for foreign technicians, supervisors, and general management may be higher than that of other TNCs. They also would tend to export little from their host country, preferring to serve export markets from their home country.

LDC firms might have a higher propensity to form joint ventures for several reasons. First, they have lower R&D expenses incorporated into their products and processes that they want to recoup via payments for technology and management fees. Second, their marketing skills may be limited and may not represent an intangible asset on which they want to earn monopoly returns. In addition, local partners could add their knowledge of local-market conditions and their access to distribution channels in the host countries and hence be an attractive joint-venture partner. Third, LDC firms may not be concerned with the quality image of their products in the local market or abroad so that they may not insist on complete control of the day-to-day management of the production process of the local firm. (As mentioned earlier, however, in order to transfer their relatively labor-intensive technology, LDC firms may find it necessary to use more foreign technicians, engineers, and supervisors in order to train and monitor the local workers.)[13] Fourth, money capital may be scarce or expensive to raise in the home country of the LDC firms, or there may be restrictions on its outflow. Hence LDC firms may welcome local capital participation. Finally, since, in general, the products of LDC firms might well be produced by locally owned firms, LDC firms may be in a weak bargaining position against local entrepreneurs who want a "piece of the action" and their governments that often desire as much local participation as possible.

Even for LDC firms that have traditionally had little or no exports to the host country, there may be reasons to invest in other LDCs. Some firms may have developed expertise in the adaption (or development) and use of small-scale, labor-intensive technology to produce goods that are suitable for the markets in LDCs. Yet trade barriers or lack of familiarity with the marketing system in other countries may have prevented them from exporting. They may see FDI in another LDC as another form of exports, but of their production and product technology rather than their final products. In addition, exports of capital equipment may be a convenient means of transferring capital from the home country and investing it in real assets in another country; that is, FDI via machinery may face fewer restrictions than portfolio investment of money capital. All the LDC firms in the sample used some machinery produced in their home countries, with an average of 38 percent of all machinery used in the production process originating in their home country.[14] Most of this machinery had either been produced by their parent firm or been substantially modified by it to be more efficient in the factor markets in LDCs than that available from developed countries. In short, the parent firms of these LDC firms may have an expertise in product and process technology that could be exploited via FDI in other LDCs.

The owners of firms in LDCs may see another advantage in making a direct investment in another LDC rather than a portfolio investment in either an LDC or a developed country. The home countries of LDC firms often have a high degree of economic and political risk for the firm as a viable privately owned entity and for its stockholders both as recipients of a continued income stream and as private citizens. FDI in another, more stable LDC not only may diversify the risk of the firm, but also may permit some of its owners or members of their families to become long-term residents or citizens of the host country. The importance of this motive cannot be easily determined. One indication that risk diversification did play some role is the finding that several parent firms of the firms in the sample made the investment in the host country specifically to strengthen the position of a member of the owner's family who was already living in the host country and acting as the firm's sales agent in the local market. Investment by firms from India and Taiwan often coincided with periods of political or economic unrest in those countries.

This analysis of some of the potential sources of competitive advantage of LDC firms, their motivations for making direct investments, and the characteristics of that investment provides a number of testable hypotheses concerning the characteristics of LDC firms and their impact on the local economies of their host countries. These hypotheses are summarized in table 3-2.

Testing the Theory of FL

In testing these hypotheses, the small sample size led to many difficulties. There were no LDC firms in the sample in industry 5, and although the sample had at least three LDC firms in each of the five ASEAN countries, they did not invest in all the remaining five industries (1,2,3,4,6) in all the countries; that is, there were substantial gaps in the data (see table 3-3). To try to

Table 3-2
Hypotheses of the Theory of FDI by Firms from Less-Developed Countries

Variable	LDC Firm Compared with Other MNCs
1. Size (S)	Smaller (−)
2. Capital intensity (K/O)	Lower (−)
3. Foreign/local employees (F/L)	Higher(+)
4. Equity participation (EP)	Lower (−)
5. Exports (X)	Lower (−)
6. Imports (M)	Lower (−)
7. Product quality (Q)	Lower (−)
8. Price-cost margin (PC)	Lower (−)
9. Profits (P)	Uncertain
10. Research and development (R&D)	Lower (−)
11. Advertising (A)	Lower (−)

Table 3-3
Distribution of LDC Firms across Countries and Industries

Country	Industry						Total
	1	*2*	*3*	*4*	*5*	*6*	*Total*
A	2	0	0	0	0	1	3
B	1	3	1	1	0	1	7
C	1	2	1	1	0	0	5
D	0	1	0	0	0	3	4
E	2	1	1	0	0	0	4
Total	6	7	3	2	0	5	23

circumvent this problem, the value of the variable under consideration for each firm in each of the twenty-five cells in the 5 × 5 country-industry matrix was put on the basis of 100, with 100 the average value for the firms in the cell. For example, if in country B, industry 3, there were six firms with capital intensity 20, 30, 50, 50, 70, and 80, on the basis of 100, their capital intensity would be 40, 60, 100, 100, 140, and 160. This rescaling procedure was carried out for all the twenty-five cells of the country-industry matrix. The average value and the standard deviations of the values of the capital intensity of the individual firms were then calculated for the two groups—LDC firms and other TNCs—across all twenty-five cells of the matrix. This procedure was followed for the eleven variables of interest: size, capital intensity, foreign/local employees, percent equity participation, exports, imports, product quality, price-cost margins, profitability, R&D, and advertising intensity. The statistical problems with this procedure are many and glaring, but given the sample size, it was the best that could be devised. One of the worst drawbacks is that it does not permit an analysis of variations in the variable under consideration between cells in the matrix or even between rows and columns; for example, comparison cannot be made between the relative capital intensity of LDC firms and other TNCs in industry 2, country B and industry 3, country B. Nevertheless, the analysis, problem plagued as it is, did support the hypotheses. The results are displayed in table 3-4. Especially note that the profits of LDC firms were *not* significantly different from those of other TNCs; in fact, they were higher, but not significantly so. The LDC firms in the sample were able to employ product strategies and process technology that enabled them to compete successfully with TNCs and locally owned firms in the ASEAN region.

Discriminant analysis was used to examine the power of the ten variables (profits were dropped) to distinguish between LDC firms and other TNCs.[15] The discriminant function was very powerful. It misclassified

Table 3-4
Comparison of LDC Firms and Other TNCs

Variable	LDC Firm[a]	Other TNCs[a]	Significance Level[b]
1. Size	46	109	A
2. Capital intensity	83	103	B
3. Foreign/local employees	120	96	B
4. Equity participation	51	108	A
5. Exports	20	114	A
6. Imports	33	112	A
7. Product quality	67	106	A
8. Price-cost margins	61	107	A
9. Profits	106	99	—
10. R&D	88	102	C
11. Advertising	65	106	B

[a]The values of the variables within each of the $5 \times 5 - 25$ cells have been put on a basis of 100, with 100 the average for the cell (see the text). The numbers in these columns are the averages for the LDC firms and other TNCs in the sample.
[b]A = significant at the 1 percent level; B = significant at the 5 percent level; C = 10 percent level.

only 4 percent (one misclassification) of the LDC firms (that is, classified an LDC firm as being based in a developed country) and 1.6 percent (two misclassifications) of the other TNCs. Given the statistical properties of discriminant analysis, this accuracy applies only to in-sample firms, but the function would have to deteriorate markedly before any of the ten variables lost significance or the discriminant function as a whole lost its accuracy if out-sample data were used.

The data lend support to a modified product life-cycle theory as a partial explanation for firms based in one LDC making investments in another LDC. The LDC firms in the sample had developed an expertise in small-scale, labor-intensive technology to produce "old," low-quality, price-sensitive goods suitable for the factor prices and income levels of other LDCs. Competitive conditions in their home-country markets and barriers to trade motivated them to exploit this expertise via FDI in joint ventures in neighboring LDCs. Before turning to the implications of these results for the impact of LDC firms on the host country, an analysis of some of the effects of LDC firms on the competitive and structural practices of other TNCs is needed.

Competitive and Structural Effects of LDC Firms

Some authors have suggested that the formation of TNCs based in LDCs may be one way for LDCs to increase their bargaining power with TNCs from developed countries and to reduce the supranormal profits they earn on their operations in LDCs.[16] As was shown previously, although LDC firms competed profitably against other TNCs, their products did not compete "head on" with those of other TNCs, even though their products were classified to the same industry. Usually the products of TNCs from developed countries competed at the "high" end of the market—R&D-intensive, high product differentiation, low price elasticity—whereas LDC firms competed at the "low" end—little product differentiation or R&D, price-sensitive, low-quality. Can the presence of LDC firms in an industry increase competition and reduce the supranormal profits of the TNCs in that industry?

Traditionally the structure-conduct-performance paradigm of industrial organization has been employed to analyze questions of this kind, that is, the relationship between the structure of the industry, the level and type of competition between firms, and the performance of the firms in allocating scarce resources efficiently. Since the "conduct" of firms is difficult to observe and quantify, most researchers have studied the relationship between various market-structure variables (or their proxies) and the performance of firms in the industry. Criticisms of this type of analysis have not deterred further analysis of the structure-performance relationship.[17] Instead, the number of market-structure variables has been increased and their measurement refined. Central to all these analyses, however, is some measure of the structure of product and sales among the firms in the industry, for example, the four or eight firms' concentration ratio, the Herfindal index, and the entropy measure. Recently, Kwoka (1979) has shown that for industries in the United States, industry profitability increased as the market share of the largest and second largest firm increased, but *decreased* as the market share of the third largest firm increased, even if the three firms together controlled a large share of the market. These statistical results imply that if only two firms dominated, they tacitly coordinated their activities in such a way as to earn supranormal profits. The presence of another large firm made coordination much more difficult, increased competition, reduced profits, and increased the efficiency of resource allocation. Following Kwoka, market-share data was used rather than some more aggregated measure of concentration.

The work of Newman (1978), Stonebraker (1976), and Porter (1979) is particularly relevant to this chapter. They have shown how the chartacteristics of firms *within* an industry—size, competitive strategy, and distinctive competence—can influence the ability of individual firms and groups of firms within the industry to earn supranormal profits. The tacit coordination of pricing, marketing, and production decisions between TNCs from different countries in the market in the host country may be more difficult than between TNCs from a single home country for several reasons. First, the competitive strengths and strategies of TNCs from different countries may differ greatly, so coordination may be difficult to achieve. Second, TNCs from different countries may have little experience competing with each other in LDCs; that is, they may not yet have learned to "dance together." As the number of TNCs from different countries (or areas) increases, the level and type of competition also may increase, since the TNCs from different countries may be unwilling or unable to tacitly coordinate their pricing, marketing, product innovation, and introduction and production strategies. The presence of LDC firms might compound this coordination problem, since their competitive strategies may markedly differ from those of other TNCs. However, the products of LDC firms may not compete directly with those of other TNCs, and hence they may have a smaller impact on the competitive environment faced by the TNCs. To test these hypotheses, the following equation was estimated:

$$P = a + bM_1 + cM_2 + dM_3 + CI + gL$$

where P is the average profitability of the firms in each of the 5×6 cells of the country-industry matrix and is measured by $P =$ (profits + interest on intercompany debt + fees and royalty payments)/(equity + intercompany loans); M_1, M_2, and M_3 are the estimated market shares of the three largest firms in the industry; I is the multinational coordination term and is equal to the number of home countries of the TNCs in the industry except LDC firms; and L is the number of LDC firms in the industry.

If Kwoka's results hold for the industries and firms in the sample, the coefficients of M_1 and M_2 should be positive, and M_3 should be negative. If the presence of multinationals from different home countries did increase the level of competition, the coefficient of I should be negative. If the presence of LDC firms also increased competition, the coefficient of L should be negative as well.

As might be expected with the few data points, the imprecise proxies used, and the restricted number of independent variables that could be introduced, R^2 was low, but the coefficients had the expected signs and were significant.

$$P = 15.3 + .213M_1 + .053M_2 - .251M_3 - .83I - .41L$$
$$(2.17) \quad (2.92) \qquad (2.17) \qquad (1.93) \qquad (2.37) \quad (2.02)$$

$$N = 30, \overline{R} = .31$$

This result supports the hypothesis that rivalry between TNCs from different countries reduced the profitability attainable by firms in an industry. It also indicates that LDC firms did not take an active a part in this rivalry (the coefficient of L is smaller than that of I). The existence of more than two firms with large market shares also reduced industry profitability.

Summary and Conclusions

The foreign subsidiaries of firms based in LDCs differed from those of other TNCs in many dimensions. In general, the LDC firms in the sample were smaller, used more labor-intensive technology, had a larger percentage of employees from their home countries, imported fewer foreign inputs, exported less of their output, and produced unbranded, low-R&D, and low-quality products that competed on the basis of price (low price-cost margins) in the host-country market. LDC firms had lower foreign-equity participation, but were more profitable (but not significantly more profitable) than other TNCs. The products of the LDC firms in the sample did not compete directly against those of other TNCs. LDC firms did not have access to the latest process technology; the large amounts of capital or the expertise necessary for large-scale, capital-intensive technology; or the marketing and product-development skills necessary for such direct competition. Even though the products of LDC firms competed on the basis of price with the products of other TNCs and locally owned firms, the presence of an LDC firm in an industry did not decrease the amount of profits earned by other TNCs in the industry as much as did the presence of another TNC from a developed country.

The major benefits of LDC firms for their host country were their expertise in the use of appropriate technology to manufacture products that were suitable to the level of income of the majority of the people in their host LDC and their extensive use of locally produced raw materials and machinery. Their major costs to the host country stemmed from their motivation to invest in order to preserve their market share in the host country; that is, they preempted local entrepreneurs who potentially had the skills and capital to enter the industry on their own. In addition, since they invested to serve the local market, their willingness (and ability) to export from the host country was low.

Based on this analysis, foreign direct investment by firms from LDCs can best serve as a complement to direct investment by TNCs from developed countries, not as a supplement. LDC firms would seem to provide only limited countervailing power against TNCs from developed countries.

Before this conclusion is accepted, however, much more data and analysis must be carried out. The limitations of this study should be kept clearly in mind. The analysis was based on data from 23 LDC firms and 130

TNCs from developed countries that had invested in six light manufacturing industries in the five ASEAN countries. Sample limitations prevented the inclusion of many of the variables of industry structure that have been shown in previous studies of both developed and less-developed countries to be important in determining industry structure, conduct, and performance. Further data collection and analysis will surely modify and extend these conclusions.

Notes

1. See Lecraw (1977), Wells (1978), and Wells and Warren (1979) and articles in Agmon and Kindleberger (1977) for some research in this area.

2. See Wong (1979) and Lecraw (1979b) for a description of the economies of these countries and an overview of FDI in the region.

3. There are restrictions or prohibitions against FDI in some of the ASEAN countries in nonmanufacturing industries such as banking, wholesale and retail trade, communications, and transportation, however.

4. In this vast outpouring of literature, see especially Vernon (1977), and the United Nations (1978).

5. Lecraw (1977), Wells (1978), Wells and Warren (1979) gave some preliminary data.

6. Vernon (forthcoming) concluded that recent FDI by TNCs from developed countries cannot be explained by the product life-cycle theory owing to homogenization of the markets in the developed countries, the rapid dissemination of product and process technology, and the reduction in trade barriers between developed countries.

7. See Wells (1972) for a concise description of the product life-cycle theory.

8. See Caves (1971).

9. Owing to concessional tariff rates, the products of firms in LDCs often face lower tariffs in developed countries than do those of TNCs from developed countries.

10. LDC firms have not invested in high-technology industries, such as heavy chemicals, petroleum refining, and so forth.

11. The noncompetitive nature of markets in LDCs have been well documented by Bergsman (1974), Lecraw (1978, 1979b), Morley and Smith (1977, 1977), and White (1976).

12. This chain of causality would not apply to the exports from LDCs to developed countries.

13. See Wells and Warren (1979) for data on Indonesia.

14. On the average, other TNCs imported 83 percent of their machinery from their home countries.

15. See Aaker (1971, pp. 115-154) for a description of discriminant analysis.

16. See, for example, Panglaykim (1972, 1977).

17. See Phillips (1976) for a discussion of the theoretical and empirical problems of the structure-conduct-performance paradigm.

References

Aaker, D.A. *Multivariate Analysis in Marketing*. Belmont, Calif.: Wadsworth, 1971.

Agmon, T., and Kindleberger, C.P., (Eds.). *Multinationals from Small Countries*. Cambridge, Mass.: M.I.T. Press, 1977.

Bergsman, J., Commercial policy, allocative efficiency, and x-efficiency. *Quarterly Journal of Economics* (August 1974).

Caves, R.E. International corporations: The industrial economics of foreign investment. *Economica* 149, February 1971.

Kwoka, J.E. The effect of market share distribution on industry performance. *Review of Economics and Statistics* (February 1979).

Lecraw, D.J. Foreign direct investment by firms from less developed countries. *Oxford Economic Papers* (November 1977).

_____ . Choice of technology in low-wage countries: A non-neoclassical approach. *Quarterly Journal of Economics* (November 1979a).

_____ . Structural and Competitive practices of TNCs in the ASEAN region. U.N. Center for Transnational Corporations, 1979b.

Morley, S.A., and Smith, G.W. Limited search and the technology choices of multinational firms in Brazil. *Quarterly Journal of Economics* (May 1977).

_____ . The choice of technology: Multinational firms in Brazil. *Economic Development and Culture Change* (January, 1977).

Newman, H.H. Strategic groups and the structure performance relationship. *Review of Economics and Statistics* (October 1978).

Panglaykim, J. The western multinational corporations with their three-sided and Japanese MNCs with five-sided power structure: Some notes. Mimeographed, 1972.

_____ . *Indonesia's Economic and Business Relations with ASEAN and Japan*. Jakarta Center for Strategic and International Studies, 1977.

Phillips, A. A critique of empirical studies of relations between market structure and profitability. *Journal of Industrial Economics* 24, June 1976.

Porter, M.E. The structure within industries and companies' performance. *Review of Economics and Statistics* (May 1979).

Stonebraker, R.J. Corporate profits and the risk of entry. *Review of Economics and Statistics* (1976).

United Nations Economic and Social Council. *Transnational Corporations in World Development: A Re-examination*. New York: Commission on Transnational Corporations, 1978.

Vernon, R. Storm over the multinationals: Problems and prospects. *Foreign Affairs* (1977):243-262.

_____ . The product cycle hypothesis in a new international environment. *Oxford Bulletin of Economics and Statistics* (forthcoming).

Wells, L.T. *The Product Life Cycle and International Trade*. Cambridge, Mass.: Harvard Univ. Press, 1972.

_____ . Foreign investment from the third world: The experience of Chinese firms from Hong Kong. *Columbia Journal of World Business* (Spring 1978).

Wells, L.T., and Warren, V'Ella. Developing country investors in Indonesia. *Bulletin of Indonesian Economic Studies* (March 1979).

White, L.J. Appropriate technology, x-inefficiency, and a competitive environment: Some evidence from Pakistan. *Quarterly Journal of Economics* 90, November 1976.

Wong, J. *ASEAN Economies in Perspective*. Singapore: MacMillan, 1979.

4 Overseas Direct Investment by South Korean Firms: Direction and Pattern

Sung-Hwan Jo

What is offered here is an *economic* analysis of the basic direction and emerging pattern of overseas direct investment by South Korean (hereafter referred to as Korean) firms from the *investing country's* point of view.[1] The basic position that this chapter takes is as follows. Overseas direct investment, whether inflow by foreign firms or outflow by Korean firms, is composed of a bundle of factors of production, including management, technology, capital, manpower, marketing information, critical materials, and so forth in variable proportions. Different components of overseas direct investment come into prominence in different phases of a less-developed country's (LDC) growth process and changing factor endowment.[2]

The first section of this chapter briefly sketeches the process of Korea's transition from import-substitution growth to export-substitution growth and relates it to the emerging direction and pattern of Korea's overseas direct investment[3] The second section presents the overall picture of the basic characteristics of overseas direct investment by Korean firms. The third section attempts to identify the types of overseas direct investment as related to varying motivations on the part of Korean investors and also considers some external and internal constraints on the future expansion of overseas direct investment.

Overseas Direct Investment as a Continuing Process of Export-Substitution Growth

Until 1962, there was neither inflow of foreign direct investment into Korea nor outflow of overseas direct investment by Korean firms. The major sources of finance for industrial sector and overhead expansion in Korea's early phase of the post-Korean war industrialization were grants-in-aid, public and commercial loans, foreign-exchange earnings, "forced" domestic savings in the form of deficit financing and inflation, overvalued exchange rates, low interest rates, and other forms of price distortions.

Inflow of foreign direct investment from its inception in 1962 steadily rose until 1967, rapidly increased from 1968 to 1973, and then gradually declined from 1974 on, as shown in table 4-1 and figure 4-1a. As of June 1979, the total number of foreign direct investment projects in Korea had reached 874, amounting to US$940,086,000 in stock value.

It was around 1967 when outflow of overseas direct investment began to be discernible as a new pattern of international operation by Korean firms. There were, however, two separate cases of forerunners of overseas direct investment by Koreans. The first case was the purchase by Korean Traders Association of a commercial building in New York City for its U.S. branch office in 1959. The purchase was financed from foreign-exchange earnings from Korean tungsten exports to the United States. The motive was to establish the U.S. base for promoting Korean exports. This case is particularly interesting in that it foreshadowed the beginning of Korean export-

Table 4-1
Direct-Investment Inflow and Outflow and Technological Licensings
(Thousands of U.S. Dollars)

Year	Foreign Direct Investment (a)	Overseas Direct Investment by Koreans (b)	Ratio (b/a)	Inflow of Technological Licensing
1962-1966	16,765 (17)[a]	—	—	777.3 (31)
1967-1970	59,838 (11)	7,453 (19)	—	—
1971	36,716 (80)	5,690 (9)	15.50	26,520.4 (326)
1972	61,232 (131)	3,183 (16)	5.20	—
1973	158,435 (239)	3,749 (18)	2.37	11,489.9 (67)
1974	162,629 (96)	22,950 (30)	14.11	17,791.0 (86)
1975	69,170 (34)	5,923 (34)	8.56	26,540.5 (99)
1976	105,574 (43)	7,878 (35)	7.46	30,423.4 (131)
1977	102,286 (46)	13,939 (62)	13.63	58,056.0 (173)
1978	100,457 (50)	40,086 (91)	39.90	85,065.4 (297)
Cumulative Total	872,812 (846)	110,851 (314)	12.70	256,663.9 (1,210)

Sources: The Bank of Korea (for overseas direct investment) and the Economic Planning Board (for foreign direct investment and technological licensing).
[a]Figures in parentheses refer to the number of cases.

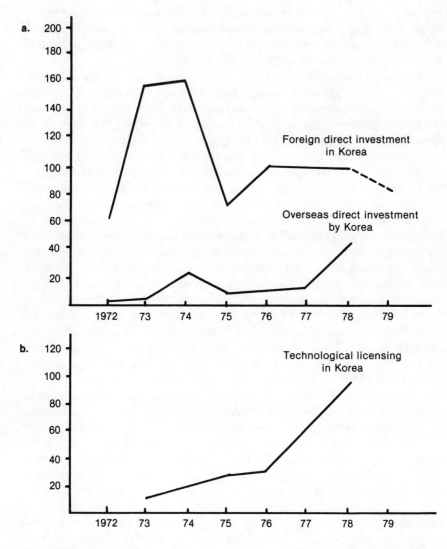

Unit: Millions of U.S. dollars.

Figure 4-1. Trend in Foreign Direct Investment, Overseas Direct Investment, and Technological Licensing in Korea, 1972-1978

related overseas investment. The predominant proportion of subsequent overseas direct investment by Korean firms falls into this category.

The second case was a timber operation in Malaysia initiated by a Korean resident in 1963. The motive was to secure a future source of supply of timber for the Korea-based plywood industry. This case foreshadowed the beginning of the import-oriented or natural-resource-related type of overseas direct investment. An increasing proportion of overseas direct investment by Korean firms in recent years is of this type.

Overseas direct investment by Korean firms started to rise steadily from 1967 and grew very rapidly during the second half of the 1970s. As of June 1979, the total number of the overseas direct investment projects had reached 314, amounting to the total value of US$110,851,000 in terms of Korean-owned equity, as shown in table 4-1.

Overseas direct investment by Korean firms can be grouped into two broad categories on the basis of the combination of trade direction and factor intensity. The first category, consisting of trading, transportation and warehousing, real estate, manufacturing, and construction, can be considered primarily export-related and labor-intensive. The other category, consisting of mining, timbering, and fishery, is mainly import-oriented and natural-resource-related. About three-quarters of the total stock of overseas direct investment falls into the first category, and the remaining one-quarter into the second category (see table 4-3 for the industrial breakdown of Korea's overseas direct investment).

It is important to note in figure 4-1a that there were distinct downward shifts in the direction of the trend between the inflow of foreign direct investment to Korea and outflow of overseas direct investment by Korea around 1974-1975. Concomitant with these shifts was the ever-increasing inflow of technological licensing (figure 4-1b). By the end of June 1979, the ratio of the cumulative total of outflows of overseas direct investment to that of inflows of foreign direct investment reached more than 12 percent.

The emerging direction of Korea's overseas direct investment can be better understood when viewed in relation to the size, changing factor endowment, and changing growth phases of the Korean economy. The initial conditions of Korea's factor endowment at the conclusion of the Korean war were characterized by a particular type of economy: an *open, dualistic* economy of a *labor-surplus* type. The Korean economy inherited a large, traditional subsistence agricultural sector relative to its commercialized nonagricultural sector, implying the dualistic structure of production. Korea is small in size, calling for a strategically important role for foreign trade. Thus, *openness* (smallness) refers to the importance of foreign trade as an essential aspect of growth. Korea's postwar transition was started with an unfavorable natural-resource endowment relative to the size of population and labor force. By *labor-surplus* is meant the presence of high population pressure on the land at the initial point of industrial growth. In addition to these basic characteristics, Korea inherited a relatively unfavorable agricultural infrastructure at the outset, but had a strong human resource base with a generally high level of education and skills.

The basic problem of Korea's transition growth after the conclusion of the Korean war was how to successfully reallocate the unemployed and underemployed labor force from the subsistence agriculture to the commercialized nonagricultural sector in order to (1) provide efficient employment for the labor force—the most abundant factor of production—and (2) increase the national product in the course of this process of intersectoral labor reallocation. With the foreign-trade sector as an important aspect of growth, such an open, dualistic economy as Korea's was bound to move gradually from traditional land-based growth and export to nontraditional labor-based growth and export.

The early phase of Korea's industrial growth for the period from the end of Korean war (1950-1953) through 1965 started with consumer-goods import-substitution activities. The immediate motive was to build up domestic manufacturing capacity with the import of capital goods and raw materials, which would produce domestically the previously imported consumer goods.

In order to induce private entrepreneurs to make investments in manufacturing industries, the Korean government took import-restrictive and industry-protective policy measures, including import prohibitions, quotas, differential tariff rates, domestic currency overvaluation, foreign-exchange controls, a multiple exchange-rate system, low-interest foreign and local loans, low grain prices, and other forms of relative price distortions.

Such a variety of policy measures for industrial protection guaranteed high profit margins by raising the *domestic prices* of industrial consumer goods and by lowering the *domestic costs* of production in terms of the low costs of equipment and raw-materials imports and low real wage rates of unskilled workers. Import substitution was concentrated into production of industrial consumer goods, starting with those items which had been imported in relatively large quantity and which could be produced with relatively simple technology (for example, flour milling, sugar refining, cotton and woolen spinning and weaving, food processing, plywood, and so forth). Import substitution was "deepened" in a small number of large-scale activities in earlier years, and it was "widened" over a large number of small-scale activities in later years.

Since import substitution was becoming a growth-propelling force operating in the early phase of Korea's industrial growth, the period from 1953 to 1965 can be called that of import-substitution (IS) growth. The characteritics of the Korean economy during the IS growth period can be summarized as follows. First, almost all industrial activities were domestic-market-oriented. Total exports occupied only a small fraction of GNP. Second, the dominant form of manufacturing production by local entrepreneurs was simple final processing or assembling of imported materials or components, using imported capital equipment. Thus the structure of manufacturing production became import-inducing and capital-intensive relative to Korea's labor-rich factor endowment. Third, Korea's exports during the IS growth period were sluggish and most were land-based or resource-based. Fourth, the traditional subsistence agricultural factor remained stagnant, and the imports of foodstuffs and raw materials continued to grow very rapidly.

It was found that nearly 80 percent of the total value of foreign direct investment made in Korea during the period 1962-1967 was concentrated in import-substituting industries, the motive being to take advantage of the sheltered local markets.[4] The idealized role of inflow of foreign direct investment in Korea during the import-substitution growth phase could be viewed as providing foreign capital, management skills, technology, and manpower training in import-substituting manufacturing industries.

The process of import substitution could not continue forever. It ended when the expanding finished-consumer-goods capacity reached the limit of the domestic market. As the domestic supply neared the limit of domestic demand, investment activities in consumer-goods industries fell sharply and the level of production rapidly declined from that of the late 1950s.

After some years of stagnation and trials, a decisive breakthrough was made in the growth of labor-intensive industrial exports by the existing import-substitution enterprises and newly established export enterprises. Some of the import-substitution enterprises initially attempted to dispose of their products in overseas markets to overcome the business stagnation at home. As time went on, the exports of labor-intensive industrial consumer goods rapidly grew, and the ratio of exports to total sales of these firms increased. A large number of those firms which had previously been domestic-market-oriented were turned into export-oriented firms within a relatively short span of time. Soon a number of new firms were established for the exclusive purpose of export processing.

With 1965 as a turning point, the Korean economy for the first time entered a new phase of rapid and continuous economic growth through the expansion of labor-intensive industrial exports. There were two important factors that led to the transition of the Korean economy to this new phase of rapid growth. One was the maturation of the entrepreneurial capability during the previous period of IS growth. Another was the shift in the government-policy package from direct controls to a more market-oriented and export-oriented system that provided the decisive impetus for the transition. A series of liberalizing measures, including devaluation of domestic currency, interest-rate reforms, partial lessening of import restrictions, and dismantling of other controls, were taken between late 1964 and 1965.

Those industrial entrepreneurs who emerged under the import-substitution policy regime and who survived the competitive environment were in a position to take advantage of the profit-making opportunities through production and export of labor-intensive industrial goods. In other words, under the liberalized market- and export-oriented policies, these businessmen came to take export activities seriously, activities from which they could make handsome profits through the proper choice of input and technology best suited to the comparative advantages of the Korean economy. The opening of overseas markets and rapid expansion of labor-intensive exports were essential preconditions for the unarrested and accelerating economic growth of Korea after 1965. The fast growth of the GDP was accompanied by a rapid rise in the export ratio from that year onward. This period is referred to as the period of export-substitution (ES) growth in that the growth of the gross domestic product was led by the continuous substitution of the "new" export of labor-intensive industrial products for the "traditional" export of land-based primary products and by that of the "new" export of sophisticated labor-intensive industrial goods for the "old" export of simple labor-intensive industrial products.

It was found that about 55 percent of the total value of foreign direct investments made in Korea during the period 1968-1974 was concentrated in labor-intensive export industries with the motive of exploiting the cheap labor.[5] The idealized role of inflow of foreign direct investment during the export-substitution growth phase could be viewed as providing the global scanning of market information and appropriate technology to be combined with the local managerial talents and the semiskilled and unskilled labor.

It was during the ES phase of growth that some of externally oriented Korean firms began to make overseas direct investment in trade-related, on-site service and processing facilities to ensure continued expansion of the industrial exports. Several prominent aspects of Korea's changing factor endowment and growth process during the period of ES growth (from 1965 on) have important implications for the international expansion of the Korean economy.

First, Korea's poverty in natural resources, together with the relatively poor performance of her agricultural sector, brought about total dependence on the importation of raw materials vital to her continuous industrial growth. The share of natural-resource-related imports in Korea's total commodity imports reached nearly 50 percent in recent years. Table 4-2 illustrates the available estimates for Korea's dependence on overseas natural resources. It was as early as 1963 when a Korean investor undertook timbering operations overseas. As already indicated, about one-quarter of the total overseas direct investments by Korean firms at the end of 1978 was of the natural-resource-oriented type. Since Korea's need for natural resources such as crude oil, coal, and other industrial raw materials will be increasing more rapidly, the relative share of natural-resource-oriented overseas direct investments is likely to increase sharply in the foreseeable future.

Table 4-2
Korea's Dependence on Overseas Natural Resources
(Percentage of Item Imported)

Year	Crude Oil	Iron Ore	Aluminum	Timber	Raw Sugar	Wool	Cotton	Rubber
1976	100.0	75.1	100.0	82.8	100.0	100.0	100.0	100.0
1981 (est.)	100.0	86.6	100.0	84.8	100.0	100.0	100.0	100.0

Second, while industrial exports grew at an annual average rate of 40 percent during the period 1970-1978, the industrial sector had to pay for the imports of raw materials and intermediate inputs as well as for the ever-increasing food imports. Such a heavy burden pushed the drive for quantitative expansion and diversification of industrial exports to its maximum. As an extended form of the export drive, the Korean government has promoted the export of Korean workers to the Middle East and encouraged enterprises to go abroad (that is, export-oriented overseas direct investments). The establishment of overseas branches, subsidiaries, and joint ventures of Korea's trading companies and banks was mainly designed to better serve their export markets. It must be viewed against the background of Korea's maximum export drive that about three-quarters of the country's total stock of overseas direct investments was designed to penetrate overseas market for labor-intensive industrial goods and to provide such on-site services as trading, warehousing, and banking to promote Korea-based industrial exports.

Third, the import substitution in the areas of consumer durables, intermediate inputs, and capital goods has been steadily expanded from the early 1970s on, with the partial return to the industrial protection system. It is important to note that both the industrial-export drive and the expansion of import-substitution industries in these new areas have been recently pursued under the same protective policy package that provided a series of incentives, including tariff reductions and exemptions for the import of raw materials and plant and equipment, preferential interest rates, direct subsidies, and so forth. To keep the process going, Korea has secured an increased inflow of foreign loans and has encouraged foreign direct investment and technical licensing arrangements.

In other words, instead of moving first to labor-intensive, then skill-intensive, and finally capital- and/or technology-intensive production and export in an orderly sequence, the Korean economy has prematurely attempted to move into some fairly technology- and capital-intensive industries. Since the minimum efficient size of import-substitution production of the new types generally far exceeds the size of domestic markets, Korea's search for export markets for these new products will be intensified during the 1980s. This will have obvious implications for the future direction of Korea's overseas expansion. The export of the intermediate inputs and capital goods would call for different marketing strategies. The overseas marketability of plant and equipment and intermediate inputs would be effectively enhanced when Korean firms participate in overseas construction and engineering-related activites, when they establish overseas subsidiaries in manufacturing activities, and when Korea offers suppliers' credit and long-term loans to overseas investors on favorable terms. Hence, in the future, the Korean government and investors will find it necessary to coordinate overseas construction and engineering activities, manufacturing investments, and financial services in a systematic way to strengthen inter-relatedness between the industrial sector and the import-substitution sector.

Fourth, in line with the changing phases of Korea's development process, there were parallel shifts in inward and outward flows of direct investment. During the import-substitution growth phase, when foreign direct investment in Korea was rising but overseas direct investment by Korean firms was almost nonexistent, foreign direct investment was heavily concentrated in import-substituting industries and the overhead capital sector. The main motive for investment was to penetrate the well-protected and growing local markets, and the prominent components of foreign direct investment in this phase were capital, managerial talent, and technology. During the export-substitution growth phase (since 1965), export-oriented foreign direct investment rose and soon became predominant. The motive was to take advantage of cheap labor, and the prominent components of foreign direct investment in this phase were global market information and appropriate technology. It was also during the ES growth phase that export-oriented Korean firms began to make overseas direct investment in on-site service facilities in export markets and processing facilities in the LDCs. The motive in this case was to better serve and protect overseas export markets, and the prominent components of overseas direct investment by Korean firms were the firm-specific adaptation of simple technology and product designs particularly suited to the LDC conditions. After a period of sustained export diversification, new import-substitution investment in consumer durables, intermediate inputs, and capital-goods industries began to increase and there was a gradual shift in relative importance from export-oriented foreign direct investment to technological licensing and turnkey contracts with the multinational corporations (MNCs).

In sum, one can make the following two points regarding the basic characteristics of Korea's overseas direct investments as related to its growth process. First, Korea's investment activities at the present phase of its growth process can be considered essentially as a nontraditional, defensive, but highly intensified form of import and export operations reflecting Korea's changing factor endowment, changing policy package, and response to the changing international economic environment. This latter response is important because the worldwide energy crisis and the growing trend towards resource nationalism on the part of resource-rich countries destroyed the basic premise upon which Korea built its industrial and trade structure during the period of the export-substitution growth—the premise that her increasing demand for vital raw materials could be met from stable overseas sources. The changing international economic environment has prompted Korean firms to intensify their efforts to secure access to overseas natural resources by establishing joint ventures with local partners in the areas of timbering, fishing, and mining. Korea's recent negotiations with the OPEC nations to directly exchange (barter) crude oil (not U.S. dollars) for construction services also should be considered as a nontraditional form of natural-resource imports. Another basic premise upon which Korea's rapid export-substitution growth was based was that the world markets would continue to purchase a constantly increasing volume of Korean industrial exports. Faced with growing protectionism in developed countries against industrial exports from the LDCs and with growing competition from other developing countries in the overseas export markets, Korean exporters have stepped up their export-marketing drive by building up their own overseas branch offices, warehousing facilities, distribution channels, and on-site processing facilities. Korean bankers also have expanded their on-site financial services to accommodate Korea's export-marketing drive. The majority of Korea's overseas direct investments can be properly considered as an extended form of export-marketing activities designed to expand home-based production. The motivation for Korea's overseas direct investments at the present growth phase was to expand, not to replace, home-based industrial production and export. Korean investors as yet do not have the aggressive motivations to realize economies of scale and/or to obtain higher factor returns than available domestically, but they are defensively motivated to acquire overseas sources of raw materials for home-based production and to strengthen export-marketing efforts in the face of growing protectionism and resource nationalism overseas.

The second point is that the growth of Korea's overseas direct investment must be viewed in the context of the dynamic process of ES growth. In this continuous process, where the export of primary goods was superseded by the export of simple, unskilled, labor-intensive industrial goods, and which may in time be replaced by the export of capital- and/or technology-intensive industrial goods, Korea's export-oriented overseas direct investment will gradually shift from simple, trade-related services to on-site processing facilities and from scattered horizontal investment to forward and backward vertical investment.

Characteristics of Korea's Overseas Direct Investment

The analysis presented in this section was mainly based on the industrywide grouped data available from the unpublished sources of the Bank of Korea. The terminal date for the data used in the tables was the end of 1978.

Industrial and Regional Distribution

It will be interesting to break down the industrial composition of the overseas direct investment into regions. Table 4-3 provides this cross-classification and highlights the following points:

Table 4-3
Industrial and Regional Composition of Overseas Direct Investment by Korean Firms
(Thousands of U.S. Dollars)

Industry		Southeast Asia	Middle East	North America	Latin America	Europe	Africa	Oceania	Subtotal
Mining	Cases	2	—	—	—	—	—	—	2
	Amount	386	—	—	—	—	—	—	386
Timbering	Cases	7	—	—	—	—	—	—	7
	Amount	20,871	—	—	—	—	—	—	20,871
Fishing	Cases	1	—	4	8	1	9	—	23
	Amount	90	—	493	881	40	6,090	—	7,594
Manufacturing	Cases	11	3	—	3	—	1	1	19
	Amount	8,847	560	—	441	—	7,000	1,348	18,196
Construction	Cases	8	6	1	—	—	1	—	16
	Amount	3,003	5,079	6,200	—	—	137	—	14,419
Transportation and warehousing	Cases	—	1	6	—	—	—	—	7
	Amount	—	800	184	—	—	—	—	984
Trading	Cases	31	3	71	2	39	2	1	149
	Amount	2,621	487	5,875	80	2,674	9,596	50	21,383
Others	Cases	4	3	2	—	1	2	—	12
	Amount	2,877	574	12,542	—	10	13	—	16,016
Real estate	Cases	2	—	—	3	1	1	1	8
	Amount	8,203	—	—	396	210	71	460	9,340
Subtotal	Cases	66	16	84	16	42	16	3	243
	Amount	46,898	7,500	25,294	1,798	2,934	22,906	1,858	109,189 (total)

1. Investment in timbering to gain access to timber supplies for the Korea-based plywood industry was exclusively confined to the Southeast Asian countries.
2. Investment in fishing was diffused all over the world except the Middle East and Oceania. About 80 percent of investments in fishing were concentrated in Africa, 12 percent in Latin America, and about 6.5 percent in North America.
3. No Korean firm made manufacturing investment in such developed regions as the United States and Europe. About 48 percent of all manufacturing investment took place in Southeast Asia, 38 percent in Africa, and 7 percent in Oceania.
4. About 43 percent of direct investment by Korean firms in construction was made in the United States, 35 percent in the Middle East, and 20 percent in Southeast Asia.
5. Investment in transportation and warehousing was concentrated in the Middle East (81 percent) and North America (19 percent).
6. Direct investment in trading was diffused throughout developed and developing regions. Korean direct investment in trading in terms of the number of cases was concentrated in North America (48 percent), Europe (26 percent), and Southeast Asia (20 percent). About 45 percent of direct investment in trading in terms of value took place in Africa, 27 percent in North America, and 12 percent in Southeast Asia.

Size Distribution

Table 4-4 shows the distribution of the sizes of the overseas direct investments. The following points are notable:

1. The number of overseas Korean firms with investments of less than US$100,000 was 155, accounting for 64 percent of all the overseas Korean firms at the end of 1978. Nearly 80 percent of the firms belonging to this group were engaged in trading.
2. The number of firms with investment sizes ranging between US$100,000 and US$500,000 was 40, accounting for 17 percent of all the overseas Korean firms. Of these 40 firms, 16 were engaged in trading, 6 in manufacturing, and 6 in construction.
3. Only 5 firms had invested between US$500,000 and US$1 million.
4. Twenty-three firms had investments of more than US$1 million. Within this group, 5 firms were engaged in timbering, another 5 in manufacturing, and still another 5 in construction.
5. The overall average size of investment was US$372,000. The average size of trading firms was US$66,000, while that of timbering firms was

Table 4-4
Size Distribution of Korea's Overseas Direct Investment
(Thousands of U.S. Dollars)

Industry	Less than US$100,000		US$100,000-US$500,000		US$500,000-US$1,000,000		More than $US1,000,000	
	Cases	*Amount*	*Cases*	*Amount*	*Cases*	*Amount*	*Cases*	*Amount*
Mining	1	80	1	306	—	—	—	—
Timbering	—	—	1	200	1	982	5	19,689
Fishing	14	502	4	1,197	1	895	1	5,000
Manufacturing	3	91	6	1,302	—	—	5	16,803
Construction	4	213	6	1,212	1	891	5	12,103
Transportation and warehousing	5	184	—	—	1	800	—	—
Trading	122	6,032	16	4,220	1	650	2	10,481
Others	5	178	2	624	—	—	3	15,214
Real estate	1	71	4	1,066	—	—	2	8,203
Subtotal	155	7,351	40	10,127	5	4,218	23	87,493

US$2,981,000. The average investment of construction firms was US$901,000, and that of manufacturing firms US$129,000.

Ownership Pattern

The ownership pattern of overseas direct investment by Koreans is presented in Table 4-5. The following points should be noted:

1. About two-thirds of the overseas direct investment was comprised of subsidiaries, 23 percent joint ventures with Korean majority ownership (more than 50 percent) and 11 percent joint ventures with Korean minority ownership (less than 50 percent). It appears that nearly 90 percent of overseas Korean investors wanted to retain effective control over the management of their overseas operations.
2. Wholly owned subsidiaries of the Korean parent firms were concentrated in such on-site service areas as trading, banking, real estate, and transportation and warehousing.
3. Joint ventures were the predominant form of overseas direct investment by Koreans in fishing, timbering, mining, manufacturing, and construction.
4. One can give several explanations about the high propensity for the Korean firms to establish joint ventures with local partners in other areas than trading and on-site trade-related services. One plausible explanation is that LDC firms, including Korean firms, that offer capital,

Table 4-5
Ownership Pattern of Overseas Korean Firms
(Number of Firms)

Industry	100%	More than 50%	Less than 50%	Subtotal
Mining	1	—	1	2
Timbering	1	6	—	7
Fishing	1	10	12	23
Manufacturing	2	11	6	19
Construction	5	9	2	16
Transportation and warehousing	4	2	1	7
Trading	134	12	3	149
Others	5	6	1	12
Real estate	8	—	—	8
Subtotal	161	56	26	243 (total)

managerial talents, and technical know-how in the production of inexpensive and undifferentiated goods using labor-intensive technology may not have much to offer (for example, such things as patent rights, monopoly profits, marketing skills, brand names, and so on) in the bargaining situation over ownership share and managerial control, while they need local partners to provide knowledge of local distribution channels and the local economic and political environment.[6] Another explanation is that some governments of the host LDCs insisted legally or informally on the majority of local ownership in specific industries (for example, mining, fishing, timbering, construction, and so on). In addition, the Korean government has explicitly stipulated in its guideline for overseas direct investment that Korean investors in LDCs should form joint ventures with local partners whenever possible and should employ as many local employees as possible.

Sources of Funds for Equity Investment and Loans

Table 4-6 shows various sources of funds for equity investments by Korean investors. From this table it can be seen that 70 percent of the total equity was paid in cash, 17 percent was locally raised by means of standby credit guaranteed by Korean banks, 10 percent was in the form of loans, 2.5 percent was contributed in kind (for example, equipment and materials made available from Korea), and only 0.2 percent was financed from profits.

Table 4-7 shows the financial sources, repayments, and balances of loans made available from the Korean side. Loans provided from the Korean sources in connection with overseas direct investments by Korean firms amounted to US$44.9 million in total at the end of 1978. Nearly 60 percent of these loans were made in the form of standby credit, 40 percent in cash, and only 0.5 percent in kind. About 18 percent of the loans were directly extended to Korean investors to finance their equity participation.

The Korean Government Policy
toward Overseas Direct Investments

The Korean government has placed a strong emphasis on the role of overseas direct investment in (1) securing access to raw materials, (2) expanding exports, and (3) promoting international cooperation with developed and developing regions. The government offers a set of incentives for overseas direct investment: (1) protection from investment risks, (2) financial assistance including loans and guarantees, (3) tax incentives, and (4) an information service.

Table 4-6
Sources of Funding for Equity Investments
(U.S. Dollars)

Industry	Cash	In Kind	Standby Credit	Loans	Profits	Total	Repatriation	Balance
Mining	386,000	—	—	—	—	386,000	—	386,000
Timbering	6,149,851	—	3,099,561	4,400,000	—	13,649,413	—	13,649,413
Fishing	4,264,651	327,000	561,985	—	—	5,159,636	65,900	5,093,736
Manufacturing	12,136,622	100,239	1,300,000	—	—	13,536,862	—	13,536,862
Construction	4,908,102	1,571,871	2,588,575	—	150,000	9,218,555	—	9,218,555
Transportation and warehousing	184,000	—	800,000	—	—	984,000	—	984,000
Trading	12,354,091	29,410	—	—	—	12,383,502	—	12,383,502
Others	12,290,481	—	—	3,696,650	29,400	16,016,531	—	16,016,531
Real estate	4,104,373	40,423	5,194,800	—	—	9,339,597	—	9,339,597
Subtotal	56,778,175	2,068,951	13,550,921	8,096,650	179,400	80,674,097	65,900	80,608,197

Table 4-7
Loans to Overseas Korean Firms from Korean Sources
(U.S. Dollars)

Industry	Cash	In Kind	Standby Credit	Total	Repayments	Balance
Mining	—	—	—	—	—	—
Timbering	260,000	—	12,837,125	13,097,125	1,475,145	7,221,980
Fishing	2,530,000	—	—	2,530,000	30,000	2,500,000
Manufacturing	—	—	8,542,719	8,542,719	3,884,000	4,658,719
Construction	2,554,366	253,384	5,200,000	8,007,750	2,807,750	5,200,000
Transportation and warehousing	—	—	—	—	—	—
Trading	9,000,000	—	—	9,000,000	—	9,000,000
Others	3,722,750	—	—	3,722,750	26,100	—
Real estate	—	—	—	—	—	—
Subtotal	18,067,116	253,384	26,579,844	44,900,344	8,222,995	25,580,699

Protection of overseas investments from losses owing to expropriation, war, civil disorder, and other causes is provided under the overseas investment insurance system. In addition, the government has made a series of bilateral agreements for foreign-investment protection with a number of countries.

Financial assistance to Korean investors is provided in the form of medium- and long-term loans and guarantees by the Korea Export-Import Bank as well as in the form of standby credit from other Korean banks.

Tax incentives are offered to Korean investors in overseas operations through such measures as deductions of taxes paid to foreign governments by Korean investors, reduction of tax rates on incomes and corporate earnings from overseas direct investment, and exemption from double taxation.

Overseas investment information has been gathered from such diverse sources as government agencies, branch offices of Korean banks, and trading companies. The basic weakness in the information-gathering activities is that there is no governmental or quasi-public agency especially designed for collection, analysis, and dissemination of overseas investment information.

Types of Overseas Direct Investment by Korean Firms and Uncertain Prospects

Types of Investment

Overseas direct investment by Korean firms can be grouped into the following five types in terms of underlying motivations.

Type 1: Investment in resource-rich countries to acquire a sure source of raw materials to serve the Korea-based industrial production complex.

Type 2: Investment in civil construction and engineering-related areas in such a region as the Middle East.

Type 3: Investment in on-site trading, warehousing, and distribution channels to serve overseas markets for Korean exports.

Type 4: Manufacturing investment in LDCs to serve the market in which the plant is located.

Type 5: Investment in research and development (R&D) firms in an industrialized nation to develop and import sophisticated technology and know-how in the place where research and technical manpower is readily available at relatively low cost.

It will be useful to relate the different types of investments to the prominence of different components of overseas direct investments, such as capital, technology, managerial talent, skilled and unskilled labor, marketing information, expertise, and so forth.

Let us first consider the type 1 investment (natural resources). A small group of larger Korean firms has established joint ventures with local partners in timbering operations in Malaysia and Indonesia, offshore fishing in Latin America and Africa, and mining operations in Thailand to secure access to these natural resources to serve home markets. The Korean firms have growing home markets for these resources, a fund of accumulated technical know-how, the machinery and equipment, and flexibility (due mainly to their relatively small size) in business dealing with local authorities and partners.

As to the type 2 investment (civil construction), it should be pointed out that Korean civil construction contractors and workers had already accumulated technical capabilities and experience in large-scale overseas civil construction projects during the Vietnam conflict before they moved into the Middle East. Korean contractors have comparative advantages over their foreign competitors in the supply of skilled and semiskilled manpower, modern labor-intensive technology for construction and engineering-related operations, the availability of sophisticated and specialized modern equipment, and flexible attitudes in dealing with local authorities. Their main reason for establishing joint ventures with local Arab partners was that local participation was a legal requirement to be eligible for competitive bidding in many classes of contracts. In some cases where local participation was not formally required, Korean contractors made arrangements with local partners in order to improve the chance of obtaining contract awards. Korean construction and engineering firms are weak in heavy-engineering and chemical-processing technology. One Korean firm recently established a joint venture with an American contractor to combine Korean manpower with advanced foreign technology and engineering know-how.

Type 3 investment (on-site services for export marketing) has been a natural outcome, as well as a cause in some cases, of the rapid and continuous expansion of Korea's industrial exports. This type of investment can be considered as a first step toward internationalization of export-oriented Korean firms. As Korea's industrial exports were rapidly growing and competition in overseas markets became intensified, an increasing number of exporting firms attempted to integrate forward in their foreign markets through the establishment of overseas branch offices, warehousing facilities, and distribution channels. A number of export-oriented Korean firms had sufficient and flexible home-based production capacity and adequate funds to purchase on-site service facilities, but were weak in marketing skills. Some Korean firms made arrangements for joint operations with local partners to combine their supply capacity with the local partners' marketing skills.

In connection with overseas investment in on-site services for export markets, it is worthwhile to note an increasing trend in overseas expansion of Korean banks. A number of Korean banks have set up their own overseas branch offices and some have established joint ventures in the world financial and trading centers. The main motivation was to tap capital sources for Korean industrial growth and to accommodate financial needs of Korean exporters and investors.

Some Korean consulting firms also have expanded their international operations, particularly in the Middle East, to meet the growing technical needs of Korean and local investors. They are playing a catalytic role in the promotion of joint ventures because they have broadened international contacts and accumulated technical expertise.

Now let us turn to the type 4 investment (manufacturing operations). Korea's overseas manufacturing investment have been confined to the LDCs in Southeast Asia, Latin America, and Africa. Typical manufactures involves apparel, cotton and synthetic cloth weaving, iron bars and wire drawings, plastic moldings, paper, tires, cement, and so forth. Korean firms were thus engaged in horizontal investment in the production of labor-intensive, standardized products.

The main advantage of the Korean firms engaged in manufacturing activities over potential local and multinational competitors seems to be derived from firm-specific adaptation of foreign technology and/or standardized process to a relatively small scale of operations and some adaptation of product designs to the LDCs' conditions.[7] Such adaptations were the result of small modifications in technology and product designs emanating from the machine shops and assembly lines of Korean plants in the labor-intensive home environment through the long process of learning by doing. Evidence from an interview-based study in which I took part indicates that most of these modifications consist of labor-using innovations peripheral to the machine or core process, including handling, packaging, storing, and so on, together with greater manual quality control (for example, plywood production), more intensive machine maintenance, and the upgrading of lower-quality raw materials into quality inputs via manual sorting (for example, wool and cotton yarn). Korean firms may have advantages over the multinationals from advanced countries in the lower labor costs of the local technicians, the semiskilled and unskilled workers, and the more flexible business attitudes associated with their small size and informal organization. The majority of manufacturing investments took place in those LDCs which the Korean firms had previously served with exports. The extent to which investment decisions by Korean firms in these cases were motivated by the desire to escape actual and potential tariffs, quotas, and other trade barriers was not investigated. However, it was apparent that the desire to be closer to the markets previously served by exports was the main motivation for making overseas investment decisions.

The predominant proportion of manufacturing investment were carried out by medium-sized Korean firms. It often has been speculated that medium-sized firms have been more active than larger firms in adapting technology and product design to labor-intensive conditions before going abroad.

As expected, some Korean firms have made arrangements with multinationals from developed countries to establish manufacturing joint ventures in an LDC. It also is conceivable that some Korean firm may soon find it attractive to use the country in which the plant is located as a base for exports to third countries.[8]

The type 5 investment (R&D) is exemplified by an interesting case. It involves the takeover of a U.S. research and development firm by a medium-sized Korean firm. The basic motivation in this case was to use the wholly owned R&D firm in the United States as an overseas base for the development, and import, of appropriate technical knowledge, new processes, and new product designs to serve the Korean market for sophisticated technology. There is a parallelism between type 5 and type 1 investments. The factor of production is technical know-how in the one case, and the factor involved in the other case is natural resources. Korea is an importer of both factors. Overseas direct investment for R&D is in contrast to investment for overseas manufacturing. Whereas overseas manufacturing investment involves the export and overseas assembling of low-cost technological components to serve overseas markets, overseas R&D investment involves the overseas assembling and import of sophisticated technical components to serve the home market. Since the process of export substitution in Korea has been rapidly shifting from the export of unskilled, labor-intensive products to that of skill- and technology-intensive products, it is anticipated that more Korean firms will follow this example of R&D-oriented investment in developed countries.

When overseas direct investment is viewed essentially as "international trade" in factors of production, Korea's investments involve trade in both directions: the import of natural resources (type 1), export-marketing know-how (type 3), sophisticated technology (type 5), and the export of skilled and semi-skilled labor (type 2) and labor-intensive modern technology (type 4).

Uncertain Prospects

Although overseas direct investment by Korean firms has expanded rapidly over a short span of time in terms of types of activities and regions involved,

Korean firms are still in the early "trial and error" stage of going multinational. The changing world economic conditions, the limited domestic resources, the high propensity to rush, and the lack of international business experience and skills are important factors that will affect the future course of international expansion of Korean firms.

Adverse World Economic Conditions. Energy-crisis-related recessions and slow growth in developed and developing countries, growing protectionism against manufactured exports from LDCs, and resource nationalism enforced by resource-rich countries will have serious implications for Korea and most LDCs and their internationally oriented firms. On the one hand, worldwide recessions and slow growth will reduce opportunities for the international expansion of Korean firms, while on the other hand, the rising tides of protectionism and resource nationalism abroad are likely to prompt Korean firms to go multinational as a defensive strategy.

Balance-of-Payments Problems. Although the balance-of-payments position of Korea improved in recent years, particularly as a result of increased foreign-exchange earnings from civil construction activities in the Middle East, Korea's current account started to show growing deficits from early 1979 on owing to sluggish overseas demand for Korean exports, domestic inflation, and "structural" recessions. It is anticipated that Korea's current-account deficit will continue for the foreseeable future, requiring increasing foreign loans for balance-of-payments reasons. Such balance-of-payments pressures would undoubtedly reduce overseas-investment activities by Korean firms.

A High Propensity to Rush. A high propensity to rush in the domestic industrial investment and export activities has been clearly visible in the process of Korea's rapid and continuous growth over the last 15 years. If such a propensity repeats itself at the international level, the prospect for natural and orderly growth of the internationalization of Korean firms along the line of global division of labor would be uncertain.

The Lack of International Business Experience and Expertise. Korea was secluded from the outside world for many centuries before her relatively recent entry into the community of modern nations. Korea has no ethnic, linguistic, or religious ties with other regions of the world. The stock of Korean managers, engineers, and skilled workers who have gained experience in doing business in overseas environment is very limited. The number of overseas Korean residents is small, and those with a business orientation are scarce. The limited stock of managerial talent and expertise in overseas operations and the limited scope of overseas business ties will become a serious constraint to the future expansion of Korea's overseas-investment activities.

Conclusion

Korean firms are in the early phase of going multinational. Overseas direct investment in the present phase of Korea's export-substitution growth can be viewed essentially as the extension of import and export activities designed to ensure continued expansion of home-based industrial production. The motivations for Korea's overseas direct investment are basically defensive in that Korean firms are seeking to secure the overseas sources of raw materials to serve their home-based production complex and to serve overseas markets for their industrial exports. These motives reflect Korea's changing factor endowment and are in response to the rising tides of resources nationalism and industrial protectionism abroad.

Aggressive motivations for overseas direct investment to realize economies of scale, to exploit technological know-how and export-marketing expertise, and to earn higher return on capital are not visible in the Korean case at the present moment. However, in view of Korea's simultaneous pursuit of export growth and promotion of new import-substitution industries (that is, intermediate inputs and capital goods), some larger Korean business groups will soon find it necessary to use overseas direct investment as a means of obtaining economies of scale. They may do this by coordinating the various overseas operations and the different activities of home-based production from within the headquarters of the business group. This process of coordination of overseas and domestic operations by common executive control would lead to vertical integration involving multinational investment pointing forward to the consumer as well as backward to raw materials.

The changing pattern of inflow and outflow of factors of production has manifested itself in the gradual shift in relative importance of foreign direct investment in Korea, overseas direct investment by Korea, and inflow of technological licensing in recent years. Overseas direct investment by Korean firms and inflow of technological licensing have gradually emerged as the important forms of "international trade" in factors of production. The direction and pattern of Korea's overseas direct investment can be characterized by the import of natural resources, export-marketing know-how, and sophisticated modern technology and the export of skilled, semiskilled labor, and labor-intensive modern technology.

Notes

1. Korean firms are still in the early phase of internationalization process. Since few Korean firms can be properly considered as multinationals,

the term *overseas direct investment* instead of multinational will be employed in this chapter. *Overseas investment*, in accordance with the provisions and definitions of article 15, section 1 of the Foreign Exchange Control Act of the Republic of Korea, covers the following five elements: (1) equity investment for managerial participation; (2) loans with maturity of more than 6 months and less than 10 years; (3) acquisition of real estate; (4) technological licensing for the duration of more than 1 year; and (5) suppliers' credit for the duration of more than 3 years. The concept of overseas direct investment as employed in this chapter will include equity investment (item 1) and the book value of real estate purchased (item 3).

2. The idea of relating inflow of foreign direct investment (the presence of the MNCs in the LDC) to the particular phase of growth process and factor endowment of the LDC in question is best expounded in Gustav Ranis, "The multinational corporation as an instrument of development," in L. Goodman and D. Apter (eds.), *The Multinational Corporation and Development* (New Haven, Conn.: Yale Univ. Press, 1976).

3. For the problem of transformation from the import-substitution growth to the export-substitution growth in the LDCs, see John C. H. Fei and Gustav Ranis, "A Model of Growth and Employment in the Open Dualistic Economy: The Cases of Korea and Taiwan," *Journal of Development Studies* (January 1975): 33-63.

4. My own estimates were based on the data presented in Sung-Hwan Jo, "The Impact of Multinational Firms on Employment and Incomes: The Case Study of Korea," (ILO WEP) Working Paper No. 13, Geneva, December 1976, pp. 12-13.

5. Ibid.

6. Professor D.J. Lecraw has made the same points in his article, "Foreign Direct Investment by Firms from Less Developed Countries, "*Oxford Economic Papers* (November 1977): 447.

7. This has been repeatedly pointed out by a number of observers. See, for example, D.J. Lecraw, ibid, pp. 445-455; and C.F. Diaz-Alejandro, "Foreign Direct Investment by Latin Americans," in T. Agmon and C.P. Kindleberger (eds.), *Multinationals from Small Countries* (Cambridge, Mass: M.I.T. Press, 1977), pp. 171-174.

8. The cases of joint-venture arrangements of the LDC investors with the MNCs from developed countries to operate in the third countries are not uncommon in Hong Kong, Singapore, and other parts of Southeast Asia. See, for example. L.T. Wells, Jr., "Foreign Investment from the Third World: The Experience of Chinese Firms from Hong Kong," *Columbia Journal of Business* (Spring 1978): 38-49.

5 Hong Kong Multinationals in Asia: Characteristics and Objectives

Edward K.Y. Chen

The establishment of multinational corporations is no longer a special phenomenon of the developed countries. In the 1970s, we witnessed the increasing importance of third-world multinationals in international trade and investment. Many multinational corporations (MNCs) today are established by the oil-producing countries, the South American countries, such as Argentina, Brazil and Columbia, and the Asian countries, such as Hong Kong, Korea (South), the Philippines, Singapore, and Taiwan. Indeed, among the 500 largest industrial corporations outside the United States listed in *Fortune* (August 14, 1978), 33 are third-world multinationals. This chapter attempts to study the phenomena of Hong Kong multinationals engaged in manufacturing. There is also foreign direct investment by Hong Kong firms in construction, entertainment, recreation, hotels, and financial services. In addition, some investment can be found in primary production, although the importance in this case is relatively small. In general, Hong Kong's direct investment overseas in nonmanufacturing activities is mostly made by individuals or groups with the objective of diversifying their present activities and business risks. In most cases, these overseas enterprises do not have headquarters in Hong Kong, or their headquarters are not in similar lines of business. However, Hong Kong's overseas investment in manufacturing activities is most frequently made by firms with experience in the same line of business in response to the changing supply and demand conditions facing them.

By *multinationals*, we mean a firm operating in more than one country. By *Hong Kong multinationals*, we therefore mean a firm with its headquarters in Hong Kong establishing subsidiaries overseas. It is, however, important to note that a firm with its headquarters in Hong Kong does not necessarily imply that it is owned by Hong Kong residents. It is commonplace to find firms in Hong Kong with largely or exclusively overseas capital that are parent firms of overseas subsidiaries. In the following pages, I shall first present a general picture of Hong Kong's foreign direct investment in manufacturing in several Asian countries. I shall then present the results of a sample survey of Hong Kong MNCs. The survey attempts to find out the motives for their investment and the reasons for their survival in the host countries. Finally, based on the general description from some secondary data sources and the information obtained from the special survey, I make some generalizations about the characteristics of Hong Kong multinationals.

Hong Kong's Foreign Direct Investment in Manufacturing: A General Description

Hong Kong began to invest overseas in manufacturing noticeably in the early 1960s, but a rapid growth in foreign direct investment (FDI) has occurred only in the past few years. At present, most of the FDI concentrates in Asia, particularly in Indonesia, Malaysia, Singapore, and Taiwan. Many Hong Kong firms also have established subsidiaries in other Asian countries, such as the Philippines, Sri Lanka, and Thailand, and in African countries, such as Nigeria and Ghana. There is also the notable example of the Hong Kong firm, Stelux, acquiring 29 percent of the U.S. Bulova Watch Company. Most important, with the pursuit of a "new" economic policy in China, a vast and so far unexploited ground has suddenly opened up for Hong Kong and other countries to invest in manufacturing projects. A brief review of foreign direct investment by Hong Kong companies in Indonesia, Malaysia, Singapore, Taiwan, and China follows. According to the information available, most of the FDI in manufacturing is made by Hong Kong-based firms and not by individuals or foreign-owned subsidiaries in Hong Kong. In this way, most of the FDI from Hong Kong can be regarded as activities of Hong Kong multinationals. It is, however, unfortunate that the Hong Kong government does not keep any record of the outflow of direct investment. In consequence, the brief analysis that follows has to rely on scattered reports and the scanty information provided by the host countries in which investment by Hong Kong MNCs is significant.

Indonesia

Hong Kong firms started to invest in Indonesia immediately after the Indonesian Foreign Direct Investment Law was enacted in 1967. During the period 1967-1976, Hong Kong's total investment in Indonesia amounted to US$210 million, which represented 11.7 percent of all foreign investment in Indonesia and was second only to Japan. Of the total US$210 million, 51.9 percent was invested in manufacturing, 18.2 percent in the primary sector, and 29.9 percent in the services sector. The United States is also an important investor in Indonesia, but much of its investment has been in mining. The other important investors in Indonesia are Singapore and the Netherlands, both of which concentrate their investment in manufacturing.

During the earlier period, say 1967-1970, Hong Kong's direct investment was concentrated in textiles. From 1967 to 1974, nineteen textile projects from Hong Kong, with an investment of US$129 million, were approved by the Indonesian government. This amount represented 59 percent of Hong Kong's manufacturing investment and 29 percent of Hong Kong's total investment in Indonesia. The only other industry of some importance was chemicals, but the investment in it represented only 4.5 percent of Hong Kong's manufacturing investment during that period. In recent years, however, while the textile industry is still dominant, the relative importance of the chemical industry has increased very rapidly. Hong Kong investment it also quite substantial in the food industry and the metal-products industry. The breakdown of the investment in the manufacturing sector of Indonesia is given in table 5-1.

In nonmanufacturing activities, investment from Hong Kong concentrates on hotels, trade services, recreational services, and timber. Some of the timber produced is sent back to Hong Kong for the making of furniture, which has become an increasingly important industry. This, however, does not imply a kind of vertical integration existing between the Hong Kong furniture firms and the Hong Kong timber firms in Indonesia because the latter are usually not subsidiaries of the former.

It is important to note that there were very few Hong Kong textile firms established in Indonesia after the earlier period. Since then, most of the investment is found in timber, chemicals, garments, printing, and food processing. In the earlier period (1967-1970), many Hong Kong textile firms shifted their location of production to Indonesia to circumvent the quotas imposed by the developed countries. With quotas on Hong Kong's textile exports, the immediate response of some firms was to move to countries where quotas had not yet been imposed. In the later years, a motive for

Table 5-1
Hong Kong Investment in the Manufacturing Sector of Indonesia, as of December 1976

Industry	Percentage of Total
Food	7.1
Textiles	55.3
Paper	1.3
Chemicals	14.6
Minerals and metals	6.5
Basic metals	4.4
Metal products	9.2
Others	1.6

Source: Bank of Indonesia.

many Hong Kong textile firms to establish subsidiaries in Indonesia and elsewhere was to find an outlet for the outdated machinery they had been using. This was also of benefit to the host countries, since the less up-to-date machinery and the less-sophisticated technology accompanying it could be more appropriate for those countries which were less industrialized than Hong Kong. In the 1970s, many proposed textile projects from Hong Kong were turned down because the Indonesian government had hoped that Indonesian entrepreneurs could take up textile production themselves. For similar reasons, one does not find firms in export-oriented industries such as electronics, watches and clocks, toys, and plastics established in Indonesia. The host government entertains the hope of developing these industries through domestic investment, thinking that Indonesia has comparative advantages in these products and will one day export them just like Hong Kong.

From this account, we can see that most of the recent investment by Hong Kong MNCs in Indonesia has been made to open up the Indonesian market for their products and not to achieve lower cost of production enabling them to export elsewhere at more competitive prices. In the case of investment in the primary and the services sectors, they are mostly made by investment companies in Hong Kong that treat FDI as a form of portfolio choice. There is little production relationship between the Hong Kong parent firm and the overseas subsidiaries in this situation.

Malaysia

In contrast to their direct investment in Indonesia, Hong Kong MNCs concentrate in the export-oriented industries, namely, textiles, garments, and electronics, when investing in Malaysia. This is made possible by the export incentives provided by the Malaysian government to foreign firms.[2] Running down the list of Hong Kong firms investing in Malaysia, we observe, on the one hand, the names of many small and unknown firms and, on the other, the names of some leading firms, such as the Atlas Electronics Corporation, the Yangtzekiang Garments Manufacturing Company, and the Textile Alliance Limited. Most of the investments are in the form of joint ventures with Malaysian companies. At the end of 1977, Hong Kong ranked fourth after Japan, Singapore, and the United Kingdom in the amount of total foreign investment in Malaysia. Hong Kong investment in Malaysia during the 1975-1977 period is given in table 5-2.

The major activities of Hong Kong firms in Malaysia are the production of textile and textile products (mainly garments), food manufacturing, chemicals, electronics, and wood products. Table 5-3 gives a percentage breakdown.

Table 5-2
Hong Kong Investment in Malaysia

Year	Millions of U.S. Dollars
1975	72.9
1976	63.5
1977	114.7

Source: Malaysian Commission, Hong Kong.

It is of interest to note that besides those products (such as textiles, garments, and electronics) which Hong Kong has long experience in producing, Hong Kong's manufacturing activities in Malaysia also include the production of products (such as food, chemicals, and wood) that are of little importance in the Hong Kong economy itself. Thus Hong Kong's investment in Malyasia can be divided into two general categories. First, there are the export-oriented industries that Hong Kong has the experience in operating and for which the objective in shifting the location of some production to Malaysia is to further minimize the cost of production to obtain a greater competitive edge when exporting to the established markets in the developed countries. The sources of lower costs are mainly derived from lower wages and lower land prices. Second, there are the industries that have not been important in Hong Kong, with their major objective being to exploit the comparative advantage of Malaysia and to develop the local market. The first type of investment, in export-oriented industries, has basically defensive motives. Facing the keen competition from other newly industrialized countries for the established markets, Hong Kong has to find ways to minimize its cost of production in the textiles, garments, and electronics industries. The second type of investment is an aggressive strategy by which new markets and new lines of activities are developed for the parent firms in Kong Kong.

Table 5-3
Hong Kong Investment in Malaysia, by Industry, December 31, 1977

Industry	Percentage of Total
Food manufacturing	9.1
Textiles and textile products	57.9
Wood and wood products	6.3
Chemicals and chemical products	8.3
Electrical products and electronics	8.3
Others	10.1
	100.0

Source: Malaysian Commission, Hong Kong.

Taiwan

Owing largely to the ethnic ties between the Chinese in Hong Kong and Taiwan, Hong Kong investment in Taiwan started immediately after the establishment of the nationalist government in 1950. Hong Kong investors began to be significant in 1964 and increasingly so after 1967. Table 5-4 shows the investment activities of Hong Kong firms during the period 1964-1978.

It can be seen that the amount of investment in Taiwan fluctuates from year to year. This is so because the decision of Hong Kong firms to invest depends on a set of factors including Taiwan's political stability and international relations, the business and economic prospects of Hong Kong itself, and the relative attractiveness of foreign investment in other Asian countries. For instance, the proportion of Hong Kong investment dropped in 1972 following Taiwan's replacement by China in the United Nations. FDI from Hong Kong during 1976-1978 was lower than that for the previous period of 1973-1975 largely because of the increasing attractiveness of the foreign-investment environment in some other Asian countries. In any case, Hong Kong is a very important investor in Taiwan. For the period

Table 5-4
Hong Kong Investment in Taiwan, 1964-1978

Year	Cases[a]	Amount[b] (US$, Millions)	As a Percentage of Total Foreign Investment in Taiwan
1964	16	2.8	14.1
1965	19	2.7	6.5
1966	29	4.6	15.7
1967	86	12.0	21.1
1968	153	17.6	19.6
1969	48	6.8	6.2
1970	51	8.3	6.0
1971	44	21.3	13.1
1972	77	12.5	9.9
1973	130	30.0	12.1
1974	45	21.7	11.5
1975	21	29.5	25.0
1976	25	17.3	12.2
1977	26	11.3	6.9
1978	22	16.5	7.8

Source: Industrial Development and Investment Center, Taiwan.
[a]Indicates the number of new projects.
[b]Indicates the total amount including new projects and expansion of existing projects.

1952-1978, this investment amounted to US$223 million, representing 11.6 percent of total FDI in Taiwan during that period. In fact, Hong Kong ranked third after the United States and Japan in the amount of foreign investment in Taiwan.

Most of the Hong Kong investment is in manufacturing activities. Earlier, textiles, garments, and plastic and rubber products were the major areas of Hong Kong interest. More recently, a large proportion of the investment is in electronics and chemicals. Table 5-5 gives a breakdown of manufacturing activities of Hong Kong MNCs during the period January 1974 to July 1979.

In general, the pattern of investment in Taiwan follows very closely the changes in manufacturing activities in Hong Kong. In the 1960s, when textiles, garments, and plastics were the major industries in Hong Kong, these industries also were the major areas of investment in Taiwan by Hong Kong firms. In the 1970s, the rapid growth of the electronics industry in Hong Kong was accompanied by the decline of textiles and plastics. At about the same time, there was an outburst of Hong Kong investment in electronics in Taiwan. The garment industry, however, has continued to grow in Hong Kong owing to its ability to diversify and improve the quality of its products. In a few cases, Hong Kong garment firms have established spinning and weaving subsidiaries in Taiwan for the supply of fabrics. While investment in the garment industry has continued, that in textiles and plastics in Taiwan by Hong Kong firms has almost come to a standstill. Indeed, during the period 1974-1979, no new textile projects were approved and the investment in textiles was only for expanding the existing capacity.

Table 5-5
Hong Kong Investment in Taiwan, by Industry, January 1974 to July 1979

Industries	Cases	As of Percentage of Hong Kong's Total Manufacturing Investment in Taiwan
Electronics and electrical appliances	15	28.8
Chemicals	8	52.9
Garments and footwear	2	4.7
Textiles	0	2.6
Machinery, equipment, and instruments	2	2.9
Metal	2	2.6
Others	5	5.5
	34	100.0

Source: Industrial Development and Investment Center, Taiwan.

One of the defensive strategies adopted by Hong Kong firms is to establish subsidiaries in Taiwan whenever the export-oriented industries in Hong Kong are being challenged by the exports of Taiwan and Korea. It is hoped that by taking up some of the opportunities otherwise available to the local Taiwanese firms and by utilizing the lower labor and land costs in Taiwan, Hong Kong firms will be in a better position to compete in the overseas markets. Since the mid-1960s, Korean and Taiwanese industries have been rapidly growing along lines similar to Hong Kong's and, in fact, producing very similar products for export. While Korea and Taiwan enjoy lower labor and land costs and greater government assistance, Hong Kong has the advantage of longer experience, higher productivity, and better management. One of the most important assets of Hong Kong manufacturing in recent years has been a plentiful supply of management expertise at relatively low costs. One can say that Hong Kong is no longer labor-intensive, but is management-intensive in the sense that Hong Kong is, at present, enjoying a relatively low factor price for management. It is thus a good idea to combine Hong Kong's relatively cheap management with Taiwan's relatively cheap labor and land through the establishment of Hong Kong-based multinationals in Taiwan. So far, Hong Kong investment in Korea has not been important despite the fact that Korea can offer cost advantages similar to those of Taiwan. This fact suggests that in making foreign direct investment, cultural and ethnic ties, familiarity with local conditions and languages, and administrative efficiency can be as important as pure economic considerations.

Besides textiles, garments, plastics, and electronics, direct investment in Taiwan by Hong Kong MNCs also can be found in such industries as chemicals, food, metal, and lumber, which have not been Hong Kong's major manufacturing activities. Of these industries, the interest in chemicals is particularly noteworthy. In the recent years, Hong Kong's investment in Taiwan's chemical industry has been by far the largest and, in fact, accounts for 9 percent of all foreign investment in chemicals. This is partly the result of the Taiwan government's encouragement of foreign investment in this area and partly due to the lack of opportunities, at present, in developing the chemical industry in Hong Kong because of environmental considerations. The Hong Kong government has made plans to encourage the development of the local chemical industry. Some chemical firms now operating in Taiwan would hope that in the near future they could use their Taiwan experience in Hong Kong. Thus, by investing in the chemical, food, metal, and lumber industries in Taiwan, the Hong Kong-based firms or individuals are following an aggressive strategy to find opportunities that are presently lacking in Hong Kong.

Singapore

There have been no published data on Hong Kong's investment in Singapore industries. However, some scattered information is available on the basis of a raw-data sheet prepared by the Singapore Economic Development Board and the results of some private studies. Hong Kong-based firms began to invest in Singapore in the early 1960s. It has been reported that Hong Kong investment in Singapore amounted to about S$12.5 million in 1966, S$46.9 million in 1970, and S$154.9 million in 1973.[3] From the very beginning, the textile and garment industry has been by far the most important industry for Hong Kong investment. The other industries of significance include food beverages, chemicals, and electronics. Table 5-6 gives a breakdown of Hong Kong FDI in Singapore by industry in 1966 and 1973.

The original objective of Hong Kong textile and garment firms investing in Singapore in the 1960s was to overcome the quantitative restrictions imposed on these exports from Hong Kong. It has been argued that it was not the export quota per se that caused the investment in Singapore.[4] The most fundamental reason was the increasing degree of categorization of the annual quota. In 1964, the original four-category U.K. quota was split into thirty-four. This change in the categorization of the quota made it difficult

Table 5-6
Hong Kong Investment in Singapore, by Industry, 1966 and 1973

Industry	As a Percentage of Hong Kong's Total Investment in Singapore Industries	
	1966	1973
Food and beverages	27.8	9.1
Textiles and garments	38.8	61.0
Chemicals	25.6	7.2
Electrical products and electronics	5.5	7.5
Others	2.3	15.2
	100.0	100.0

Sources: For 1966, P. Luey, "Hong Kong Investment," in Hughes and You (eds.), *Foreign Investment and Industrialization in Singapore* (Canberra: Australian National Univ. Press, 1969), table 5.2; it refers to Hong Kong investment in pioneer industries, which in 1966 represented about 75 percent of Hong Kong's total direct investment in Singapore. For 1973, K. Yoshihara, *Foreign Investment and Domestic Response* (Singapore: Eastern Universities Press, 1976), table 7.3; it is based on his list of foreign firms in Singapore worked from the Registry of Companies and information supplied by the Economic Development Board and trade associations. Data derived from the two sources are not directly comparable, but indicate some broad trends.

for the local firms to adjust and adapt within a short period of time. Their solution was to establish subsidiaries abroad where either the quota had not yet been imposed or was less severe. At that time, there was a choice between Taiwan and Singapore for Hong Kong's textile and garment firms investing overseas. Owing to the fact that the U.K. market was then the largest, that Singapore still enjoyed the benefit of commonwealth preference, and that Singapore had better shipping and financial facilities, Hong Kong firms in general preferred Singapore to Taiwan. The rapid increase in Hong Kong investment during 1966-1968 was mainly due to political factors. The riots in Hong Kong in 1966 and 1967 led to an exodus of capital from Hong Kong to Singapore. Taiwan was not preferred because the political futures of both Hong Kong and Taiwan were considered to be closely related. In the 1970s, the continuous increase in investment by Hong Kong firms was due mainly to economic considerations of costs. Since 1970, the industrial wage level in Hong Kong has remained higher than that in Singapore.[5] In addition, land prices are much lower in Singapore and the Singapore government gives especially favorable considerations to the use of industrial land by foreign investors. In absolute terms, the industrial wage level in Singapore is still higher than that in other Asian countries, such as Taiwan, Indonesia, Korea, Thailand, and the Philippines, that also are trying to attract foreign investment. However, it is generally the case that workers in Singapore are more productive than those in the other countries. In the past few years, the growth of Hong Kong investment in Singapore has declined. This is due in part to the increasing attractiveness of other Asian countries as host countries and in part to the fact that the Singapore government is now interested in more capital- and technology-intensive industries in which Hong Kong firms are not yet ready to take part.[6]

Over time, the proportion of Hong Kong investment in food processing and chemicals has declined, while that in electronics has increased quite rapidly. In electronics, many of the larger firms in Hong Kong have subsidiaries in Singapore. However, in other industries, the Hong Kong parent firms with subsidiaries are only medium in size. Inasmuch as Hong Kong investment concentrates on textiles, garments, and electronics, which are the basic export-oriented products of Hong Kong, the objective of the investing firms is largely a defensive one. Hong Kong-based MNCs facing competition in the export markets would naturally like to exploit the lower labor and land costs in Singapore. However, in the near future, it is expected that Hong Kong firms will engage in joint ventures in more capital- and technology-intensive industries in Singapore. This will enable these firms not only to develop new lines of activities overseas, but more important, to acquire modern technology and skills and bring them back to Hong Kong. It is now necessary for Hong Kong to diversify its industries owing to its overconcentration in a few products that other Asian countries, such as Korea and Taiwan, can now produce at a lower cost. It is intended that the direction of diversification will be toward more capital- and technology-intensive industries.

China

With the downfall of the "Gang of Four" in 1976 and the subsequent declaration of a "new" economic policy, China has just begun to invite foreign investors to take part in the modernization programs. It is certainly not a surprise that Hong Kong-based firms, with their familiarity with Chinese "ways" and their geographic proximity to China, are among the earliest and largest investors in China. There are no official statistics on the exact amount of the Hong Kong investment, but Chinese officials in Hong Kong have indicated that about 500 Hong Kong-based firms are presently engaged, under different arrangements, in various activities. Many firms still have reservations about the business prospects of operating in China and are also very concerned with the questions of political stability. Hence the amount of investment per project is rather moderate, usually less than US$1 million. There are, however, a number of much larger projects. For example, the investment by Asia International Electronics (which also has subsidiaries in other Asian countries) amounts to US$4 million; Stelux (which is also an investor in the United States and Switzerland) has plans to invest US$30 million in China in the production of electronic watches; and a printing firm with an intended investment of US$6 million (divided into 3 years) will begin production in China early next year. It is, however, expected that the announcement of China's Law on Joint Ventures on July 8, 1979 will lead to more large projects in the form of joint ventures in the near future.[7]

At present, involvement by foreign firms (including those from Hong Kong) in China can take one of the following three forms. First, foreign firms can arrange for subcontracting work done in Chinese factories. The Chinese factories will perform the processing in accordance with the specifications of the foreign firms, which would supply the material and/or intermediate products. Many small- and medium-sized Hong Kong firms are very interested in this kind of subcontracting, because this scheme enables them to obtain many parts and semimanufactured goods at a much lower cost than they can get from local firms.[8] Indeed, most of the foreign firms engaged in this kind of subcontracting are Hong Kong-based, and almost all the factories are in the Kwangtung province, many in Shumchun, the border district nearest Hong Kong.

Second, foreign investment in China can be in the form of compensation trade. This first began in early 1978 and is intended for larger industrial projects. Under this scheme, factories are set up under cooperative arrangements between China and foreign firms. China supplies land and workers and foreign firms supply raw materials, parts, machinery and equipment, and technical and managerial personnel. In addition, the investors are responsible for training the Chinese workers. This scheme requires substantial initial investment, but it also means that the foreign firms' activities are no longer limited by the existing level of skill and technology. China in this case is able to acquire modern technology and management skills, one of the most important motives for opening its doors to foreign trade and investment. Many of the existing projects in textiles, garments, watches, and electronics taken up by Hong Kong firms are set up in the form of compensation trade.

Third, to further the promotion of foreign trade and investment, the Chinese government enacted the Law on Joint Ventures.[9] This law enables foreign investors to actually invest in China's industries and share the profits for an indefinite period of time. The law is a very general one, but details have to be worked out for individual cases. Nevertheless, the law gives some general guidelines and assurances to the potential investors that China is sincere and anxious to invite foreign participation in its modernization programs. Faced with keen competition at home and abroad, and considering the vast potential of the Chinese market, many foreign firms (including Hong Kong firms) undoubtedly have keen interest in making joint-venture applications. It is still too early to predict the final outcome of the operation of joint ventures in China, but there is no doubt that we shall be seeing increasing foreign participation in the Chinese economic scene in the near future.

While many American, European, and Japanese firms come to China for the trade in capital goods and raw materials at present and for the opening of the vast Chinese market for consumer goods in the future, the objective of most Hong Kong-based firms investing in China is certainly the maximization of their short-run profits through the benefits of lower labor and land costs. Perhaps the lower land cost is a more important consideration. The shortage of industrial land in Hong Kong has become increasingly severe, resulting in very high land prices that many cannot bear. Given the physical features of Hong Kong, there is no solution to the land problem in the near future. It is, of course, true that wage rates in China are much lower than in Hong Kong, but foreign firms do not employ workers in the free market in China. Very often the processing charges fixed by the Chinese authorities are only marginally below the cost for the same job in Hong Kong, while workers in China generally are less productive.

The operation of Hong Kong-based firms in China has one characteristic that is not normally shared by Hong Kong investment elsewhere. This is the close relationship between the Hong Kong parent firm and the subsidiary in China. In particular, the parent firms attempts to build a vertically integrated structure with the Chinese subsidiaries. Elsewhere, the Hong Kong-owned subsidiaries might be producing different classes of products (usually less-sophisticated products) from those produced by the parent firm, but the subsidiaries, in most cases, are responsible for producing the complete products, which are ready for export or for sale in the local market.[10] However, it is typical that the Chinese subsidiaries are responsible for only one stage of the production process, usually the labor-intensive stage. This is very similar to the investment of many U.S. and European multinationals in the developing countries and very unlike Hong Kong investment in other countries.

Motives for Investment and Reasons for Survival: Some Survey Results

In view of the fact that any theory of foreign investment must have the power to explain the motives for a firm to invest in another country and the reasons for the overseas subsidiary surviving the competition from local firms and subsidiaries of other countries, a preliminary survey of a small sample of Hong Kong multinationals was carried out to probe into these issues. Included in this small sample were twenty-five firms, ranging in size from large to medium, producing garments and electronic, metal, and textile products, and investing in Taiwan, Singapore, Indonesia, China, Sri Lanka, Malaysia, and the Philippines. The sample firms were chosen on the basis of the management being known to us directly or indirectly, since it was thought that only by establishing some personal relationship could we obtain genuine answers to the questions. Nonetheless, considering the small number of firms in the sample, one must be very cautious in interpreting the results. In addition, the sample primarily covers the defensive type of investment, that is, investment overseas in those industries which are already well-developed in Hong Kong.

In conducting the interviews, among other things,[11] we asked the managements for their opinions on the motives for making direct investments abroad, the criteria for selecting a host country, and the reasons for surviving the competition from local firms and from other countries' multinationals. We asked the managers to rank the importance of a list of factors we supplied to them on a scale of 0 (no importance) to 10 (extremely important).[12] The rank for each factor reported in the following sections is the average rank of all the firms in the sample. The higher the number indicated in the rank column, the greater the importance of that factor as considered by the managements of the firms.

Motives for Investment

A list of seventeen factors was presented to the managers for ranking. This list of factors included many of the concepts contained in the current theories of foreign investment and some a priori reasons for foreign direct investment. The factors listed were not mutually exclusive and included motives of a firm investing abroad and characteristics of host countries. The results of the survey are shown in table 5-7.

The results of the survey are largely in line with our a priori interpretation of the phenomenon of Hong Kong's foreign direct investment. The pursuit of a lower cost structure, especially land cost, seems to be the most important factor. However, a lower cost structure does not imply a higher rate of profits, only greater profits. This is so because a lower price goes with a lower cost, so that the competitiveness in developed-country markets can be maintained. It is of interest to note that making use of outdated machinery is quite an important motive for investment overseas. It is a little unexpected that the firms ranked diversification of risks so high. This indicates that Hong Kong firms do have reservations about the political and

Table 5-7
Motives for Hong Kong Foreign Direct Investment

Motive	Rank
1. Higher rates of profits	3
2. Diversification of risks	5
3. Lower land costs and rents	7
4. Lower labor costs	5
5. Lower capital costs	2
6. Availability of technical and skilled labor force	1
7. Availability of management manpower	1
8. Availability of higher levels of technology	3
9. Defending the existing market by directly investing there	2
10. To open up new markets by directly investing there	1
11. To build up a vertically integrated structure	2
12. To make use of the outdated machinery in the Hong Kong firm	4
13. To circumvent tariffs and quotas imposed by developed countries	2
14. To make fuller use of the technical and production know-how developed or adopted by your Hong Kong firm	5
15. Availability of raw materials and/or intermediate products	1
16. To avoid or reduce the pressure of competition from other firms in Hong Kong	5
17. As a means of managing the financial assets of your Hong Kong firm (that is, establishing a subsidiary overseas is similar to investing in the financial markets overseas)	2

economic stability of Hong Kong, especially as the year 1997 draws closer.[13] It is also of interest to note that the pressure of competition does constitute an important motive for FDI. It seems that even in the context of third-world multinationals, some support for the notion of foreign investment as oligopolistic reaction also can be found.[14]

Criteria for Selecting a Host Country

It is of interest and importance to understand how firms make decisions on the selection of host countries. Of course, from the criteria ranked by the firms, we also obtain information on the motives for investment. The results reported in table 5-8, therefore, also serve to cross-check and supplement those reported in table 5-7.

The results again suggest that land and labor costs are very important considerations for making foreign direct investment. Of course, it is of no surprise that political stability is a prerequisite. The results also indicate that production in overseas subsidiaries is mainly intended for exports. Tax concessions, financial facilities, language, and business and family connections are not as important as one would have expected. In addition, firms place greater importance on technical manpower than on technology.

Table 5-8
Criteria for Selecting Host Countries

Criterion	Rank
1. Political stability	7
2. Government efficiency	4
3. Good infrastructure (for example, good transportation and communication networks)	2
4. Cheaper land	7
5. Cheaper labor	6
6. Loan availability	3
7. Tax concessions	3
8. Availability of advanced technologies	3
9. Availability of technical and skilled manpower	5
10. Size and potential of the host country's market	1
11. Geographic location	3
12. Business and family connections	4
13. Absence of foreign-exchange control and the possibility of repatriating profits	5
14. Possibility and facility for exporting to the developed countries	6
15. Language problems	4

Competition with Local Firms in Host Countries

The benefits that an overseas subsidiary derives in a host country must be greater than the disadvantage of being less familiar with the local conditions than the local firms. What, then, are the most important advantages that Hong Kong-owned subsidiaries enjoy in the host countries? The ranking by the firms in our sample of this information is reported in table 5-9.

The factors numbered 1 to 6 in the table are characteristics of a foreign subsidiary and the last factor refers to a characteristic of the host country. The survey results indicated that the firms considered better management skill and longer experience as their greatest advantages over local firms. In general, however, they did not consider that they were more flexible and used more appropriate technologies. They also did not consider that host-country policies were in their favor.

*Competition with Other Multinationals
in Host Countries*

Evidently, multinationals from the developed countries have even better management skills and longer experience than Hong Kong-based firms. What competitive edge do they have over such multinationals?

Firms agreed unanimously that they did not have longer experience in production and they did not receive preferential treatment from the host countries. As shown in table 5-10, they considered lower costs for managerial and technical personnel as their most important advantage over the other multinationals. They also thought that they used more appropriate technologies and understood the local conditions better.

It is clear that there is no way for us to discriminate between one particular theory of foreign investment and another on the basis of the empirical evidence we have. A more "general" theory of foreign investment

**Table 5-9
Advantages over Local Firms in Host Countries**

Advantage	Rank
1. Better management skill	7
2. More advanced technologies	5
3. More appropriate technologies for the local conditions in the host countries	3
4. Longer experience in production and operation	6
5. Better connections with the export markets	4
6. Greater flexibility and adaptability	2
7. Government policies in the host countries in favor of foreign firms	1

Table 5-10
Advantages over Other Multinationals in Host Countries

Advantage	Rank
1. Lower costs for managerial and technical staff	7
2. More appropriate technology for the local conditions in the host countries	5
3. Longer experience in production and operation	0
4. Greater flexibility and adaptability	3
5. Better understanding of the conditions in the less-developed countries	6
6. Better connections with export markets	2
7. Government policies in the host countries prefer overseas firms from developing countries to these from developed countries	0
8. Better local connections in the host countries	4

is perhaps called for in explaining the behavior of third-world multinationals. This means that basically we do not need an entirely new theory, but a skillful synthesis of the existing theories.[15]

Characteristics and Objectives:
Some Generalizations

After an examination of the general patterns of Hong Kong investment in the major host countries and some survey results, we are now in a position to generalize some of the characteristics and objectives of the Hong Kong-based multinationals.

First, the fundamental reason for most Hong Kong firms to invest abroad was the search for a lower cost structure, so that they could export their products to the established markets (mainly in developed countries) at a more competitive price. The rising labor and land costs and the increasing competition from other newly industrialized countries exerted great pressure on firms to invest overseas. In most cases, the objective of foreign investment was not to open up, maintain, or expand the market in the host countries, but to maintain or expand the market in the developed countries, as mentioned earlier. We can call this the *defensive* type of foreign investment. For the developed countries, the experience was investment following trade. When these firms found that their exports were meeting increased competition from products of local firms, they began to establish subsidiaries in the overseas markets. For Hong Kong, the pattern was somewhat different. When faced with competition from other developing nations in the markets of developed countries, Hong Kong firms began to establish subsidiaries in other developing countries (which may or may not have been its competitors) and to export these products to the established markets. The cost-saving effect was derived from combining the relatively cheap management skill of the parent firm with the relatively cheap labor and land in the host countries.

Second, the other major reasons for Hong Kong investment abroad included (1) evading the quota restrictions by locating some of their production in countries not yet under such restrictions, (2) internalizing the use of technology and capital goods in the sense of economies in the use of technology and as an outlet for outdated capital goods,[16] and (3) overcoming the competitive pressure arising from an oligopolistic market structure.

Third, there were also some firms that invested overseas for the purpose of taking up opportunities not presently available in Hong Kong. Investments in chemicals, wood and wood products, and food processing in other Asian countries are examples. We can call this the *aggressive* type of foreign investment. They established subsidiaries in wood and wood products to be near the resources and invested overseas in chemicals because of the concern in Hong Kong about environmental deterioration. In these cases, the form of ownership is usually joint venture. The Hong Kong MNCs contributed capital and management skills, while the partners supplied the necessary technical skills.

Fourth, technology transfer might occur in different directions for the aggressive and defensive types of foreign investment. By investing in well-established industries such as textiles, garments, and electronics, Hong Kong-based firms perform the function of transferring their relatively more advanced and sometimes more appropriate technologies and management skills to the host developing countries. However, when Hong Kong firms invest overseas in industries such as chemicals, opticals, and machinery, which are not yet well-developed at home, there is sometimes a "backflow" of technology from the host countries to Hong Kong. This is made possible through the formation of joint ventures with the developed-country or host-country firms that have already acquired considerable technology in those industries.

Fifth, the Hong Kong-based firms usually do not attempt to build a vertically integrated structure with their overseas subsidiaries. In addition, if there are several overseas subsidiaries, usually no attempt is made to integrate the subsidiaries. However, the recent Hong Kong investment in China has developed a significantly different pattern. There is usually a vertically integrated structure between the parent firms and the subsidiaries in China in the sense that the subsidiaries are only responsible for the more labor-intensive operations of the entire production process. This is very similar to the type of relationship existing between the parent firms in developed countries and their subsidiaries in developing countries.

Sixth, when making defensive investments overseas in the industries well-established in Hong Kong, it is generally true that the foreign subsidiaries are smaller in size and lower in technology level than the Hong Kong parent firms. This usually means that those products which are more labor-intensive and less-sophisticated are taken up by the subsidiaries. This is not true of aggressive FDI in the industries not well-established in Hong Kong. In this case, the overseas subsidiaries are usually much larger than the Hong Kong parent firms.

Seventh, not many of the Hong Kong companies making foreign investments can be considered large firms. This is somewhat different from the case of the developed-country multinationals, which are generally large. During the period when developed-country MNCs first began to appear, this was especially true, although today the evidence on the size of multinationals is rather mixed. For some countries, foreign direct investment is dominated by large firms, but for others, multinationals comprise mainly medium- or even small-sized firms. In the case of Hong Kong, a large proportion of its MNCs is medium in size, employing 200 to 1,000 workers. This can perhaps be explained by the fact that the keenest competition in Hong Kong is among these medium-sized firms. The lack of opportunities to expand locally vis-à-vis the large firms drives these medium-sized companies to look for opportunities overseas. Another reason why most of the Hong Kong-firms that invest abroad are medium-sized is a circumstantial one. Many of the larger businesses are foreign-owned subsidiaries and as such, they do not fall into the category of Hong Kong multinationals.

Eighth, the competitive edge of Hong Kong firms over local firms and other multinationals is mainly accounted for by the high quality and relatively low cost of their management personnel.

This list of generalizations indicates that Hong Kong multinationals, and probably other third-world multinationals as well, are not very different from those of the developed countries. However, the evidence on the importance of management skills as a factor of production, the possibility of a two-way technology flow, and the set of complex factors affecting the motives of foreign investment is significant enough for us to reconsider the existing theories of foreign investment when applied to third-world multinationals. To reiterate, we may not need a completely new theory, but a more general theory synthesizing the existing theories is certainly called for.

Notes

1. See Palmer (1978, p. 106).

2. For a description of the export incentives, see Federal Industrial Development Authority, *Malaysia: Your Profit Center in Asia* (Malaysia, 1976), p. 14.

3. See Luey (1969, p. 114); Tang (1973, Table 5); and Yoshihara (1976, Table 7.3).

4. See Luey (1969, p. 123).

5. Before 1970, the wage level of Singapore was about 20 percent higher than that of Hong Kong.

6. Nonetheless, we can find some Hong Kong-based firms investing in the machinery and equipment industry in Singapore.

7. For an unofficial translation of the law, see *Taikung Pao (Hong Kong)*, July 9, 1979.

8. It is said that the cost of parts and materials supplied from China is usually 10 to 20 percent lower than that which can be obtained from Hong Kong firms even after allowance for transportation costs.

9. Some major points of the law are (1) the proportion of foreign investment shall not be less than 25 percent and can in fact be 100 percent; (2) the technology or equipment contributed by any foreign participant as investment shall be truly advanced and appropriate to China's needs; (3) a joint venture shall have a board of directors with the chairman appointed by China and the vice-chairman by the foreign investors; (4) business decisions shall be made on a joint consultation basis; (5) there are provisions for a tax holiday of 2 to 3 years; (6) a joint venture can export the products directly or sell the products in the Chinese market; (7) profit and wages may be remitted abroad; and (8) the provision for an arbitral body in case of disputes.

10. There are a few exceptions, one of which is Hong Kong's investment in timber in Malaysia and Indonesia. The semimanufactured wood products are shipped back to Hong Kong for further processing. A few Hong Kong textile firms in Taiwan supply fabrics to their parent garment firms in Hong Kong.

11. The sample survey also asked questions related to technology transfer, labor training, research and development, ownership, production costs, and marketing. Owing to limitation of space here, these aspects are kept for future studies.

12. This is similar to Lecraw's study of multinationals in Thailand. See Lecraw (1977).

13. The lease of part of Kowloon (the peninsula opposite Hong Kong Island) and the New Territories (the area between Kowloon and the mainland) will expire in 1997 according to the "unequal" treaty in 1898. For most of the time, the Chinese government in Peking denied all unequal treaties, and this means that the expiry data of 1997 has no meaning. Recently, however, a Chinese official in the foreign office mentioned the year 1997 and said that a solution will be made in due course in the coming 18 years.

14. For discussion on foreign investment as oligopolistic reactions, see Vernon (1971) and Knickerbocker (1973).

15. For an attempt to synthesize the existing theories, see chapter 1.

16. For an exposition of a theory on foreign investment based on the notion of internalizations of imperfect markets, see Buckley and Casson (1976).

References

Buckley, P.J., and M. Casson. 1976. *The Future of the Multinational Enterprise. London: Macmillan.*

Heenan, D.A., and W.J. Keegan. 1979. The rise of third world multinationals. *Harvard Business Review* (January-February).

Knickerbocker, F.T. 1973. *Oligopolistic Reaction and the Multinational Enterprise.* Cambridge, Mass.: M.I.T. Press.

Lecraw, D. 1977. Direct investment by firms from less developed countries. *Oxford Economic Papers* (November).

Luey, P. 1969. Hong Kong investment. In H. Hughes and P.S. You (Eds.), *Foreign Investment and Industrialisation in Singapore.* Canberra: Australian National University Press.

Palmer, I. 1978. *The Indonesian Economy Since 1965.* London: Cass.

Pennant-Rea, R. 1979. Foreign investment in Asia. *The Economist* (June 23).

Streeten, P. 1979. Multinationals revisited. *Finance and Development* (June).

Tang, S. 1973. *International Investments in Singapore.* Singapore: Malayan Law Journal.

Vernon, R. 1971. *Sovereignty at Bay.* London: Longman.

Wells, Jr., L.T. 1977. The internationalization of firms from developing countries. In T. Agmon and C.P. Kindleberger (Eds.), *Multinationals from Small Countries.* Cambridge, Mass.: M.I.T. Press.

_____ 1978. Foreign investment from the third world: The experience of Chinese firms from Hong Kong. *Columbia Journal of World Business* (Spring).

Wells, Jr., L.T., and V. Warren. 1979. Developing country investors in Indonesia. *Bulletin of Indonesian Economic Studies* (March).

Yoshihara, K. 1976. *Foreign Investment and Domestic Response.* Singapore: Eastern Universities Press.

6 Direct Investment and Technology Transfer from Taiwan

Wen-Lee Ting and
Chi Schive

This chapter focuses on foreign direct investment from Taiwan. In the first section, the general pattern of the outward flow of investment, including its technology-transfer aspect, is discussed. Illustrating this process in the later part are two cases of Taiwan corporations that have internationalized.

Taiwan's Outward Investment

The Trend of Taiwan's Outward Investment

Officially, the first Taiwanese outward investment was made in 1959 when a local firm invested $100,000 worth of machinery in a Malaysian cement plant. After a lull of 2 years, a jute-bag manufacturer restarted Taiwan's capital outflow in 1962 by setting up a plant in Thailand. Throughout the 1960s, Taiwan's annual foreign direct investment (FDI) hovered around the $800,000 level, as shown by the near horizontal line in figure 6-1. The outward investment has been increasing at the annual rate of 23.78 percent since the early 1970s, however.

By the end of 1978, Taiwan's Investment Commission approved a total of 124 investment applications, of which 27 were later withdrawn partly as a result of the end of the Vietnam war. Among the 89 local firms whose applications had been approved during the previous decades is a partly government-owned trading company with twelve subsidiaries around the world. A plastic products company with six foreign ventures is the Taiwanese manufacturing firm with the largest number of subsidiaries. Six other local firms had at least three foreign subsidiaries.

In general, Thailand, Malaysia, and Singapore attracted more than 50 percent of Taiwan's outward investment in the 1960s, while the main host countries of Taiwan's FDI in the 1970s were the Philippines, Indonesia, and the United States (table 6-1). In addition to these six countries, Taiwan's investors have located their capital in twenty-one other countries.

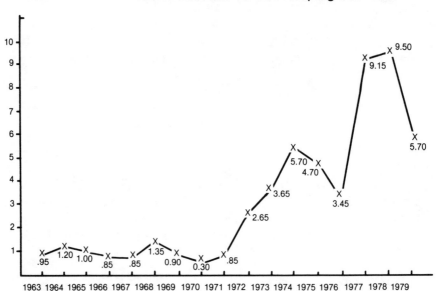

Note: The figures were moving averages over 2 years.
Unit: Millions of U.S.dollars

Figure 6-1. Taiwan's Outward Investment, 1963-1979

Motivations for Outward Investment

Taiwan's investors went abroad primarily for three reasons: (1) to secure supplies of raw materials, (2) to pursue profits by supplying host-country markets, and (3) to facilitate exports. The first category of investors are in the agricultural, forestry, fishery, lumber, and bamboo products industries. More exactly, investors in these industries are plywood producers, a fishing company, and a canned pineapple producer. Thailand, Malaysia, Indonesia, and Costa Rica are the host countries to these ventures. Table 6-2 shows the Taiwan FDI by industry in the ASEAN countries and the United States.

Firms in the food and beverage, textile, plastic and plastic products, and nonmetallic materials industries were motivated to invest overseas by the desire to supply the domestic markets of the host countries. Within the food and beverages industry, the major investors are monosodium glutamate (MSG) producers, while those in the textile industry are involved in synthetic fiber processing. Several investors in the plastics industry are also interested in foreign ventures. One PVC plastic products processor has six foreign subsidiaries. Most of the firms in the nonmetallic materials industry are cement manufacturers. To make this type of investment, the parent

Table 6-1
Destinations of Taiwan's Outward Investment
(Percent)

	Thailand	Malaysia	Singapore	Philippines	Indonesia	United States	Others
1959-1970	26.23	11.68	14.37	3.08	—	1.23	42.29
1971-1978	5.40	2.42	6.32	20.03	18.40	17.36	30.06
1959-1978	8.57	3.76	7.49	17.58	15.74	15.03	31.82

Source: *Statistics on Overseas Chinese and Foreign Investment, Technical Cooperation and Outward Investment, the Republic of China* (Investment Commission, Ministry of Economics Affairs, 1978).

Table 6-2
Taiwan's Outward Investment, by Industry and Country, 1959-1979

Industry	Thousands of U.S. Dollars (Percent of Total FDI)	Thailand	Malaysia	Singapore	Philippines	Indonesia	United States	Others
							Percentage of Industry FDI	
1. Forestry, fishing, lumber products	4,523 (8.06%)	8.38	25.07	—	—	22.33	—	44.22
2. Food and beverages	7,340 (13.02%)	19.30	—	—	3.42	20.53	—	56.86
3. Textiles	7,460 (13.30%)	12.36	1.74	9.48	—	51.14	—	25.28
4. Garments and footwear	749 (1.33%)	—	—	75.43	8.01	—	—	16.55
5. Paper	1,960 (3.49%)	—	—	—	—	100.00	—	—
6. Plastic and plastic materials	13,449 (24.06%)	2.27	0.59	6.87	68.52	2.00	3.70	16.10
7. Nonmetallic minerals	7,052 (10.57%)	—	2.04	13.57	1.47	—	6.54	76.80
8. Primary metal and machinery	2,401 (4.28%)	33.78	14.54	5.54	—	11.66	8.33	26.16
9. Electronics and electrical appliances	4,505 (8.03%)	17.40	4.93	20.24	2.22	—	47.39	7.81
10. Trade	6,279 (11.19%)	3.30	0.29	—	1.59	—	79.63	15.19
11. Construction, finance, service, and others	376 (0.67%)	—	17.28	—	—	—	37.23	45.48
Total	56,108 (100.00%)	—	—	—	—	—	—	—

Source: *Statistics on Overseas Chinese and Foreign Investment, Technical Cooperation and Outward Investment, the Republic of China* (Investment Commission, Ministry of Economic Affairs, 1978).

firm must have the necessary experience and technology to compete with local firms and other MNC subsidiaries. The Taiwan investors in these four industries have the common characteristic of a long period of development and experience in their special areas. For example, the MSG and cement industries were established by the 1950s and the PVC and PE plastics industries were well developed in the late 1950s and late 1960s, respectively. It was in the late 1960s also that the synthetic fiber industry experienced rapid growth until it was supplying up to 90 percent of the local demand.[1] Thus the investing firms in the four industries were equipped with the necessary technology and experience before entering the relatively risky foreign market.

The third type of investment was aimed at facilitating exports of Taiwanese goods. FDI in the electronics and electrical appliance and trade industries can be classified in this category. Table 6-2 indicates that the United States attracted 47.3 percent of the outward investment in the electronics and electrical appliance industry and 79.63 percent of that in trade activities. With the U.S. market absorbing around 40 percent of Taiwan's total exports in the 1970s, it was seen that any import quota imposed on Taiwanese goods would impede that country's trade. As a result, the establishment of subsidiaries in the trade partner for bringing in the semifinished products, which are not as tightly restricted, became an effective way to penetrate the trade barriers. The three largest Taiwanese electronics and electrical appliance producers all have ventures in the United States. Other large exporting manufacturers are eager to set up trading offices in their major export markets. For instance, Taiwan's largest sewing machine maker organized a trading company in the United States in the middle 1970s.

Exports of Machinery

Another aspect of Taiwan's FDI, especially the second type aimed at the host-country markets, is the significant proportion of capital transmitted in the form of machinery. Table 6-3 shows that by the end of 1979, about 25 percent of the capital for valid investments was contributed as machinery, worth approximately $12 million. By deducting the investment in trade activities, exports of machinery increases to 31.4 percent of the total investment capital. The use of machinery as capital in foreign investment is not unique to the Taiwanese investors. In 1965, 50 percent of the foreign direct investment transmitted to Taiwan was in the form of machinery.

One explanation of this phenomenon is that the machinery exported as capital is not new. Although we lack conclusive data to verify this statement, studies in other countries shed some light on the issue. In the early

Table 6-3
Capital Composition of Taiwan's Outward Investment, 1959-1979
(Percent)

	Foreign Currency	Machinery	Materials	Technical Know-How	Total
Taiwan's valid outward investment	64.89	25.72	8.15	1.24	100.00
Taiwan's outward investment withdrawn	45.42	43.41	11.00	0.17	100.00
Total	62.69	27.71	8.47	1.12	100.00
FDI in Taiwan in 1965	28.60	50.00	21.40	—	100.00

Sources: Investment Commission of Taiwan; and M.C. Liu, "Overseas Chinese and Foreign Enterprise and Economic Development in Taiwan" (in Chinese), *Bank of Taiwan Quarterly* 20(1971):51.

1960s, Stressman found that "among American subsidiaries, 79 percent of those in Mexico and 57 percent of those in Puerto Rico used second hand machines."[2] Moreover, three-fifths of the foreign firms used second-hand machines, while only one-third of the national firms did so. Given the fact that the used-machinery market is imperfect and there are biases against using such machines, the economic value of used machines can be higher than their book value.[3] Besides, the use of second-hand machines may reduce costs if the worker has greater familiarity with them and operates them more easily and efficiently. Sometimes, the limited local market size may be too small to justify using a newly developed machine designed for a large market. In addition, the technological level of the recipient may be too low to absorb more sophisticated new machinery. All these factors indicate that investors both from abroad to Taiwan and from Taiwan to other countries also might use second-hand machines as capital in their overseas ventures.

A further investigation of Taiwanese investors going abroad reveals that the six cable and wire manufacturers capitalized a total of $571,000 worth of machinery, accounting for 85.86 percent of their total outward investment. Three out of the five cement companies used exported machinery as capital, and four out of seven of the monosodium glutamate manufacturers did so. Generally speaking, capitalization of machinery for FDI was more popular in the 1960s than in the 1970s. During the 1970s, the number of instances of using machinery as capital decreased, while the value of the machinery brought out by the investors increased. Two examples can be found in the paper and synthetic fibers industries. Two local paper producers formed a joint venture with Indonesian overseas Chinese to manufacture paper. The total capital committed was $1,960,000, all in the form of machinery. Another case is the Indonesian investment by Tuntex, which is to sell a plant for $26 million, of which 13.85 percent will be used as investment capital (see the case study of Tuntex). Given the rapidly growing local machinery industry (Taiwan exports of machinery increased 14.5 times during the period 1970-1978 and reached $541 million in 1978) and the size of each investment made recently, the latest investments involving machinery are unlikely to export depreciated machinery. If this is so, outward investment is an effective way to stimulate home-country machinery industry exports, as it did in the developed countries.

Export of Technical Know-How

From table 6-3 we also observed that some investors carried out their overseas ventures by providing technical know-how directly. The capitalized technical skills accounted for 1.12 percent of the total capital outflow. After mastering a particular technology, some Taiwanese investors tried to maximize the returns from their rent-yielding assets. For instance, when a Taiwanese PVC producer established a plastics plant in 1975, which, with an annual capacity of 240,000 tons, made it the fifth largest plant in the world at that time, it was well-qualified to sell the technology to any other firm in the world. This company then sold its technical know-how to a Puerto Rican firm and the receipts were capitalized as equity in that firm. Acceptance of technology from Taiwan also may be due to the preference for an arms-length transaction or for the lower price of the Taiwan firm's technical know-how.

From the limited data just presented, we can infer that when a firm accumulated experience in processing a certain product and gradually built up the capability of maintaining and even modifying the process, it increased the value of its old machinery by capitalizing it when investing abroad. A few firms went a step further, using their technical know-how in the same manner or exporting a complete plant if the home-country machinery industry was capable of producing it.

The following brief case studies of two Taiwanese firms provide further examples of some of the motivations and operational and technological characteristics we have just mentioned. Data used in the case studies were obtained through personal interviews with management personnel and from secondary sources.

Gamma Corporation

Gamma Corporation,[4] a leading electrical and electronics manufacturer in Taiwan, is a multidivisional company with a wide range of product lines ranging from consumer household appliances, telecommunications equipment, electronics products and computers, to heavy electrical equipment and instruments, steel, machinery, and chemicals. In 1978, the company's gross sales amounted to US$340 million. Founded 60 years ago, it has steadily progressed, with domestic success, to become a major industrial corporation in Taiwan and, with later foreign investments, also achieved the status of a technologically competent multinational firm.

Beginning in the early 1970s, it established a network of manufacturing subsidiaries abroad in Japan, Singapore, Hong Kong, and the United States, in addition to a global network of sales and purchasing offices in Europe, the Middle East, and Africa. By 1977 it had reached a level of overseas investment totaling about US$5 million. Gamma's entry into international business followed the classic pattern of development. Its success in exports led to technical cooperation and licensing of technical know-how and, subsequently, into direct investment in wholly owned manufcturing subsidiaries. Gamma's subsidiaries in Japan, Singapore, and the United States primarily manufacture and assemble products, such as household appliances and electronic goods, with which it had attained domestic success.

Besides the manufacturing subsidiaries and the network of sales offices to service export markets, Gamma also entered into technical-cooperation agreements and joint ventures with local manufacturers in several LDCs. Examples include technical-assistance agreements and equity joint ventures in electrical household appliances in the Philippines and Thailand and manufacturing electronic products in Indonesia and Malaysia. A summary of Gamma's diverse international business ventures is shown in table 6-4.

Motivations for Internationalization

A combination of factors seems to have spurred Gamma's multinationalization. The success Gamma found in its domestic market appears to have provided the initial thrust by both conferring upon it the ability to invest abroad as well as engendering a need for it to internationalize in order to maintain the image of leadership and prestige among its competitors. A closely parallel reason is the reinforcement of its brand name in the international markets to which it had already been exporting. The immediate motive of circumventing tariffs and quota restrictions of markets in the European Economic Community (EEC) and high-tariff LDCs also may have contributed to Gamma's internationalizing its production. As West European protectionism went up against Asian electronics exports, many of those firms moved their production plants to excess-quota countries in order to maintain their European sales from these locations. For instance, Gamma's television plant in Singapore was established to circumvent the EEC's quota and also to supply completely knocked-down units to high-tariff countries in the surrounding region.

Table 6-4
Gamma's Overseas Investment, Technical Cooperation, and Sales Servicing, 1978

Country	Investment[a] (Thousands of U.S. Dollars)	Form of Business[b]	Products	Capital-Labor[c] (Thousands of Dollars per Worker)
Japan	102.8	WOS, SST	Television, Washing Machines, Cookers, Refrigerator reassembly	2.7
United States	1,353.0	WOS, SST	Color televisions, electric fan mfg.	12.3
Hong Kong	108.3	WOS, SST	Color television, mfg.	9.5
Singapore	1,143.5	WOS, SST	Television picture tube mfg., television assembly	7.76
Indonesia	Technical fees	TA, EJV	Television, transistors, stereos, transformers,	N.A.
Thailand	Technical fees	TA, EJV	Televisions, refrigerators	N.A.
Philippines	100.0	TA, EJV	Washing machines, rice cookers, electric fans, meters	N.A.
West Germany	—	SST	Electrical household products, televisions, audio	—
Korea	—	SST	Electrical household products, television, audio	—

[a]Investment includes plant, machinery and equipment, working capital, and land.
[b]WOS = wholly owned manufacturing subsidiary; TA = technical assistance; EJV = equity joint venture; SST = sales servicing, import/export, and retailing.
[c]Capital-labor ratios are based on investment in fixed assets, such as plant, machinery, and equipment, but excluding land.

Coinciding with these internal stimuli to internationalize was the formulation by the Taiwan government of a policy to encourage an outward flow of investment to diversify the economy. As a highly export-dependent economy in the midst of growing uncertainty in the world export markets, the government embarked on a strategy of diversifying from product flows to capital flows. Therefore, both inward investment and overseas investment were encouraged in order to further strengthen Taiwan's international economic links. The flow of outward investments was mainly to LDCs in Southeast Asia in the intermediate technology industries as well as to other newly industrializing countries and the United States and Japan.[5] Thus Gamma's move overseas was a response to both internal and external imperatives.

Operational Profile

Organizational and Personnel Policies. As would be expected of a multinational from a newly industrializing country (NIC) in the Asia-pacific region, Gamma Corporation is ethnocentric in its approach to the management of its subsidiaries. Most of the planning and control decisions are centralized in the Taipei headquarters. Out of necessity, only day-to-day operational decisions are localized in the various subsidiaries. The company's personnel policies are also characterized by an ethnocentric orientation. Virtually all management and technical personnel in its foreign subsidiaries are home-country nationals. This is due to the firm being both culturally predisposed and economically motivated to use managers and technicians from Taiwan. The costs of maintaining its overseas personnel are much lower than those of the advanced countries' multinationals. In addition, the nature of Gamma's investments in less-capital-intensive, small-scale and general-purpose technology in its subsidiaries requires a greater number of skilled personnel capable of improvisation to substitute for the lack of specialized production equipment usually found in capital-intensive technology. Thus, even operating-level technicians in the subsidiaries are home-country nationals.

Marketing Orientation. In contrast to MNCs from developed countries, Gamma Corporation is less sophisticated in its marketing and is more production- and process-oriented. However, compared with many other local firms, it has demonstrated a high degree of marketing orientation. It has, for instance, carefully developed an internationally reputable image through the use of a well-designed brand name and logo. Brand recognition and awareness are relatively high in many of the LDCs in Southeast Asia and Europe, where many of its household and electronic products are selling competitively against other well-known foreign brands in the local markets.

Although lacking in any original R&D and new product innovations, Gamma nevertheless pursues a relatively sophisticated product-modification strategy. In the field of consumer electronics, for instance, Gamma's product strategy involves the "scaling up" and "scaling down" of product features and designs to meet the specific needs of different levels of consumer sophistication. It has therefore a rather substantial department dealing with adaptive R&D and product modification.

Production and Technology. As an NIC, Taiwan has acquired the capability of providing production technology to other NICs and LDCs. Technology transfers by firms from newly industrializing nations usually gravitate toward the intermediate-technology industries of the recipient economies. They are usually more efficient providers of products and processes at the lower and intermediate stages of the technology spectrum.[6] The NIC firm's technological compatibility with the recipient stems from the proximity in the stage of general economic development and similarity in the level of technical compatibility. It is often more efficient to transmit technology to LDCs via the more advanced developing countries rather than directly from advanced countries to LDCs because of the wide technological gap between them. Thus Taiwan has been perceived as a bridge in the technology-transfer process. It receives, absorbs, and adapts advanced technology from the industrialized countries and then transmits the technology in a scaled-down and modified form to other developing nations.

NIC multinationals are more efficient suppliers of modified or intermediate technology because of their cost economics in the transfer process. Their investments usually are small-scale and less-capital-intensive than those of their advanced-country counterparts. They also incur lower overheads in terms of less-expensive overseas personnel and facilities.[7] On the side of consumption technology, multinationals from NICs may have superior market knowledge, especially in standardized, mature, and less-sophisticated products vis-à-vis the industrialized-country firms.

In the same vein, Gamma Corporation served as a conduit in the technology-transfer process. In its early stages, Gamma was the recipient of quite advanced technology in household appliances and consumer electronics from the United States and Japan through technical assistance with limited capital participation from a few key firms in those countries. Recently, it has assumed the role of the transmitter of this technology both through direct investment and technical-cooperation agreements with manufacturers in Southeast Asia. Through greater cost economics and better market knowledge of consumption technology in LDCs, Gamma has an advantage over advanced-countries' multinationals in the transfer of such technology.

Tuntex's Investment in Indonesia

Tuntex Fiber Company, a synthetic fibers producer established in 1973, started operation in 1975 with a daily capacity of 42 tons. By 1979, it was ranked as eleventh among the twenty-seven producers in the industry. Originally, Tuntex was organized with a Japanese investment that was later withdrawn. The total investment of Tuntex amounted to $46.4 million in 1979, and the total revenue was $24.7 million in the same year. Tuntex exported 43 percent of its total product, valued at $10.7 million in 1978, which accounted for 3.4 percent of Taiwan's total exports of synthetic fibers.

Before planning the Indonesia venture, Tuntex had applied for permission to go to Singapore, but this project was not realized. Although Tuntex was neither a foreign firm nor a multinational corporation before the proposed Indonesian investment, the company had a firm relationship with local businessmen in Japan and the Southeast Asian countries owing to the fact that the chairman of the board of Tuntex, Mr. Y.H. Chen, had resided in Singapore for several years. During that period, he helped organize a cement-factory project in Indonesia receiving technical assistance from a Taiwanese cement producer.

In 1979, the company, with three overseas Chinese groups, applied for an investment permit in Indonesia to set up a polyester fiber plant. The total capital of the Indonesian plant was $12 million, in which Tuntex and its subsidiary, Tuntex Engineering Company, owned 30 percent, the Indonesian partners owned 45 percent, and the remainder belonged to a Hong Kong-based overseas Chinese group.

The most distinctive characteristic of Tuntex's investment is not related to the amount of capital committed, but the total value of the machinery to be exported with the investment. In the proposed project, Tuntex Engineering would sell a complete $26 million polyester fiber plant to the newly organized company, which is about 7.2 times of the total capital committed. Therefore, an obvious rationale behind Tuntex's investment is, among others, to facilitate the sale of synthetic fiber processing equipment.

Motivations of Tuntex's Indonesian Investment

Although Tuntex has a relatively short period of development experience, it has been running at near full capacity since its establishment. Tuntex acquired its technology by purchasing the equipment from a developed-country MNC. From another report, Tuntex was known to have improved the technology significantly through process changes made by its engineering group. Tuntex's overall performance led it to consider maximizing its rent-yielding assets through direct foreign investment. The Indonesian venture is just the beginning; Tuntex is working on a second project in an African country.

Another reason for Tuntex's investment is to provide a secure export market for its intermediate production. Tuntex uses petrochemicals to produce polyester chips, and from these the fiber is made. In 1978, the production of chips accounted for 80 percent of the company's total output by value. Once the Indonesia plant is in operation, Tuntex will supply all the chips it needs, which is roughly 30 percent of the Tuntex chip production. Thus Tuntex is looking for a multipurpose investment project.

Operational Profile

In addition to the machinery and materials offer, Tuntex is fully responsible for the implementation of the project from the very beginning. A sixty-person team comprised of management personnel and engineers will be sent to construct the plant. According to Mr. Chen, the cost of this team is very competitive if compared with those from Japan or the United States. An equally important factor in Tuntex's favor is that its local partners are Indonesian overseas Chinese. In this case, no serious cultural and/or language obstacle is foreseen.

Looking from the host country's point of view, the investment is also favorable in many ways. First, the plant will create about 600 jobs. Tuntex's initial large involvement in terms of personnel is bound to decrease as the plant starts functioning well. Second, the local overseas Chinese are interested in diversifying their activities, especially in developing certain manufacturing industries. Part of the reason may be for creating a better image. Third, all synthetic fibers produced are to supply the local market. In spite of the fact that there are so many unfavorable arguments against the import-substitution strategy, the synthetic fibers industry is vital to the downstream fabrics industry in which Indonesia has a comparative advantage. However, Indonesia is in a favorable position to develop its petrochemical industry owing to its large oil deposits. In short, the artificial fiber industry has strong forward as well as backward linkages that may justify the heavy capital outlay for its development.

Conclusion

The trend of Taiwan's outward investment shows that the country has entered the multinational stage of international business for various purposes: to secure supplies of raw materials, to pursue profits by supplying host-country markets as well as transferring technology, and to facilitate its exports. Both Gamma's and Tuntex's outward ventures point to one thing; that is, we should start paying attention to the multinational corporations from the third world, more specifically, from the NICs and the role these

MNCs play in the technology-transfer process. Further study is also needed to determine the different effects of direct investment from developed and new industrializing countries.

Notes

1. For details, see C. Schive, "Direct Foreign Investment, Technology Transfer and Linkage Effects: A Case Study of Taiwan", Unpublished dissertation, Case Western Reserve University, 1978, chap. 5.

2. W.P. Stressman, *Technological Change and Economics Development, The Manufacturing Experience of Mexico and Puerto Rico* (Ithaca, N.Y.: Cornell Univ. Press, 1968), p. 211.

3. For details, see D.D. James, *Used Machinery and Economic Development* (M.S.U. International Business and Economic Studies, 1974), chaps. 2, 4, and 7.

4. A fictitious name has been used to preserve the anonymity of the firm.

5. The term *intermediate technology* as used here should not be confused with the popular meaning it has acquired in the media and elsewhere, connoting usually a small-scale, non automated, and indigenous process. It is rather a measure of the R&D intensity of a production process or a product.

6. See W.L. Ting, "Transfer of Intermediate Technology by Third World Multinationals," in *Academy of International Business Conference Proceedings* (Honolulu, December 1979).

7. See L.T. Wells, Jr., and V'Ella Warren, "Developing Country Investors in Indonesia," *Bulletin of Indonesian Economic Studies* 15(1); and Wells, "Foreign Investment from the Third World: The Experience of Chinese Firms from Hong Kong," *Columbia Journal of World Business* (Spring 1978).

7

Third-World Joint Ventures: Indian Experience

Ram Gopal Agrawal

The postwar world has witnessed a series of developments in the field of international trade and investment. The pure theory of international trade specifies the nature and direction of world trade from the principle of comparative costs. These are analyzed in terms of factor endowments and demand conditions that produce relative advantages in different markets. Originally, the flow of goods could be understood in these terms, but this has to be extended to the flow of capital. The rationale of comparative costs has found equal application in the analysis of foreign investment, which has reflected itself in the growing trend toward internationalization of firms. This trend appears natural and transcends conventional trading mechanisms. The giant conglomerates, mainly of the developed countries, with enormous capital base, sophisticated technology, and efficient management, have been continually extending their operations on the basis of comparative costs.

These *multinationals*, or *transnationals*, are defined as those which "directly control the deployment of resources in two or more countries and the distribution of the resulting output generated between these countries." The MNC represents a key force in the international business world and now a major influence in the conduct of world affairs. Its basic goals are to operate a vigorous, growing, diversified, and profitable business. This corporate organizational form promised to increase world welfare by its ability to combine the use of internationally mobile and immobile factors of production effectively. Its advantages lay in allocating capital and technology, along with management skills in organizing production and sale on a global basis. However, in some cases, the MNC acquired a bad image, for it failed to relate itself well to the problems of host nations. In other cases, it transgressed certain limits, making it socially and even economically detrimental to the interests of the host nations.

Origin and Growth

It is against this backdrop that one has to view the emergence of joint production and marketing enterprises of the third world. These also have been christened multinationals—miniature multinationals—because their opera-

115

tions extend to more than one country. Since the term *multinational*, or *transnational*, has generally come to be associated with large corporations of developed countries, it is desirable to characterize joint-venture operations of the third world somewhat differently. In the search for a new nomenclature, one could think of corporate enterprises of the third world. These would include commercial and industrial enterprises in which two or more parties from two or more developing countries share the responsibility for operation by providing risk capital, goodwill, know-how and management, natural resources, and access to national markets in an agreed manner. Mere movements of capital between nations, as occurring from oil-rich OPEC to other developing countries, would not fall within the purview of such ventures. It may be mentioned that such enterprises can contribute significantly to the expansion of the production capacity, trade, and technological capability of developing countries as well as to the mobilization of their financial resources in a way that is not subject to domination by transnational corporations.[1]

In Asia, the Middle East, Latin America, and parts of Africa, a number of local firms are moving abroad to establish manufacturing plants in other developing countries. Indian companies have set up joint ventures in Malaysia, Thailand, Kenya, Indonesia, and even the United Kingdom, the United States, and West Germany. Argentine firms have established production facilities in Brazil, Chile, and Uruguay. For some developing countries that are looking for technology or management from abroad, investment from other developing countries appears to offer an economically and perhaps politically attractive alternative to the traditional linkup with multinational corporations of the developed world.

It may be mentioned here that these joint ventures play a catalytic role in promoting the trade transactions among the developing countries, both qualitatively as well as quantitatively. Although the magnitude of trade creation cannot be measured in view of limited experience, its potential cannot be ignored. Needless to emphasize that the fallout has its impact in total economic relations. The growing volume of capital exports from the developing countries indicate, albeit obliquely, its contribution (see table 7-1).

Motivations

The factors that encourage foreign investment and technology transfers by a wide range of firms from the developing countries are many and varied. The motivations in promoting inter-developing-country ventures arise from one or more of the following factors by the investing country:

Table 7-1
Value and Growth of Exports of Capital Goods from Developing Countries

Exporting Countries and Territories	Value of Capital Goods Exported (US$ Million)		Average Annual Rate of Export Growth, 1968-1976 (Percent)		Share of Capital Goods in Exports, 1976 (Percent)
	1968	1976	Capital Goods	Total Exports	
1	2	3	4	5	6
Argentina	24.3	292.8	36.5	14.1	7.5
Bahrain	0.0ᵃ	46.9	627.3	26.5	3.1
Brazil	32.1	542.5	42.4	23.4	5.4
Colombia	2.2	29.0	38.0	14.9	1.7
Hong Kong	18.7	176.6	32.4	21.9	3.1
India	20.4	139.9	27.3	14.5	2.7
Indonesia	—	41.3	—	37.0	0.5
Iran	1.1	34.7	54.3	37.5	0.1
Ivory Coast	6.3	23.7	17.9	18.2	1.1
Kuwait	5.8	98.4ᵇ	42.4	27.4	1.1
Malaysia	5.3	193.7	56.6	19.3	4.9
Mexico	15.7	119.7	28.9	12.8	3.6
Pakistan	2.5	22.3	31.4	6.0	1.9
Republic of Korea	6.7	624.9	76.2	42.5	8.1
Singapore	46.4	703.2	40.5	22.8	10.7
Thailand	0.18	11.8	73.2	20.8	0.4
Trinidad and Tobago	5.4	15.3	13.8	21.3	0.7
Yugoslavia	202.4	891.7	20.4	18.4	18.3
Total	395.3	4008.4	33.6	24.2	3.7

Sources: UNCTAD Secretariat, based on *Handbook of International Trade and Development Statistics*, UNCTAD (various issues); *Commodity Trade Statistics, Series D*, United Nations (various issues); and *Non-Series D United Nations Trade Tapes*, TD/B/739, 9 March 1979.
ᵃLess than US$50,000.
ᵇ1975.

1. Sharing of experience and expertise in fields where adequate capabilities have been developed in the home country.
2. Setting up enterprises of a comparatively medium/small size in industries in which transnational corporations did not evince interest.
3. Safeguarding of markets to which goods have been exported and using the venture for promoting exports.
4. Expectation of a reasonable return on investment coupled with technical know-how fees and royalties.
5. Participation as a means to secure larger orders for machinery and components.
6. An assured supply of raw materials.
7. Diversification of business risks among two or more countries.

However, the motivations of the host country include the following:

1. Obtaining investment without use of own foreign exchange.
2. Acquiring technology best suited to its needs.
3. Setting up of import substitution and export-oriented industries.
4. Participation in management.
5. Stronger bargaining position vis-à-vis transnational corporations.

Other factors that govern the decision to invest abroad include the dynamic desire to make a name abroad, use of the joint-venture country as a production base for the supply of components to the investing country, indirect fringe benefits such as easy foreign travel on behalf of the joint venture, creation of an outpost through the joint venture for commercial intelligence, using it as an instrument of trade development on a two-way basis, demonstration of a dynamic spirit of enterprise in carrying out a job outside one's own country, and absorbing new ideas through such operations in a competitive environment.[2]

One of the major impulses of the investing company of a developing country in venturing abroad can be explained by the growth theory of the firm. If restraints on expansion of an enterprise are placed at home, growth can be achieved by diversifying risks across the borders through transfer of appropriate technology suited to the needs of the host country. The acceptability of joint ventures among developing nations has been increasing, for they often tend to have a competitive edge over multinationals of developed countries whose practices of transfer pricing, earning excessive profits, underbidding the domestic producers, and so forth have come in for a certain degree of criticism. Other factors that interact to promote the internationalization of LDC firms are the stimuli provided by the policies of the investing country by viewing such effort as an important instrument of export promotion and sharing relevant technology with codeveloping countries. Firms of developing countries investing abroad particularly thrive in such segments of the market where they can withstand cost competition on their own economic strength because of the relatively low cost of their operations inclusive of the low prepromotional expenses, such as the preparation of feasibility reports, offering consultancy services, and the like. The DC investors have an in-built advantage by adapting technology for manufacturing products where the total size of the operation is relatively small. In other words, they have concentrated on finding a niche in areas where small-scale technology is ideally suited to the needs of the host country. The transfer of management technology and other personnel is also very economic. Low cost of management and other technical skills enhance the advantage of LDC investors over the multinationals of developed countries. Further, this trend is often regarded as a complementary factor for promoting overall economic cooperation among developing countries.

Economic Cooperation among Developing Countries (ECDC) and Third-World Joint Venture Enterprises

Following the Nairobi Conference in 1976, UNCTAD set up a Committee on Economic Cooperation among Developing Countries (ECDC). One major dimension of the issue relates to the need for extending and expanding trade and other linkages among them. Several studies have been undertaken on matters such as evolving a global system of trade preferences among developing countries and cooperation between state trading organizations and multinational marketing enterprises.[3] As for multinational production enterprises, a number of ideas have been generated for formulating a clear definition of the concept and for promoting projects that have either significant linkages with new or existing facilities in more than one country or projects involving the location of complementary facilities in one or more countries. Recommendations have been made for preparing an indicative list of sectoral investment possibilities in production of social goods based on complementarity, rational development of nonrenewable resources, optimal exploitation of natural resources for the efficient development of agro-based projects, and development of basic industries, engineering industry, and so forth. The concept of collective self-reliance implies an active approach toward creation of additional productive capacity, and the multinational production enterprises of developing countries have an important role to play.[4]

The resolution adopted by UNCTAD refers *inter alia* to the need for intensification of activities by it in collaboration with United Nations Industrial Development Organization (UNIDO), leading to action-oriented conclusions in the field of multinational production enterprises among developing countries [Resolution 127(V), adopted on June 3, 1979]. There are suggestions for the setting up of arrangements for joint technological research and development, design and engineering in areas of common interest, and even establishment of preferential arrangements for development and transfer of technology inter se developing countries.[5]

These initiatives may be said to reflect, to a degree, a "growing questioning of Western models of industrialization and urbanization, together with a renewed emphasis on rediscovering one's own cultural heritage, as well as the need to have the economic capacity to be able to follow a genuinely independent development path."[6] Along with other measures, joint ventures among developing nations are an essential component and instrument for bringing about structural changes for stimulating the growth process in the third world. At the national level, total integration of economic planning, even within small sub regions, is difficult to achieve. Such integration at the intercountry level has posed even more problems, for such programs of integration tend to be inflexible and limit interregional initiatives. It is in this context that one has to view the initiatives taken at the

Asian trade ministers' meeting held in New Delhi (August 16–23, 1978) that also emphasized the role of "trade-creating" joint ventures as providing scope for promotion of intraregional trade. At the micro level, the joint-venture enterprises, which bring together partners having common objectives and interests, seek to concretize such cooperation for mutual benefit. Because of limited specific objectives, they do not require a higher degree of political commitment and economic adjustment involving a large number of related projects and general industrial policy. They thus become suitable and flexible vehicles for cooperation on a bilateral or trilateral basis within economic regions as well as between countries belonging to different regions.

In terms of promotion and ownership, multinational enterprises fall into some general patterns: ventures involving mainly private-equity participation and market development; broader public-sector initiatives on a bilateral or multilateral basis, but outside the framework of regional or subregional groupings; and multinational enterprises utilizing finance from those developing countries with surplus liquidity in a manner likely to yield commercial returns on their investments while strengthening third-world solidarity in production and trade.

In terms of their operational objectives, these production enterprises fall into three main categories:

1. Regionally oriented ventures inspired by and contributing to a broader set of cooperation and integration strategies.
2. Sectorally oriented ventures resulting from and contributing to sector coordination among two or more third-world countries located in the same or different regions.
3. Essentially ad hoc enterprises that serve a particular bilateral or multilateral common interest but which do not form part of a broader framework of collective self-reliance.

The overall contribution of the joint-venture enterprise to third-world development is likely to be greater in the case of initiatives falling into the first two categories. They provide a framework within which practical issues can sometimes be resolved over a period of time on a case-by-case basis and which avoids the problems of broad industrial allocation and the forecasting of the distribution of benefits between the participating countries.

Among specific economic objectives that can be achieved through such undertakings, the following may be noted:

1. The utilization of resources not likely to be developed on the basis of a single national market.
2. Integration of different production stages through the utilization of regional resources and market complementarities.

3. The organization of production lines so as to achieve economies of scale and specialization within branches of industry, while providing a mutually acceptable dispersion of production facilities and pooling of markets.

4. The enhancement of opportunities for intra-third-world trade through the creation of transportation and commercial enterprises devoted to that purpose as well as the establishment of third-world consultant firms.

5. Strengthening the bargaining power of developing countries in their trade relations with developed countries through the creation of multinational export and import enterprises owned and controlled by developing countries.

It has been found that establishment of joint ventures of the third world has considerably enhanced third-world bargaining power in negotiating with multinational enterprises of the developed world in obtaining capital and relevant technology. The sharing of talent and expertise has resulted in a great degree of confidence and credibility concerning each other's capabilities. Thinking also has been generated that such sharing should not be deemed to constitute "brain drain," for it benefits the giver as much as the taker. The need for cooperative exchange of skills among developing countries is being increasingly recognized.[7] Such skilled manpower transfer from one developing country to another can be absorbed in an expanding industrial society with a modern value system. In general, the corporate cultures and management styles interact better in the ethos prevailing among developing countries. For promoting joint ventures, this is of considerable importance. Support action for such enterprises can be given through a proper information referral system that can be set up on a regional or global basis.

It is equally important to conceive of joint-production enterprises, wherever possible, with buy-back arrangements so that the interests of the host country become better protected. The concept of joint-production enterprises also must be enlarged by mutual help in setting up industrial estates and workshops. Other areas where greater awareness must be created are in the service sectors, including banking, insurance, shipping, transport, and communications. The financial institutions in the developing countries can be strengthened by exchange of personnel and by creation of suitable training programs. The exchange of experience of investment-promotion agencies in developing countries is also of relevance for promoting joint-production enterprises.

In this context, reference may be made to the suggestion made for the creation of a preinvestment fund for the setting up of joint-venture projects of the third world made in the paper entitled "Monetary and Financial Cooperation to Support the Programme of Trade Preferences among Developing Countries."[8] The nonaligned countries also have been discussing the need for strengthening the technical-cooperation and consultancy-services arrangements among them, including the feasibility of setting up a project development facility (PDF). A decision on this was finally taken at the Ministerial Meeting of the Coordinating Bureau of Nonaligned Countries held in Colombo from June 4 to 9, 1979. This will promote the use of technical skills and know-how available among these countries for the preparation of feasibility studies and project reports and encourage the use of equipment available in executing projects and programs. This will involve the organization of a "user-oriented system" encompassing multiple routes for participation and flow of requisite technical expertise and technological services. It will need sound information-collection and dissemination mechanisms responsive to the needs of the developing countries. A selective approach will have to be adopted to concentrate on a few specific areas to demonstrate the impact and contribution which alone can have spinoff effects.

A cognate idea that has been processed separately relates to the establishment of an industrial development unit within the Commonwealth Fund for Technical Cooperation. This unit would mobilize capabilities to help solve specific industrial problems and provide continuing assistance to commonwealth developing countries in their industrialization effort. This would include preinvestment services.[9] A study of the Indian experience of establishing joint ventures would be relevant to concretize the components of the ECDC as was outlined earlier.

Indian Joint Ventures Abroad

India has emerged as one of the third-world countries taking a lead in setting up joint-venture projects abroad. Today India has nearly 200 operating joint enterprises spread over 35 countries. Of these, 110 have already gone into production and 87 are in various stages of implementation. The countries in which Indian joint-venture projects are being established are shown in table 7-2.

Most of the ventures are spread over the developing regions of Asia and Africa. A few projects, numbering 22, are in advanced countries, such as the United States, the United Kingdom, Canada, West Germany, and Switzerland. India's labor-intensive technology has found acceptance in developing countries mainly because of the similarity in socioeconomic conditions. The developing countries, as is well known, are handicapped owing to the scarcity of capital, although they have an abundance of resources—both material and manpower—that remain either underutilized or unutilized. Collaboration with a country like India is welcome in these countries primarily because it helps optimize the use of available factors of

Table 7-2
Analysis by Country of Indian Joint Ventures Abroad, as of July 31, 1979

Country	In Production	Under Implementation	Total Operative Joint Ventures
Afghanistan	1	2	3
Australia	—	1	1
Bahrain	1	—	1
Bangladesh	—	1	1
Canada	1	1	2
Fiji	1	1	2
France	1	—	1
Hong Kong	1	1	2
Indonesia	9	9	18
Iran	1	2	3
Kenya	8	6	14
Kuwait	1	1	2
Libya	—	1	1
Malaysia	27	9	36
Mauritius	8	1	9
Netherlands	1	—	1
Nigeria	5	7	12
Nepal	1	6	7
Oman	3	2	5
Philippines	3	3	6
Qatar	—	1	1
Saudi Arabia	1	6	7
Seychelles	—	1	1
Singapore	6	2	8
Spain	—	1	1
Sri Lanka	3	2	5
Switzerland	—	1	1
Thailand	5	3	8
Uganda	1	—	1
United Arab Emirates	9	8	17
United Kingdom (including N. Ireland)	4	2	6
United States	6	4	10
West Germany	1	—	1
Yugoslavia	—	1	1
Zambia	1	1	2
Total	110	87	197

production and thereby creates a basis for an orderly growth of their economies.

The efficacy of Indian collaboration, particularly in the developing countries, has been mentioned in a study of the operational characteristics of LDC firms in Thailand: "LDC firms, especially Indian firms, often used absolutely efficient technology; they operated . . . with costs below the theoretical minimum cost."[10]

The joint-venture projects set up by India cover a fairly wide range of fields and encompass a large number of engineering products, capital goods, shipping, and the like. A breakdown of Indian joint ventures abroad by broad industrial sectors is given in table 7-3.

Indian projects in the advanced countries are largely concentrated in service ventures, such as hotels, restaurants, and food processing. Only a few are manufacturing enterprises, such as asbestos cement production in the United Kingdom, oil engines and rice milling machines in West Germany, plastic and polyethylene products in the United States, and bicycle tires and tubes in Canada. By contrast, in developing countries, the Indian projects are fairly diversified and include sophisticated items, such as steel foundry, engineering steel files, steel rolling, assembly of tractors, shipping, paper, chemicals and pharmaceuticals, synthetic textiles, viscose, and cotton as well as apparel, to mention just a few by way of illustration.

The scope for venturing overseas is also steadily becoming varied and diversified. Over the last decade, a number of nonindustrial ventures, such as marketing,construction, and consultancy, have come up. Lately India has entered into a new field, namely, transport. For instance, a collaborative transport service has come up in Kuwait, an air cargo transport service in United Arab Emirates, and a joint shipping line in Nigeria. In addition, India also has offered technical collaboration. In Argentina, for instance, an Indian firm has supplied technical know-how for manufacturing reactive dyes. A similar arrangement has been made with a U.S. firm for manufacturing reactive dyes in the United States for ultimate use in Brazil.

Table 7-3
Analysis by Industry of Indian Joint Ventures Abroad, as of July 31, 1979

Industrial Sector	In Production	Under Implementation	Total
Engineering products	30	17	47
Contruction, trading, and consultancy	16	18	34
Hotels, restaurants, and food products	15	11	26
Textiles	17	7	24
Chemical products and pharmaceuticals	7	12	19
Oilseeds, crushing, refining, and fractionations	7	8	15
Pulp, paper, and paper products	3	2	5
Cement, cement products, sugar, and sugar products	1	3	4
Shipping	1	—	1
Others	12	10	22
Total	110	87	197

Similarly, Indian technical know-how has been extended to manufacturing bicycles and parts in Bangladesh, Guyana, Iran, Sudan, Tanzania, and Zambia.

Operation of Some Ventures

Of the many and varied projects that have been undertaken by the Indians, quite a few are noteworthy. The operation of some of them is analyzed in the following paragraphs.

Kenya

There is a noteworthy venture set up by the Birlas, the second largest industrial house in India, in Kenya. The project is known as Pan African Paper Mills. The enterprise, formed in 1970 and jointly sponsored by the government of Kenya, International Finance Corporation, and Orient Paper and Industries Limited, a Birla unit, is the only integrated paper pulp plant in Africa. The project went into production in November of 1974. Initially conceived to cater to the integrated market of the East African Community, the project faced tough marketing and financial problems. However, with World Bank assistance, which was made available in view of the efficacy and viability of the Indian offer and its relevance and importance to the economy of Kenya, the project turned the corner. Its products are marketed in neighboring African countries as well. The Pan African Paper Mills not only manufacture high-quality paper and newsprint, but also caustic soda, chlorine, and so forth. Now the Birlas have been offered another contract in Nigeria to supply know-how and technical services for an integrated pulp and fine-paper mill costing $250 million with a capacity of 60,000 tons of fine paper and 100,000 tons of pulp per year.

Malaysia

In Malaysia, where India has the largest number of joint ventures, one project for manufacturing electric motors, diesel engines, and alternators (set up by Kirloskar Electric Company Ltd., another leading industrial house) is doing well. In this joint venture there is no collaboration as such. The company has been set up jointly with Malaysian interests. The work, from the purchase of the land, contacting investors, raising share capital, obtaining various approvals in Malaysia and India, to installation and commissioning of the plant, was done entirely by the Indian party. The project, initiated in November of 1970, went into production in January of 1972—just 14 months later, which is a record considering the types of products involved. The project is manufacturing products that were previously imported by Malaysia. Managed by a board consisting of eleven directors, of which eight are Malaysians and only three Indians, the project has gotten pioneering status and also has been granted a 10-year tax holiday. Since 1975-1976, the unit has been regularly declaring dividends. The Indian party has been able to earn royalties and selling agency commissions worth US$200,000, which have been repatriated to India.

Singapore

There is yet another plant, the first of its kind in Singapore, manufacturing precision instruments and tools. This project was promoted by the Tatas (India's largest industrial house) in 1972. Its equity came from the earnings received in Switzerland. The Tatas are presently responsible for running and managing the plant. The unit, since going into production in September of 1973, has earned a good name. A training center known as Tata–Government Training Center has been started in Singapore as an integral part of the enterprise. The project was conceived mainly as an export-oriented enterprise. Only 2 percent of its total production finds markets locally; the balance is exported. Initially, the project plans were based on the assumption that it would receive sizable orders for tools from the well-established multinationals, such as GEC, Philips, and so forth. However, this did not materialize. The unit had to seek markets for its products elsewhere. What is noteworthy is that the products manufactured in this plant, particularly tools and dies for semiconductors, are exported back to India. The customers include public-sector units, such as Bharat Electronics Limited, Hindustan Machine Tools, and Hindustan Aeronautics.

Thailand

There is a multidimensional project for paper and pulp in Thailand in which, apart from India, entrepreneurs from France, Belgium, and Austria, with equity holdings of 12 percent each, are participating. In spite of the Thai government's effective participation in the $60 million project, the Indian company (namely, Ballarpur Industries Pvt. Ltd., an enterprise of the Thapar group, which is one of the large industrial houses) has been assigned the responsibility of managing it. The project is under implementation.

Most of the joint-venture projects have been set up by the large industrial houses, although not large by international comparison. These industrial houses have resources in terms of capital and technology, experience in setting up varied enterprises, and of course, good business contacts abroad. These undoubtedly have given them an edge over the medium-and small-scale enterprises. Nevertheless, a few small-scale firms—their number is very few indeed—also have started venturing overseas of late. They have invested mainly in those sectors which are highly labor-intensive, requiring a minimum of capital resources. The mosaic tiles and rolling shutters plant, one of the successful ventures in Mauritius, is a case in point.

It is true that the initiative for setting up joint ventures abroad emanated primarily from private-sector units and they account for the bulk of Indian ventures. However, a few public-sector units, or in other words, government-owned enterprises, too, have started looking for opportunities abroad. As of July 31, 1979, only one project, an electric repair shop undertaken by a state-owned unit, has gone into operation and the other six are under various stages of implementation. They cover such areas as consultancy, tendering and bidding of contracts, insurance, road construction, manufacturing machine tools, and so forth. The public-sector units have, of course, made sizable headway in establishing high-value turnkey projects that are now becoming larger and more diversified. For example, a $250 million integrated township contract has been undertaken by Engineering Projects (I) Limited in Kuwait, and the contract covers not only laying down the plan of an integrated township, but also the construction of dwelling units, sewerage, a road network, schools, hospitals, and other public facilities. Moreover, there are several other projects, such as the construction of an airport terminal, a thermal power project, a water treatment plant, and a grain storage facility—mostly in the Middle East countries.

Thus the industrial progress and diversification that India has achieved over the three decades of its planned development are fully reflected in the type of joint enterprises that have been undertaken abroad.

Indian Overseas Projects vis-à-vis
Multinationals of Developed Countries

Notwithstanding the large number and diverse nature of Indian projects, developing Indian ventures are different from those established by the multinational corporations of the developed market economies. First, Indian projects are not subsidiaries nor extensions of the Indian companies, but are collaborative enterprises where the Indian entrepreneur is largely a minor partner, leaving the major shareholding in the hands of the local collaborator. As a matter of policy laid down in the guidelines issued by the government, Indian entrepreneurs are encouraged to go in mostly for minority participation. Major equity holding by Indians is allowed only in exceptional cases where the host country has a marked preference on this count. If one looks at the list of Indian overseas projects, the examples of entrepreneurs having more than 50 percent shareholding are few and far between. There is only one example where the Indian partner accounts for 97 percent of the equity. The West German project is for assembly of oil engines and rice-milling machines. The Indian collaborator in this case purchased most of the German shares in an already running concern.

Second, the size of the Indian investment in the joint ventures is small, judged by any yardstick. The total investment in the 200 effective joint ventures abroad is about $85 million. Of this, the investment in the 110 projects that have already gone into production is $35 million. The investment, taken in its entirety, would not match that of a developed-country MNC in one venture. In fact, with comparatively little capital, India has made good progress through plowing back and reinvesting profits and dividends. What is more, the question of ownership and management control, which has been one of the most controversial issues with MNCs, does not apply to ventures emanating from a country like India. The Indian entrepreneurs are encouraged to initiate training programs with a view to enabling the local partner, in course of time, to take over the responsibility of running and managing the project.

In spite of these basic positive factors, India's investments abroad and establishment of joint overseas ventures are questioned or criticized on many accounts. Eyebrows are often raised as to how a capital-scarce country such as India, dependent on foreign aid and assistance, involves itself in capital exports. Joint ventures in the eyes of such critics are a sheer "capital drain." The answer to this criticism is not difficult to find if one were to look at the nature and form of Indian equity participation. The very concept of joint ventures in India's case implies participation largely in the form of supply of capital goods, machinery, equipment, basic materials, technical know-how and managerial services, and so forth. Only in a very few cases, and those only recently, has the Indian government allowed cash remittances or financial participation. This has been done mainly with a view to making the Indian offer competitive, enabling entrepreneurs to weather financial problems in the initial stages, running the units efficiently, and meeting the problems arising out of cost escalation.

India also has been criticized that the projects set up abroad, like "tied aid," are "tied" ventures—tied to the supply of machines and know-how. The foreign partners can get a feeling that Indian entrepreneurs, as a result, have little or no stake in the successful running of the venture. In order to meet this criticism and in view of the present comfortable foreign-exchange position, the Indian government has agreed to consider financial participation in exceptional cases. It may be reiterated here that a tied investment on its own is not anathema if it provides the best terms of the given offers.

Then there is another objection. Are Indian entrepreneurs, through joint ventures, not affecting the domestic production and consumption? When the rich natural resources which India is endowed with remain underutilized and when there is widespread unemployment, instead of optimizing production at home, is it rational to venture overseas? This criticism also seems to be misplaced. A look at the list of industries or fields taken up abroad by Indian entrepreneurs would reveal that most of them are those in which India has either excess or underutilized capacity. Many of the manufacturing industries connected with Indian joint ventures are presently running much below their installed capacity. Textiles and engineering projects are obvious examples in this regard. Some of the industries are handicapped on account of lack of demand at home. In fact, joint ventures in such cases not only help boost production, but strengthen the industrial structure as well. Above all, the challenge of successful implementation of joint ventures under the pressure of keen foreign competition tones up the efficiency of its own industries at home—both in the fields of production and marketing.

The joint-venture projects are an important source of earning foreign exchange, accruing through dividends, royalties, technical know-how fees, and so forth. However, the Indian projects have not made any marked achievement on this score. By and large, the earnings that have so far been repatriated to India are estimated at $10 million.[11] It is undoubtedly not a big sum, particularly in view of the fact that 110 projects have gone into production. The earnings repatriation, however, has to assessed or judged on a different footing altogether. Viewed in the context of the quantum of Indian investments, the earning and repatriation of $10 million is not a very significant amount. It also needs to be emphasized that many of the Indian ventures, both in terms of number and investment, have become operational only very recently. More than 75 commenced production only after 1973, which means that they have not had enough time to overcome the initial difficulties and to stabilize production. The setting up of joint ventures across national frontiers by a developing country such as India presents uncertainties and risks of a scale not encountered in the home market, and hence it would not be reasonable to expect immediate and spectacular results from such ventures. In many cases, it must be remembered, Indian entrepreneurs have reinvested their earnings in order to raise their equity to a desired level. In some other cases, technical know-how fees have been capitalized. A few units that went on stream quite sometime back had to be given up in the wake of the nationalization policy of the country concerned or as the local partners purchased the Indian shares. Projects in Canada, Ethiopia, Nigeria, and Libya are examples of this. While making an assessment of the overall performance of the Indian joint ventures in terms of the cost and benefit, these factors have to be taken into account.

At the same time, one cannot overlook the fact that many sanctioned Indian joint ventures did not get off the ground. For example, 80 of the 105 projects approved in 1970 remained unimplemented—the abandoned projects being 76 percent. The percentage of failure, however, came down to 6.3 in 1977 and only 0.9 in 1978. This is a reflection of the improvement in the procedures for clearances of projects by the Inter-Ministerial Committee, which now requires the intending entrepreneurs to prepare feasibility reports prior to grant of sanction.

The significance and success of Indian joint ventures have to be viewed in terms of their contribution to the export-promotion effort. In fact, the major motivating force for Indian joint ventures has been to provide a new thrust to the export effort. Indian ventures have been conceived mainly as a means of promoting export of Indian goods and services, and the gains on this score have not been insignificant. For instance, the Indian equity investment—\$35 million in operating ventures and \$50 million in the projects under various stages of implementation—is largely through supply of machinery, equipment, and the like, which constitute immediate export. Moreover, it has been estimated that additional exports worth \$65 million to \$70 million have been generated directly through these projects. This is certainly not a small gain. What is more significant is their contribution in creating markets for Indian goods and services. Sharp rise in exports of engineering goods, particularly machinery and capital equipment, is a case in point. For instance, export of engineering goods, which was just about \$15 million in 1970–1971, shot up to \$860 million in 1978–1979, and it is during the seventies that a large number of joint ventures fructified. Thus the part played by Indian joint ventures in creating ground for making a breakthrough in exports cannot be overemphasized. In addition, these ventures have helped project the industrial image of India as having wide-ranging technological capability of relevance to developing countries. The efficacy and relevance of Indian joint ventures has to be judged against these broad parameters.

Notes

1. See *Report of the Group of Experts on Economic Cooperation among Developed Countries,* convened by UNCTAD at Geneva, October 27 to November 4, 1975. This report considers *inter alia* four reports on joint ventures among developed countries (TD/B/AC.19/1, dated December 17, 1975).

2. For an elaboration, please see the author's study, "Joint Ventures among Developing Countries," prepared on the basis of a field survey as consultant for UNCTAD (TD/B/AC.19/R.7, dated October 1, 1975).

3. These are elaborated in the Arusha Programme for Collective Self-Reliance and Framework for Negotiations, adopted in February 1979 (TD 236, pp. 7–24, May 1979, published by UNCTAD).

4. See *Paper on Economic Cooperation among Developing Countries: Priority Areas for Cooperation, Issues and Approaches,* prepared for UNCTAD V (TD 244, May 1979).

5. Some of these issues are expected to figure in the Third General Conference of UNIDO in New Delhi, January 21 to February 8, 1980.

6. See *1978 Review: Development Cooperation—Efforts and Policies of the Members of the Development Assistance Committee of Organization for Economic Cooperation and Development*, Paris, November 1978, pp. 36-37.

7. See TD/B/C.6/AC/4/8Rev. 1 brought out by UNCTAD entitled *Cooperative Exchange of Skills among Developing Countries—Policies for Collective Self-Reliance,* 1979.

8. TD/B/C.7/27, dated March 22, 1979 by UNCTAD.

9. The proposal was originally agreed upon at the commonwealth ministerial meeting on industrial cooperation held at Bangalore (India) on March 5-7, 1979 and accepted at the meeting of the commonwealth heads of governments held in Lusaka, August 1-8, 1979.

10. D. Lecraw, "Direct Investment by Firms from Less Developed Countries," *Oxford Economic Papers* 29 (3).

11. The earnings are considered inadequate by the government of India as reflected in the discussions on the subject see *Report of the Workshop on Indian Joint Ventures and Project Exports,* organized by the Federation of Indian Chambers of Commerce and Industry, February 16, 1979. The Committee on Controls and Subsidies, which reported in May 1979, has in its chapter on exchange control recommended that the functioning of Indian joint-venture units abroad and the gain therefrom should be continually evaluated and an annual statement in this regard presented to Parliament (p. 100).

8 Indonesia as a Host Country to Indian Joint Ventures

Kian-Wie Thee

In a recent article on third-world investors in Indonesia, it was stated that 22 percent of the foreign-investment projects in manufacturing activities were made by firms based in developing, rather than developed, countries.[1] The figures presented in that paper indicated that over the period 1967-1975, 64 projects were initiated by firms from other developing countries out of a total of 288 realized foreign manufacturing projects. Out of these 64 ventures, 48 were classified as Chinese (meaning that they originated in Taiwan, Singapore, or Hong Kong), 10 projects came from other Southeast Asian countries, while the origin of the remaining 6 was not mentioned.

Although the country of origin of these six projects was not specified, there is reason to believe that at least a few of them were Indian projects. In fact, an interesting development during the past few years has been a modest upsurge in direct investment by Indian firms as well as by people of Indian origin who are residing in Indonesia or other countries. In the following pages a short overview will be given of some aspects of direct foreign investment by Indian firms in Indonesia. Since no comprehensive survey has as yet been conducted on the foreign-investment activities in Indonesia by developing-country firms, this chapter is mainly exploratory in nature, trying to highlight some interesting aspects and characteristics of the Indian direct investment.

Overseas Indian Direct Investment

Although there was some Indian overseas investment during the early 1960s, notably in Eastern Africa, direct investment by Indian firms only began to pick up since the late 1960s. With the steady progress India has made in the industrial field, several Indian firms found themselves in a position to undertake direct investment in other countries, particularly, but not exclusively, in other developing countries. Having embarked earlier on the process of industrialization than most other other developing countries,

I would like to thank Mr. Ahmad Marzuki, of the Capital Investment Coordination Board, Mr. J.C. Sharma, First Secretary (Commercial) of the Indian Embassy in Jakarta, and Mr. A. Sivaram, Birla International Private, Ltd., for the valuable information they provided on Indian direct investment in Indonesia. I alone, however, am responsible for any errors in this chapter.

India has acquired sufficient industrial and technological expertise to share its experiences with other countries. India is in several respects more suitable to undertake direct investment in other developing countries than most industrialized nations, particularly with the considerable experience Indian firms have gained in adapting and modifying advanced technology to suit the country's peculiar conditions and requirements.

In addition to this technological advantage, some Indian investors also felt that the management of their overseas enterprises would perhaps be psychologically more appropriate to the social-psychological conditions of a developing country. Having a greater understanding of the needs and demands of a traditional society because of their own background, Indian managers are likely to display a greater tolerance and understanding toward their employees than would be the case with Western managers. Possibilities of conflict between management and employees also might be minimized in this way.

The reasons that India has undertaken overseas direct investment are quite similar to those of other investing countries. For one thing, foreign ventures have been earning precious foreign exchange for India. Earnings from these ventures in the form of dividends, royalties, technical know-how fees, engineering service fees, and others have been considerable, amounting to Rs 25.9 million up to December 1975.[2] With the recent increase of new ventures abroad, the earnings from these ventures are expected to rise even further.

Another expected benefit from these Indian investment ventures is the increase of exports of capital goods, components, and raw materials needed by these ventures. By December 1975, exports of Indian-made machinery amounted to Rs 148.8 million against Indian equity participation overseas, whereas exports of components and raw materials amounted to Rs 183.5 million. With many successful Indian investment projects the value of exported machinery, components, and raw materials on a sustained basis has considerably exceeded the initial equity holdings.

Applying the categories used by Heenan and Keegan to describe the economic soil in which third-world multinationals are taking roots, India can be categorized as a *market-rich, rapidly industrializing country*.[3] Like other big countries, such as Brazil and Mexico, India's route to multinationalism has probably been by initial industrial success in its own large and growing domestic market which subsequently led to exports abroad. With the rise in protectionism in other developing countries, it was only natural that Indian firms would gradually turn to setting up their own investment projects in these countries to safeguard their foreign markets.

Another motivation for Indian firms to invest abroad is the policy of India's government to restrict monopolistic tendencies in its home market. Thus its large business houses have begun to seek foreign markets for their investments. This hypothesis is also confirmed by Lecraw, who found that some of the developing-country firms investing in Thailand had been motivated in part by interventionist policies of their own government to restrain their monopolizing behavior in the home market.[4] Determining what motivated Indian firms to invest in Indonesia, however, would require a more comprehensive survey.

Policies of the Indonesian Government toward Foreign Investment

The Indonesian government under Soeharto has pursued an open-door policy that is based on a firm belief that private foreign investment could play an important role in the economic development of the country, particularly in the exploitation and development of its vast natural resources and in the industrialization process. As part of this new economic policy, a Foreign Investment Law was enacted in 1967 to attract new foreign investment. The law provided for several tax concessions as the major inducement, including a tax holiday on company profits, exemption from import duties on initial capital equipment and on raw materials, and accelerated depreciation allowances. In addition, the Foreign Investment Law contained provisions about the transfer of after-tax profits and a portion of the earnings of expatriate personnel. It also guaranteed that the government would not summarily nationalize a foreign company. The response of foreign investors to the new open-door policy turned out to be quite gratifying. By 1970, 3 years after the enactment of the law, 235 new investment projects (excluding oil and banking), involving an amount of $1.2 billion, had been approved by the government.[5]

However, as time passed it became evident that the Foreign Investment Law contained a number of weaknesses that gave rise to various difficulties. One weakness was the relative brevity of the law. Because the law was general rather than specific, various important details were left to be handled by government regulations and departmental policies.[6]

To meet the complaints of foreign investors, an improved Foreign Investment Law was enacted in 1970 that provided for better facilities for the prospective investors. Subsequently, in 1973 the government simplified the time-consuming procedures for foreign-investment applications by reorganizing the agency dealing with foreign investment. The reorganized agency, called the Investment Coordination Board (Badan Koordinasi Penanaman Modal or BKPM), was granted more coordinating authority.

In order to improve the investment climate even further, the Investment Coordination Board (BKPM) announced a priority list (Daftar Skala Prioritas or DSP) in early 1977 for all new foreign and domestic investment projects. Actually, the guidelines contained in the DSP did not represent a basic change in the approach, but were intended only to further speed up the existing processing procedures for investment applications that had contributed to a slow-down in investment activities.[7]

In 1978, a revised priority list (DSP) was issued in which economic activities were classified according to four distinct categories, three of which were open to foreign investment, each with different provisions regarding fiscal incentives. In line with the heightened public concern about raising the welfare of the so-called economically weak groups in society, the revised DSP contained a provision that required foreign as well as domestic investors to enlist the capital participation of these groups in the venture.

Indian Joint Ventures in Indonesia

Size of Investment

Indian direct investment in Indonesia is quite understated in the reported data of the Capital Investment Coordination Board (BKPM) and the Bank of Indonesia, since some foreign ventures are not registered as foreign. With a sizable resident Indian community, it can be expected that some Indian investments in Indonesia, like some of the overseas Chinese investments, are registered as domestic rather than foreign-investment projects.

Official data from the Bank of Indonesia provided by the BKPM reveal that on December 31, 1978, Indian direct investment numbered only four projects, amounting to US$2,644,000, of which only one had been realized. One project was in agriculture, while the other three were in manufacturing. Table 8-1 presents data on these investments as provided by the BKPM.

However, in the Financial Memorandum and Draft State Budget of the Minister of Finance, data on foreign direct investment indicate that Indian investment projects over the period 1967-1979 numbered five, with a total amount of approved investment of US$11.4 million. Of this amount, only US$1.4 million was realized by October 1978.[8]

Information provided by the Indian embassy in Jakarta presents an entirely different picture than the one provided by the BKPM or contained in the Financial Memorandum. According to this source, Indian direct investment in Indonesia at present amounts to approximately US$76 million. This is still less than Japanese, American, and even Hong Kong investment, but considerably higher than the BKPM data or the Financial Memorandum data.

One of the reasons for this large discrepancy may be the differing interpretations of what actually comprises Indian direct investment in Indonesia.

Table 8-1
Indian Direct Investment in Indonesia, December 31, 1978
(U.S. Dollars)

			Intended Investment					Realized Investment		
			Own Capital		Loan			Own	Loan	
Sector	Activity	Location	Indonesia	India	Capital	Total		Capital	Capital	Total
1. Agriculture:	Rubber cultivation	Central Java	—	694,000	—	694,000		—	—	—
2. Manufacturing:	Chemicals	West Java	400,000	600,000	1,900,000	2,900,000		—	—	—
	Metal products	West Java	125,000	375,000	1,200,000	1,700,000		71,000	340,000	411,000
	Metal products	West Java	525,000	975,000	2,700,000	4,200,000		—	—	—

Source: Badan Koordinasi Penanaman Modal.

Unlike the BKPM or the Financial Memorandum, both the Indian embassy and the Economic Cooperation Association of India and Indonesia (BKII) include direct investment by Indian-based firms as well as by Indian-owned or Indian-controlled firms based in other countries, such as Hong Kong, Singapore, and even as far as Bermuda. In addition, the BKII included under Indian direct investment ventures that are officially listed as domestic investment projects by the BKPM. These projects were undertaken by people residing in Indonesia who are of Indian origin.

Another reason for the big difference is the fact that the figures of the BKPM/Financial Memorandum include only equity capital as Indian investment. The Indian embassy, however, counted loan capital as part of the investment made by Indians. Since this broader interpretation is more realistic, we will use the data as provided by the Indian embassy and the BKII.

Time Pattern of Investment

Since several planned projects are in the process of being implemented, Indian investment in Indonesia is expected to reach the quite considerable figure of US$180 million to US$200 million by the end of 1980, particularly if two synthetic fibers projects (each with an intended investment of US$35 million), a fiberglass project (with an intended investment of US$20 million), and a chemical project (with an intended investment ranging between US$15 to 20 million) are implemented.

The preceding total-investment figure might rise even further in the coming years because quite a few large Indian companies have indicated their interest in investing in Indonesia. Table 8-2 shows that the number of Indian joint ventures (all in the field of manufacturing) has grown relatively fast during the past few years, particularly since 1974. Although, again, figures on the exact number of Indian joint ventures differ somewhat from source to source, the following figures of the Federation of Indian Chambers of Commerce and Industry (FICCI) show that as of January 31, 1979, eighteen Indian joint ventures had been approved. Of these eighteen, however, only eight projects have commenced production, while of the remaining ten approved projects, nine are still under implementation and one project has yet to start implementation.[10]

With the largest market in Southeast Asia, political stability, and the absence of a significant source of political conflict between the two countries, Indonesia seems to offer quite a hospitable climate to Indian investors. Since there is also considerable public concern about the "over-presence" of Japanese investment, Indian joint projects could be viewed as a possible counterweight to the former.

However, according to some Indians, officials and private businessmen in Indonesia have thus far shown a lukewarm interest in attracting more

Table 8-2
Year of Approval and Initial Production for Indian Industrial Joint Ventures

Year of Approval	Number of Projects	Year of Production	Number of Projects
1972	1	—	—
1973	1	—	—
1974	3	—	—
1975	3	1975	1
1976	2	1976	3
1977	4	1977	2
1978	4	1978	2
Total	18	—	8

Source: Federation of Indian Chambers of Commerce and Industry.

Indian investment. As a consequence, the number of projects is expected to rise steadily but not dramatically during the next few years. With the recent removal by the Indian government of its restrictions on the exportation of liquid capital, Indian overseas investment, including that in Indonesia, is expected to get an additional stimulus because these restrictions were a major limiting factor.[11]

Nature of Investment

Like Japanese investors, those from India prefer to set up joint ventures with host-country partners rather than fully owned subsidiaries. Since their preference also accords with the policies of both governments, all Indian investment projects in Indonesia are joint ventures.

From the Indonesian point of view, joint ventures are a suitable channel for the transfer of technology and managerial and technical skills. In addition, they enable Indonesia to exert some degree of control over the operation of foreign forms.

From the Indian point of view, the establishment of joint ventures is a way of earning foreign exchange through the transfer of dividends, interest, royalties, management fees, technical license fees, and the export of Indian-made machinery and equipment, components, and raw materials. They also provide opportunities for its young managers to gain experience in overseas operations and first-hand knowledge of foreign markets. In addition, Indian joint ventures in Indonesia are seen as further strengthening the existing good political relations between the two countries.

Even though joint ventures are the preferred form of organization in Indonesia, Indian investors, like other foreign investors, experience great difficulties in finding suitable local partners. In fact, since Indian investors are latecomers on the Indonesian scene, they experience even greater difficulties than the others. The Indonesian government requires not only majority shareholding by Indonesian nationals, but also majority participation by indigenous Indonesians, making it very hard for the Indian firms to find suitable local partners whose capital is not already tied up in the Japanese or other foreign ventures.

The Indian investors often try to overcome this problem by resorting to the Japanese investors' practice of using "nominal" or "dummy" shareholders.[12] Under this arrangement, the foreign investor lends its local partner money to buy shares. The loan is then repaid out of future dividends. Whether some Indian investors also resort to under-the-table payments to Indonesian nationals for the use of their names, as some Japanese investors have been doing, could not be verified.

In accordance with the policies of the government, Indonesian shareholding in Indian joint ventures has gradually increased during the past few years. Whereas during the period 1972-1975, Indonesian equity ownership in Indian joint ventures ranged from 10 to 20 percent, it gradually rose to 20 to 25 percent after 1975. With the common practice of "nominal" shareholding, however, Indonesian majority shareholding may be more apparent than real and not reflect an actual increase in local ownership and control of the Indian joint ventures.

Distribution of Indian Investment
by Location and Industry

Table 8-3 shows the geographic and industrial distribution of two categories of projects: (1) those involving Indian-based firms, and (2) those owned or managed by Indians. From this table it is evident that out of fourteen Indian joint ventures operating in Indonesia, all but one are located in Java. The only joint venture outside of Java, a textile plant, is located in Padang, capital of the province of West Sumatra.

Comparing the regional spread of Japanese investment projects with the Indian joint ventures, we see that out of 197 Japanese ventures, 154 projects, or 78 percent of the total number of projects, were located in Java, of which not less than 128 projects, or 65 percent of the total number of projects, were located in the Jakarta Capital Region and the adjacent province of West Java.[13]

In the case of Indian joint ventures, thirteen out of fourteen, or 92 percent of the total number of projects, are in Java. In contrast to the Japanese ventures, however, only one Indian project, or 7 percent of the total number of projects, is in Jakarta and six projects, or 42 percent of the total number of projects, are in Surabaya, in the province of East Java.

Table 8-3
Location and Industry of Indian Joint Ventures and Indian-Associated Ventures, August 1979
(Number of Projects)

Industry	Java				Outside Java	Total
	Jakarta	*West Java*	*Central Java*	*East Java*	*West Java*	*Total*
Joint ventures						
1. Food and beverages	—	—	—	1	—	1
2. Textiles	—	3	1	1	1	6
3. Basic metals, nonferrous and pelican	1	1	—	3	—	4
4. Chemicals	—	1	—	—	—	1
5. Paper industry	—	—	—	1	—	1
6. Pharmaceuticals	—	1	—	—	—	1
Total	1	6	1	6	1	14
Ventures with Indian owners or management						
1. Textiles	1	5	4	—	—	10 / 24

Source: Economic Cooperation Association of Indonesia and India (BKII).

This difference in the regional spread between Japanese and Indian ventures can be attributed to the fact that the Indian investors were latecomers to Indonesia, when Jakarta was already closed to new investment. As a result, many Indian investors turned to the next best location, Surabaya, which, after Jakarta, has the best infrastructure and urban amenities in Indonesia.

A look at the distribution of Indian investment by industry also shows that all joint ventures involving Indian firms and ventures owned and managed by Indians are in manufacturing. The latter type of ventures are in textiles only. Since many merchants of Indian origin are in the textile trade, Indian-financed textile plants are assured of large and reliable marketing outlets.

Looking at the industrial distribution of Indian joint ventures, we see that most of them manufacture light consumer goods (such as food and beverages and textiles), light engineering goods (such as steel files and rasps, pipe fittings, ribbed torsteel, and office equipment), chemicals (such as dyestuff), writing paper and coated art paper, and pharmaceuticals (antibiotics). Judging from their products, Indian direct investment in Indonesia can be described as a *market-oriented* type of investment, producing mostly light consumer goods for the domestic market.

Average Investment by Industry
and Total Employment

Table 8-4 presents the average total of Indian joint ventures by industry. The table shows that the total investment of the paper plant is the highest, amounting to US$9 million, whereas the plants producing basic metals, nonferrous and pelican, have the lowest average total investment, amounting to US$2 million.

Table 8-4
Average Total Investment by Industry

Industry	Average Total Investment (Millions of U.S. Dollars)
1. Food and beverages	3.0
2. Textile	6.7
3. Basic metals, nonferrous, and pelican	2.0
4. Paper	9.0

Source: Economic Cooperation Association of Indonesia and India (BKII).

A comparison of the average total investment of the Indian textile ventures with that of other countries reveals that the average capital investment of Japanese textile ventures is somewhat lower than that of the Indian textile ventures (US$5.3 million as compared with US$6.7 million). Data from the Bank of Indonesia indicate that the average total investment of Hong Kong textile ventures is less than one-half that of the Indian textile ventures, that is, US$3.0 million as compared with US$6.7 million. Without data on the volume of production, however, it would be difficult to conclude that Japanese and Hong Kong textile ventures in Indonesia are smaller than the Indian textile ventures.

As far as employment in Indian joint ventures is concerned, no detailed information is available about the number of workers employed in each venture. Roughly speaking, it is estimated that the twenty-four ventures of both categories employ between 7,000 and 7,500 workers. This is quite a sizable number, if compared with the 45,191 Indonesian workers employed by the 203 Japanese joint ventures.[14] They also have about 150 to 160 expatriate staff personnel, mostly Indian, but also including some Japanese and Koreans.

In the preceding pages some aspects of Indian joint ventures have been highlighted. These first glimpses of the phenomenon of investment projects initiated by Indian firms and individuals suggest issues that call for further research and analysis.

Notes

1. Louis T. Wells, Jr. and V'Ella Warren, "Developing Country Investors in Indonesia," *Bulletin of Indonesian Economic Studies* 15(1):69-70, 1979.

2. Indian Investment Center, *Joint Ventures Abroad* (New Delhi, 1976), p. 15.

3. David A. Heenan and Warren J. Keegan, "The Rise of Third World Multinationals," *Harvard Business Review* (January-February 1979):101-103.

4. D. Lecraw, "Direct Investment by Firms from Less Developed Countries," *Oxford Economic Papers (New Series)* 29(3):444-445, 1977.

5. M. Sadli, "Foreign Investment in Developing Countries: Indonesia," in Peter Drysdale (ed.), *Direct Foreign Investment in Asia and the Pacific* (Canberra: Australian National Univ. Press, 1972), pp. 205-207).

6. Ibid., p. 216.

7. Robert C. Rice and Hall Hill, "Survey of Recent Developments," *Bulletin of Indonesian Economic Studies* 13(2):14-15, 1977.

8. *Nota Keuangan dan Rancangan Anggaran Pendapatan dan Belanja Negara Republik, 1979/1980,* financial memorandum and the draft state budget of the Republic of Indonesia for the fiscal year of 1979-1980, Jakarta, January 1979, Table VIII, 6, p. 249.

9. Indian Investment Center, *Joint Ventures Abroad,* p. 16.

10. Federation of Indian Chambers of Commerce and Industry, *Report on Workshop on Indian Joint Ventures and Project Exports, February 16, 1979* (New Delhi, 1979), pp. 50-53.

11. Indian Investment Center, *Joint Ventures Abroad,* p. 3.

12. Franklin Weinstein, "Multinational Corporations and the Third World: The Case of Japan and Southeast Asia," *International Organization* 30(3):389, 1976.

13. L. Siahaan, Thee Kian-wie, Ahmad Hamid, and J.L. Tamba, *Japanese Direct Investment in Indonesia-Findings of an Experimental Survey* (Tokyo: Institute of Developing Economies, 1978), p. 74.

14. Ibid., p. 67.

9

Third-World-Country Firms in Nigeria

C.N.S. Nambudiri,
Olukunle Iyanda, and
D.M. Akinnusi

The emergence of multinational firms based in third-world countries that operate in other developing countries is a growing phenomenon. The literature on multinational corporations (MNCs), focusing on investment from the developed countries, is yet to catch up with this new trend. The few studies to date indicate that this new category of multinationals has several characteristics that distinguish it from the multinational firms based in developed countries.[1] These new MNCs do not seem to have the patterns of multinationl behavior usually associated with the latter, namely, strategies associated with exploiting a technological lead, a strong trade name, advantages of scale, access to large capital, or even, a scanning capability.[2] However, they seem to thrive on their ability to innovate adaptively in mature technologies and to manufacture efficiently to serve small national markets at a price advantage.[3]

The growth of such multinational companies points to the differences in the degrees of development that third-world countries have reached and assumes importance for four reasons. First, there is a considerable body of opinion today in favor of greater economic and technological cooperation between developing countries. Second, there is greater emphasis on learning from the developmental experiences of third-world nations, experiences not available from the developed world. Third, there is an increasing realization that the gap, in terms of relevance, between postindustrial societies and the developing world is increasing. Finally, there is a greater awareness of the value of appropriate technology—a common theme for most developing countries—which third-world nations are better able to provide. This chapter focuses on the experiences of third-world firms operating in Nigeria. The purpose is to analyze their character and to attempt an explanation of their competitive success against multinationals of the developed countries.

Data on Third-World Investments and Companies

The data on third-world firms operating in Nigeria were limited because their investments were smaller than those of firms from developed coun-

145

tries, particularly those from the United Kingdom. Of the net capital inflow into Nigeria during the years 1967-1973, the investment from countries other than the United Kingdom, the United States, and Western Europe amounted to nearly 10 percent.[4] A survey of the *Industrial Directory* (1975) showed nearly fifty-four organizations operating in Nigeria with owners coming from one or the other of the third-world countries. There were twenty-four firms from Asia, nine from other African countries, and twenty-one from the Middle East. Country-wise, Lebanon (nineteen), India (twelve), and China (eleven) led in number of companies.[5] The industrial activities in which these organizations participated are given in table 9-1. It will be noticed that they operate in fields of mature technologies.

Our study focused on eight firms in the following industries: fabricated metal products (one), textiles (two), paper (one), furniture (two), and plastic footwear (two). We used a structured questionnaire for the interview. Managing directors, and other senior officers where necessary, were

Table 9-1
Fields of Investment by Third-World Countries in Nigeria

SIC No.	Description	Number of Companies with Foreign Ownership	Number of Companies with Third-World-Country Ownership
3119	Cocoa, chocolate, and sugar confectionary	6	3
3211	Spinning, weaving, and finishing textiles	19	11
3213	Knitting mills	3	2
3230	Weaving apparel	5	2
3212	Make up textiles	2	2
3240	Footwear (leather)	5	3
3320	Furniture and fixtures (except metal furniture	7	4
3411	Paper	1	1
3521	Paints, varnishes, and lacquers	3	1
3523	Soap, cosmetics	6	1
3529	Miscellaneous chemical products	4	4
3559	Other rubber products	6	1
3560	Plastic products	6	2
3620	Glass and glass products	2	1
3812	Metal furniture	4	2
3813	Structural metal products	10	4
3819	Fabricated metal products	12	2

Source: *Industrial Directory*, 7th ed., 1975.

interviewed. Of the respondent firms, the earliest was established in 1955, the latest in 1970. The nationalities of ownership were Indian (three), Kenyan (one), Syrian (three), and Lebanese (one). In most of the cases studied, firms from developed countries operated as competitors; the exception was the paper manufacturer, which was the only one of its kind in the country. Sales ranged from ₦1 million (US$1.6 million) for the smallest to ₦20 million (US$32 million) for the largest. The fabricated metal products company was the largest in Nigeria as far as its first and principal product was concerned. The furniture manufacturing firms were the biggest in the industry by employment. One of the two textile units studied was among the largest in this industry. The other manufactured specialized textile products such as braids, shoe laces, lamp wicks, and sewing thread. In the Nigerian textile industry—the largest industrial sector and the one with the largest number of third-world-country operations—these firms seemed to form an intermediate sector in size (defined in terms of employment) between the larger companies from the developed countries and the smaller indigenous ones (see table 9-2). The two shoe manufacturing enterprises were second and third in size to a large multinational firm, while there were numerous smaller footwear manufacturers.

Three types of companies were distinguishable among the firms studied. The first category consisted of companies that had manufacturing bases in their home and other countries and brought their experience to Nigeria. This category was multinational in the traditional sense. The second category included those firms which had manufacturing bases in the home country, but had no operations in Nigeria. They brought only their managerial and technical expertise to Nigeria to run companies on a management-contract basis. This group, although limited in number, was

Table 9-2
Distribution of Textile Firms in Nigeria by Size

Size (Number of Employees)	Developed-Country Units	Third-World-Country Units	Indigenous Units
Over 2000	5	2	0
1000-1999	2	0	4
500-999	2	2	6
	—	3	12
200-499	—	4	10
100-199	—	1	10
50-99	—	—	—
25-49	—	—	18
10-24	—	—	32
Total	9	12	92

significant to Nigeria inasmuch as management and technological skills had greater priority over capital inflow. One of these companies had a joint venture in manufacturing appliances with a state government in Nigeria. The management contract led to the multinational investing in a very large expansion project based on the operation it had previously managed. The third category consisted of firms that had manufacturing operations in Nigeria but did not have them elsewhere. The owners had earlier been traders in Nigeria and subsequently integrated backwards to become manufacturers. In this category were cases of export of entrepreneurship from one country to another.

Operating Characteristics

Investment Drives

There were three types of investment drives that motivated the firms to invest in Nigeria. The first was a defensive strategy: the firms operated in many countries to reduce the risk of nationalization and takeover. For example, one of the companies studied had operations in several African nations and suffered the consequences of nationalization in two of them. The defensive strategy was, of course, combined with an aggressive one of searching for an opportunity to participate in one of the largest markets and richest countries in Africa.

The second investment drive also could be described as a defensive one. The firms had earlier operated in Nigeria as importers and distributors. The later government policies of promoting "indigenization" of retail trade and offering incentives for industrialization forced these firms to set up manufacturing units and close down their trading operations.

The third motive is the aggressive strategy of exploiting the opportunity to operate in the largest country in Africa. This motive led to the establishment of new units as well as the takeover of unsuccessful firms. In two cases, they took over firms from a developed country.

Technology

Technology consists of three components: the equipment used in production, the technical managers making the technological decisions, and the training given to the employees. The first two components are discussed in the following paragraphs.

Equipment. With one exception, the companies studied imported machinery from developed countries. The machinery was installed without any special adaptation except tropicalization. In the textile industry, one of the firms studied, a large one, had imported automated machinery that was considered uneconomic in its home country but not in Nigeria. Factors such as the boom condition in the market, the absence of any governmental guidelines on the choice of highly automated equipment, the unions' passive attitudes toward the matter, and the low productivity and high cost of labor favored the choice of automated over labor-intensive machinery. Prospective investors in Nigeria from third-world countries preferred to have machinery imported from developed countries to compete with other firms so equipped.[6]

In the exceptional case, the machinery was imported from Thailand, Hong Kong, and India. This equipment suited the level of skills of the operators and conformed with the less-sophisticated product that was believed to be in keeping with the market as well as with the firm's operating experience in these Asian countries.

The Technical Decision Makers. Although most of the machinery was imported from developed countries, the men who make the operational decisions were invariably from third-world countries. The machine operators were Nigerian, but the technical managers were from other developing nations. Decisions on plant size, layout, choice of machinery, and expansion were taken by the latter. Consultants from the third world were also used, for example, Indian textile consultants in setting up textile mills. It may be noted that the third-world firms brought with them not only their experience in operating the machinery, but also knowledge about its availability. This might not have been much of an advantage in a developed country where information was available from consultants or manufacturer's representatives through personal visits or even telephone calls. It was, however, very useful to entrepreneurs in a developing country who had no idea about the sources of the machinery to be used.

One of the characteristics of third-world-country investors identified in earlier studies elsewhere was their adaptation for small-scale operations. The smaller-scale operations of third-world firms in Nigeria was considered a positive advantage. The distribution of the size of textile mills operated by firms from developing nations seemed, however, to indicate their capability to operate economically over a wide range. While one of the two textile mills in our sample was among the largest in Nigeria, a plant of similar size would be considered a medium-sized mill in its home country. However, a metal fabrication company's operation is several times larger than those in its home country or in a developed country. A key factor in the paper manufacturer getting a management contract was his experience in operating a small, nonintegrated (pulp imported) paper mill, experience gained in his home country where such plants were now considered uneconomic. These observations indicated an ability to adapt the scale of operations over a wide range.

The general strategy of third-world multinationals was to enter on a small scale and gradually expand and diversify. For example, one of the firms studied introduced a single line of collapsible tube, becoming the first manufacturer of the product in Nigeria. Later it added aluminum roofing sheets to its product line in an extension of its main building. This seemed to be in sharp contrast to the approach of companies from developed countries, who preferred sophisticated and expensive technology and tried to be self-sufficient for their services (providing their own tool room, maintenance, and so forth), all of which contributed to larger-scale operations. The strategy of entry, expansion, and even diversification by the third-world firms, combined with their small-scale operations, enabled them to open up industries not considered viable for entry by the developed-country multinationals or to establish an earlier foothold in an industry.

Price-Cost Advantages

All firms in the study mentioned price-cost advantages of the third-world-country businesses over developed-country MNCs. The price advantages were not, however, made use of during the time unsaturated, seller's-market conditions prevailed in the country. In other words, the third-world firms could have used competitive pricing as a strategy had the conditions required it.

The third-world firms did have cost advantages in comparison with developed-country MNCs, particularly in terms of the lower cost of their managerial and technical manpower. One company estimated that its managerial and technical personnel costs would have doubled had it hired personnel from developed countries. Apart from the cost, the firms from developing nations seemed to require fewer managers, each of whom assumed a broader range of responsibilities, than their counterparts from developed countries. The advantage of lower personnel costs was much more significant in the case of the smaller third-world companies than the larger ones. The developing-country firms also indicated that their overheads were lower than those of the developed-country MNCs.

Little cost advantage was felt in the areas of raw materials, machinery, or wages. Almost all raw materials and machinery were imported. Owing to the scarcity of trained labor, wage levels did not differ between businesses of the same size, although they did between the largest and smallest. In comparison with indigenous firms, the third-world enterprises rated their cost as higher, but pointed out the advantages of greater managerial efficiency.

Marketing

Little or no strength in marketing has been ascribed to third-world firms.[7] However, the multinationals from the developed countries have been generally credited with the advantages of a strong trade name and economies of scale in some marketing functions, such as advertising. In a resource-rich developing country with a substantial number of poor people, the power of a strong trade name associated with a sophisticated product developed primarily for a developed market may be questionable. Our study indicated that third-world-country firms had some advantages derived from their experience with similar markets in their own countries. These advantages existed in areas such as product selection and distribution and catering to the special requirements of the local market.

For example, an aluminum hollow-ware manufacturer discontinued a line of high-quality, in terms of polish and finish, hollow-ware to produce lower-priced and more-functional items. It successfully grew into what may be the biggest production line for that product, and with little advertising. An Indian textile firm attributed its success to its product choice—cotton material dyed in African prints—and its continued attention to new design. The cotton prints better catered to a price-conscious market than other textile products. Two manufacturers, one from India and the other from Syria, who were producing plastic shoes for the low-income groups in competition with a larger multinational claimed special suitability of their products for the local markets. Their products were not advertised, but were sold largely through the local outlets. A Lebanese furniture manufacturer competed with the bigger firms from developed countries located in the south of Nigeria. He claimed as advantages his location nearer the markets in the north and better quality and design. Every one of the respondents claimed special knowledge of the local market as a distinct advantage. One may conclude, then, that third-world-country firms operating in Nigeria had specialized knowledge of the market that enabled them to identify market segments that they were specially competent to satisfy.

Advantages and Disadvantages

The firms from developing countries had several advantages over the indigenous ones. These included access to capital from abroad, from local branches of home-country banks (Bank of India, The Arab Bank, and so forth), and from a small body of influential ethnic nationals. More significant in terms of industry was the technical and managerial expertise brought in by these firms from the home countries. Their knowledge about the type of machinery needed, its possible sources, and the availability of experienced technical and managerial manpower proved to be useful.

The third-world MNCs also had several advantages over the multinationals from developed countries. Some of them are their ability to select and manufacture for less-sophisticated, price-conscious markets, their experience in operating economically on a smaller scale with lower overhead and managerial and technical personnel costs, and their greater adaptability and experience contending with internal and external constraints, such as the relatively poor infrastructure. The developed-nation MNCs, however, were considered to have advantages of economies of scale, access to sophisticated technology, and larger capital funds. The support they received from the home-country governments, national airlines, and banks was certainly superior to that received by third-world-country firms.

Other Characteristics

None of the firms studied paid royalties or licensing fees. Nor did they borrow from outside the country. Repatriation of funds was confined to dividends paid out to home-country shareholders. In general, the firms seemed to enjoy considerable independence as far as operations in Nigeria were concerned.

Conclusions and Discussions

The firms from third-world countries were attracted to Nigeria by the greater opportunities, the larger returns, the available incentives, and the lower rates of taxation. They had brought with them technological and managerial expertise, knowledge of marketing in less-developed countries, and entrepreneurial skills. They had the advantages of lower operating costs, smaller-scale operations, and less-costly capital equipment. However, they do not seem to have utilized their low costs as a competitive advantage during the prevailing seller's-market conditions. Their ability to initially operate on a small scale and gradually expand may provide them an advantage in "indigenizing" manufacturing in those areas where MNCs from developed countries are less likely to enter. These skills could be effectively used by the host country to open up medium-scale consumer industries through joint ventures between indigenous and third-world-country firms. The import of machinery is not necessarily tied to the home country, as is generally the case with the developed-country multinationals. This may open better opportunities for the acquisition of technologies that are more suitable for the host country. The relatively autonomous operations and loose ties with the home country point to the lack of a global strategy on the part of the third-world MNCs. Such a situation can make their operations more compatible with governmental policies of the host country in areas such as exports, employment, "indigenization," and so forth in the future. The relevance of the marketing experience of the firms from third-world countries in exploiting situations in other developing countries seems to be much more significant than hitherto considered. This may be greater in some fields, such as agricultural machinery and fertilizers.[8]

While the importance of third-world solidarity in the rise of third-world multinationals is being stressed and there is greater awareness of what third-world countries have achieved and are capable of, there seems to be little evidence to suggest that these have been recognized by host countries.

Notes

1. Louis T. Wells, Jr., "The Internationalization of Firms from Developing Countries," in Tamir Agmon and Charles Kindleberger (eds.), *Multinationals from Small Countries* (Cambridge, Mass.: M.I.T. Press, 1977); Louis T. Wells, Jr., "Foreign Investment from the Third World: The Experience of Chinese Firms from Hong Kong," *Columbia Journal of World Business (Spring 1978); Louis T. Wells, Jr. and V'Ella Warren, "Developing Country Investors in Indonesia,"* Bulletin of Indonesian Economic Studies* (March 1979); and David A. Heenan and Warren J. Keegan, "The Rise of Third World Multinationals," *Harvard Business Review* (January-February 1979).

2. Raymond Vernon and Louis T. Wells, Jr., *Manager in the International Economy* (Englewood Cliffs, N.J.: Prentice-Hall, 1976).

3. Wells, "The Internationalization of Firms from Developing Countries."

4. A.M. Ndioma, "Foreign Private Investment in the Manufacturing Sector in the Nigerian Economy, 1966-70," *Economic and Financial Review* 12(1), June 1974. Also see "Foreign Private Investment in Nigeria 1971-73," *Economic and Financial Review* 14(1), 1976.

5. Investment Promotions Centre, *Industrial Directory*, 7th ed. (Lagos: Federal Ministry of Industries, 1975).

6. See Wells, "Foreign Investment in the Third World."

7. Wells and Warren, "Developing Country Investors in Indonesia."

8. Heenan and Keegan, "The Rise of Third World Multinationals."

10 The International Projection of Firms from Latin American Countries

Eduardo White

Significance and Trends

One of the most remarkable trends in the present stage of development in Latin America is the emergence of a widespread phenomenon of internationalization of local firms actively engaged in direct investments abroad and exports of technology.

The significance of this phenomenon is not reflected in the statistics of Latin American countries. The share of intraregional foreign investment appears to be less than 1 percent of the total stock registered by the central banks. However, the real volume of these flows is normally underestimated in both source and host countries of the region. It is underestimated in the source nations because much of the direct investment abroad has been unreported by the investing firms to avoid foreign-exchange and tax controls, and it is underestimated by the central banks to avoid publicity about a phenomenon still considered ambiguous. In the host countries, the volume is underestimated because of the excessive aggregation of the foreign-exchange registers or the decision of certain investors to keep secret their operations in both home and host countries.[1]

Yet information gathered through different sources revealed more than 300 cases of direct investments among countries of the region in the period 1970-1976. Several projects involve huge volumes of investment; apart from the spectacular hydroelectrical binational joint ventures in the Plata Basin, there are other costly projects in the steel, petrochemicals, pulp, and paper sectors, as well as joint development of a transportation infrastructure.[2]

The internationalization of Latin American firms also seems to take place through ways and mechanisms that differ from those of the direct-investment form. For example, the Brazilian government reported that the value of contracts for export of technology (namely, construction and consulting services) exceeded US$4 billion at the end of 1978.[3] In addition, a

This chapter is based on the research carried out at the Institute for Latin American Integration by a team in which the author took part. The results of this work are published in the book *Las Empresas Conjuntas Latinoamericanas*, by E. White, J. Campos, and G. Ondarts (INTAL), 1977). Other information has been collected through the information center of INTAL and partially published in the *Boletin de Inversiones y Empresas Latinoamericanas*.

155

study of Argentine exports of technology through turnkey contracts and technical-service arrangements detected thirty-four cases in the period 1973-1977, amounting to $341 million.[4]

The evidence about this phenomenon is still largely impressionistic, but there is no doubt about its increasing importance. Despite their problems, the available statistics on direct investments serve at least to show that during the recent period, registered flows among countries of the region grew at a high rate. In fact, the stock of Latin American foreign direct investments (LAFDI) in four countries of the region (Brazil, Colombia, Ecuador, and Venezuela) more than doubled during the 1970-1975 period, reaching US$127.5 million in 1975, with the registered annual flows increasing from only US$1.5 million in 1971 to US$36 million in 1975.[5]

Furthermore, for some nations of the region, the contribution of capital and technology from firms of other Latin American countries has already become significant. In smaller countries such as Ecuador, direct investments from other Latin American countries increased at a much higher rate than those which originated in industrialized nations during recent years and today represent a relatively significant part of the FDI stocks (table 10-1).

Table 10-1
Foreign Direct Investment Accumulated in Ecuador, Percentage Variances, 1973-1977
(Thousands of U.S. Dollars)

Countries of Origin	1973	1977	Percentage Change, 1973-1977
Andean Pact	$9,182	$17,058	86%
Colombia	5,410	10,347	91
Venezuela	3,729	5,525	48
Peru	43	1,186	2,658
Bolivia	—	—	—
Rest of America[a]	$10,746	$69,960	551
Argentina	30	10,846	36,053
Brazil	—	4,752	—
Chile	1,626	11,097	582
Mexico	1,185	4,771	303
Panama	6,571	28,718	337
Other	1,334	9,776	633
Rest of the World	551,345	670,829	22
Total	571,273	757,847	33

Source: Banco Central del Ecuador, Subgerencia de Balanza de Pagos.
[a]Does not include the United States.

Main Patterns

To appreciate the real dimensions of the present LAFDI trends, it is necessary to take into account existing differences among countries, sectors, and organizational forms.

Participating Countries

The More Advanced Countries. In Latin America, the different levels of development among countries coincide with their different positions and roles with regard to the outflow and inflow of intraregional FDI. Argentina, Brazil, and Mexico are the most important source countries of the region. In the case of Argentina (the only country with available statistics on this subject), the annual average of registered outflows was around $4 million during the 1973-1978 period (in 1978, authorized outflows reached US$8 million). More than 90 percent of the Argentine projects were located in other Latin American countries, and more than half of them were in manufacturing, particularly the metallurgical, machine tools, food, and automotive sectors. About fifty firms, the majority in the private sector, appeared to be responsible for these operations. However, different sources indicate that other important investments were carried out decades ago, when there was no register. Some of the 120 Brazilian firms reported as belonging to 60 Argentine economic groups are from this earlier period. Three of the larger Argentine firms, the conglomerate Bunge y Born, the textile company Alpargatas, and the metallurgical firm Siam Di Tella, expanded to Brazil and other Latin American countries at the end of the last century or during the first decades of the present century. The present influence of Argentine firms is particularly evident in the neighboring and smaller economies of Uruguay and Paraguay, where six of the largest fifty firms (1977) and two of the ten largest companies (1974), respectively, are Argentine subsidiaries. However, as has already been noted, several projects in other countries have taken the form of exports of technology, accounting for exports of industrial plants valued at several hundred million dollars.

Brazil is probably the most impressive case of aggressive internationalization of domestic firms in Latin America. The emergence of Brazilian enterprises in the world arena is reflected in the appearance of eight of these companies among the 500 largest concerns outside the United States listed in 1978 by *Fortune*. Despite the lack of official information on investments abroad and the limits of statistics of host countries (in nine Latin American countries, the Brazilian foreign investments amounted to $60 million in 1978), there is clear evidence of the importance and diversity of Brazilian involvement in projects abroad. As in the case of Argentina, several domestic companies have expanded to other less-developed Latin American countries. A salient feature of the Brazilian experience is the entrance into the markets of developed nations, such as the United States, France, and other European countries,[6] and into the African markets. In Nigeria, for example, some forty Brazilian companies are starting to assemble a wide range of consumer goods.[7]

In comparison with Argentina and other Latin American countries where foreign investment has been largely made by private companies following the market impulses, the Brazilian performance seems to be closely linked to the role of some public corporations, such as the trading company INTERBRAS, the oil-exploration company BRASPETRO (both subsidiaries of the state oil corporation PETROBRAS), the Banco de Brazil, and other major state corporations such as the iron and steel concerns SIDERBRAS and Vale do Rio Doce Company. INTERBRAS, exploiting the bargaining power resulting from the huge oil imports of PETROBRAS, and the Banco de Brazil, with a network of fifty-one agencies in foreign countries and a program of special financial incentives and guarantees, serve as channels for promoting Brazilian business abroad. These ventures include the sale of technology and construction and consulting services to Latin American, Asian, and African countries. One such operation, involving the building of a railroad in Iraq, is the biggest contract for export of services, and it totals US$1.2 billion.

The BRASPETRO overseas operations range from association with other companies for oil exploration, as in Iran and the Philippines, to equity participation in oil-exploring companies in other countries, such as in Colombia. The steel enterprise SIDERBRAS is participating in a joint venture with the government of Colombia for the exploration of Colombian coal deposits.

As with Brazil, foreign investments by companies from Mexico are not adequately reflected in official statistics. The registered stock of Mexican foreign investment in nine Latin American countries amounted to only US$62 million in 1978. However, a business organization revealed in 1976 that approximately thirty Mexican firms were engaged in more than fifty projects in eight South American countries, involving wholly owned subsidiaries and equity and contractual joint ventures for the production of steel, petroleum, chemicals, paper, electronics, and construction and engineering services.[8] Mexican companies are also active in Central America and the Caribbean, where several large projects were launched or negotiated in recent years, including a steel mill and a pulp and paper project in Honduras, a bauxite project in Jamaica, a fertilizer plant in Costa Rica, and a multinational merchant fleet with the Caribbean countries.

Some Mexican firms and groups seem to have become truly multinational in their orientation. Among such firms, the most important cases can be found in the steel, newsprint paper, oil, construction, and engineering sectors, including (1) Hojalata y Laminas, S. A. (HYLSA), one of the biggest private concerns, which developed a sponge-iron process already exported to Brazil, Venezuela, Indonesia, Iran, Iraq, and Zambia; (2) Bufete Industrial-Cusi, which has sold its technology for turning waste material from sugar cane into newsprint to Argentina, Peru, Venezuela, Pakistan, and Egypt; (3) PEMEX, a state corporation that developed a process for oil refining thereafter spread to Colombia, Jamaica, and other countries; (4) the building company ICA, established in eleven Latin American countries and participating in projects ranging from hydroelectrical works to railroads and hotels; and (5) Tecnimexico, an association of thirty-two consulting and engineering firms that since its creation in 1974 has promoted fifty-six projects in other countries, mostly in Latin America.

Less-Developed and Middle-Sized Countries. The present significance of Latin American direct investment also can be appreciated by looking at the host countries, particularly those with small or less-developed economies in the region. It has already been mentioned that Argentine firms are traditionally important in Uruguay and Paraguay. More recently, the Brazilian presence has increased in the two countries, particularly through big engineering and consulting firms participating in the development of physical and industrial infrastructure projects. In Ecuador and Bolivia, the smaller countries of the Andean Group, Latin American direct investments represent an important percentage of the total stock. In Ecuador, the figure was 11.5 percent in 1977 (or 7.7 percent if the Panamanian investments are excluded) and was even higher for the manufacturing industry. In Bolivia, 9 percent of all foreign investments approved by the government during 1972-1976 originated in other Latin American countries.

Finally, the middle-sized, intermediate countries, such as Chile and Colombia, seem to play a more balanced role as sources and recipients of regional foreign investment. During the period 1974-1978, twenty-four firms of seven Latin American countries were authorized to invest US$17 million in Chile, and between 1976-1978, about twenty Chilean companies registered investments in other Latin American countries amounting to US$12 million. In the case of Colombia, the registered stock of investments abroad was $41 million in 1976, with Latin America as the host of 77 percent of the projects. However, the stock of direct investment from the region to Colombia amounted to approximately 6 percent of the total (in 1968 the percentage was less than 2 percent). Table 10-2 summarizes the intraregional direct investments.

Table 10-2
Intraregional FDI in Latin America: Registered (by Host Countries) Accumulated Flows, Latest Available Data
(Thousands of U.S. Dollars)

Countries of Origin	Host Countries									
	Argentina[a] 8/1976	Bolivia[b] 1976	Brazil[c] 6/1978	Colombia[d] 12/1978	Chile[e] 8/1978	Ecuador[f] 12/1977	Mexico[g] 12/1978	Peru[h] 12/1977	Venezuela[i] 12/1978	Total
Argentina	—	441	20,031	1,062	662	10,846	986	1,771	2,058	37,857
Bolivia	2,605	—	17	5	133	—	—	431	49	3,240
Brazil	16,889	1,301	—	2,404	13,969	4,752	734	949	338	41,336
Colombia	22,043	—	244	—	50	10,347	218	695	1,499	34,878
Chile	355	271	273	195	—	11,097	—	1,240	82	13,731
Ecuador	—	—	148	17,620	100	—	—	825	21	18,714
Mexico	762	—	7,650	4,142	2,552	4,771	—	1,156	1,846	22,879
Paraguay	—	—	1	—	—	—	—	—	77	78
Peru	8	594	14	1,719	47	1,186	133	—	193	3,894
Uruguay	7,930	—	16,475	1,110	300	—	—	2,256	3,812	31,884
Venezuela	10,090	—	13,333	26,123	5,697	5,525	1,205	2,011	—	63,984
Others Central America	—	—	194	278	82	—	—	38	731	1,323
Total	60,682	2,607	58,380	54,659	23,592	48,524	3,276	11,372	10,706	273,798

[a]Declared investments until August 1976. Subsecretaria do inversiones Externas, Ministerio de Economia. Not available period 1/9/1976 to 1/3/1977. From September 1976 to September 1979 a total amount of US$ 27.426 (always in 1000 dollars) was approved (Brazil, 20.632; Uruguay, 4.917; Venezuela, 829; Costa Rica, 848; Guatemala, 200).

[b]FDI approved by industrial promotion agency (INI) only for 1972-1976 and covering only a fraction of DFI in industrial sector.

[c]Boletin del Banco Central de Brasil, December 1978.

[d]Oficina de Cambios, Banco de la Republica. Petroleum investment not included.

[e]Comite de Inversiones Extranjeras, Period 1974-11-8-1978.

[f]Banco Central del Ecuador, Subgerencia de Balanza de Pagos, FDI accumulated, direct research.

[g]Direccion General de Inversiones Extranjeras y Transferencia de Tecnologia: "Sociedades mexicanas con participacion de capital de paises de la ALALC." An exchange rate of 22,767 pesos per dollar was applied, corresponding to the average for 1978 (FMI, International Financial Statistics).

[h]CONITE, Ministerio de Economia y Finanzas. An exchange rate of 83,81 soles per dollar was applied, corresponding to the average for 1977 (FMI, International Financial Statistics).

[i]Superintendencia de Inversiones Extranjeras, Ministerio de Uacienda. Not including investments in oil, tourism, banks, and insurance. An exchange rate of 4,29 bolivares per dollar was applied, corresponding to the average for 1978 (FMI, International Financial Statistics).

Sectors, Firms, and Forms

The Latin American FDI is diversified in a wide range of activities, including manufacturing, mining petroleum, agriculture, building, consulting, trade, banking, and insurance services. The information available for a group of four host countries indicated a strong concentration in manufacturing (44.5 percent of the stock), followed by trade and banking, together responsible for 3 percent of the Latin American investments (see figure 10-1). Within the manufacturing industry, there are certain specializations that are consistent with the general pattern of industrial production in Latin America, as seen in table 10-3. A high proportion of the investment is backward or forward linked with agribusiness (agrochemicals, agricultural machinery, textiles, and food products).

Latin American foreign direct investment and transfers of technology are almost completely limited to nationally owned firms of the investing countries. Despite their great contribution to exports, particularly of manufactures,[9] subsidiaries of transnational corporations from developed nations play only a minor role in these operations. Only a few foreign companies have used their Latin American bases for setting up subsidiaries in other countries of the region. Among the few cases, mention could be made of the investments of the Argentine subsidiaries of Fiat, Peugeot, and Citroen in other LAFTA countries made on the basis of binational trade arrangements for the automotive sector.

The majority of cases of FDI and transfer of technology involve medium or large (in Latin American terms) private firms, although public corporations are also active, particularly in projects in the basic industries, such as steel, mining, and petrochemicals, where the role of state enterprises is important in Latin America, as well as in physical integration projects, such as hydroelectrical or transport ventures.[10]

Joint ventures with local partners or associates are the most frequent organizational form of LAFDI. Among the 313 cases identified by the INTAL study, around 65 percent adopted such an arrangement. The percentage was higher for the manufacturing sectors and lower for banking, building, and trade.[11] The joint-venture preference is corroborated by the official country records. Of the Argentine firms that registered investments abroad in 1967-1976, 60 percent declared that they had local partners in the host countries. Nearly 80 percent of all companies with Latin American capital registered in Ecuador during 1974-1976 had local partners, which in more than half the cases controlled 50 percent or more of the capital.

Other nonequity forms of exporting technology are also very common in the Latin American experience. Among contractual forms, licensing agreements are frequently used by Latin American firms for doing business abroad, but the most significant development is the growing trend of ex-

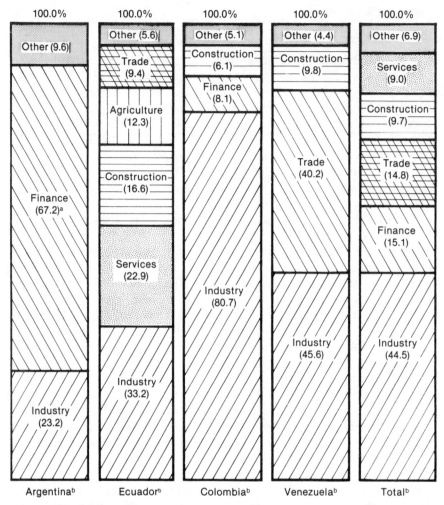

Source: Argentina: Ministerio de Economía; Ecuador: Banco Central; Colombia: Banco de la República; Venezuela: Banco Central.

[a]Includes a Brazilian investment in the financial sector explaining 77.1 percent of this subtotal.

[b]Period 1971-1974; stock in 1974.

Figure 10-1. Sectoral Distribution of LAFDI in Some Latin American Countries

porting consulting and engineering services and turnkey plants by firms in Argentina, Brazil, and Mexico, as was mentioned earlier.[12]

Factors and Forces

Although the emergence of the first Latin American international firms goes back to the turn of century when some Argentine firms started moving

Table 10-3
LAFDI in Manufacturing Sectors

Sector	Percent
Food products	16.2
Textiles	8.1
Agrochemicals	4.1
Agricultural equipment	8.1
Printing	5.4
Chemicals and pharmaceuticals	10.8
Steel and inputs for steel production	4.8
Electromechanical	10.8
Automaking and components	8.1
Others	21.6
Total	100.0

Source: Seventy-seven cases identified in the study by INTAL, E. White, J. Campos and G. Ondarts, *Las Empresas Conjuntas Latinoamericanas* (INTAL, 1977), p. 26

abroad, this phenomenon grew into a significant, sustained trend only during the last two decades.

The Maturing and Expansion of
Industrial Capacities

Several developments took place during the past 20 years that led to growth of factors conducive to internationalization among domestic firms. During the 1960s, Latin America as a whole achieved high rates of growth. Between 1965 and 1973, real output increased over 7 percent annually, and the economic structures experienced an accelerated process of transformation. The process of industrialization, initiated in countries such as Argentina, Brazil, Chile, and Mexico well before World War I and in other less-advanced countries of the region after World War II, began to bear fruit and gave rise to a diversified and relatively advanced manufacturing base during the 1960s, growing at an average rate of 6.9 percent in 1960-1965 and 7.5 percent in 1965-1970. Manufactured exports increased by an average of 26 percent for the region during the 1965-1973 period, and by 30 percent for Brazil, Mexico, Argentina, and Colombia (the four most important exporters of manufactures in Latin America) covering products ranging from textiles to chemicals and transport equipment.[13] The expansion of manufactured exports was particularly significant within Latin America, increasing from 21 percent of intraregional trade in 1961 to 43 percent in 1974.

The process of transformation and deployment of productive forces throughout the region was coupled with a significant diversification of the actors participating in such developments. Transnational enterprises occupied dominant positions in the most dynamic industries, particularly in capital-intensive sectors employing advanced technology, and as mentioned earlier, they accounted for a high share of exports of manufactures. However, domestic enterprises, both private and state-owned, also took part in the process.

Latin American firms attained or preserved a significant role in several medium-sized industries, such as food, textiles, and metal-working, in traditional branches of chemicals and electronics, and in certain basic industries, such as steel and petrochemicals.[14] Today most of these sectors account for an important share of the industrial exports. In Argentina, for example, local firms were responsible for 71.8 percent of manufactured exports by mid-1970.[15] In Colombia at about the same time, national participation in exports was 85 percent for food products, 71 percent for nonelectrical machinery, 90 percent for furnitures, and 55 percent for professional equipment.[16]

As a result of these developments, there are many industries in the industrial sectors of Latin American countries that have considerable experience and technical capacity, based on human and institutional resources, to cope with the challenges of international competition. During the late 1960s, when Latin American governments became aware of the limits and problems of import substitution as an industrial strategy and decided to promote the diversification of exports through incentive programs and changes in their exchange rate policies, many local firms responded to the new objectives.

Regional-Integration Programs

During the last decade, the regional-integration schemes and their trade-liberalization measures offered a wider scenario to the Latin American firms. Although subsidiaries of transnational corporations from developed nations took greater advantage of the opportunities provided by tariff cuts and complementation agreements than domestic enterprises, regional groups such as the Latin American Free Trade Association, the Andean Group, and the Central American Common Market stimulated the awareness of local firms about the possibilities available in the regional market.[17]

In broader terms, integration programs also helped to encourage the formation of Latin American multinational enterprises as an effective tool for achieving objectives of common interest in the region.[18] The Andean Group enacted a special statute (decision 46 of 1971) to regulate and promote such joint ventures, and the SELA (Latin American Economic System) gave priority to the formation of regional multinationals in various sectors. These institutional developments were not always effective (for example, decision 46 has never been applied), but indirectly they were instrumental in lessening the traditional distrust of Latin American governments toward domestic foreign investments and their disdain for FDI coming from Latin American countries. These developments also explain in part the greater knowledge now available in this field and, more significantly, the gradual institutionalization, through special government offices and regulations, of foreign investments as a "normal" activity of local firms.[19] At the same time, during the last several years, some countries have included special tax and financial incentives for the export of technology within their export-promotion programs.

The availability of a wide regional market is also important in the case of LAFDI because of the different levels of economic development that exist among Latin American countries. In terms of industrial modernization and technological capacity, there are, in fact, significant gaps among (1) the larger, semi-industrialized countries (Argentina, Brazil, and Mexico); (2) the smaller economies with relatively experienced industrial sectors (Chile, Colombia, Peru, and Venezuela); and (3) the rest of the less-developed countries of the region. Such gaps and the corresponding non-synchronism of the industrialization process in the different economies provided, together with other factors, a major force for the intraregional flow of investments and technology from firms of the more-developed countries and sectors to other less-advanced sectors and countries of Latin America.

Changes in the External Sector

The changing conditions of the external sector are also important factors explaining the trends of LAFDI. During the last decade, the balance-of-payments performance for the region as a whole was strong and the foreign-exchange constraint became less binding, so that a more flexible governmental attitude toward investment was possible. For example, the net international reserve holdings of Colombia increased from US$95 million in 1966 to US$800 million in 1976, owing to the continuous favorable situation in the balance of trade.[20] Without this progress it would be hard to explain the increasing flow of Colombian FDI authorized by the government since 1968. Similarly, the rapid growth of Argentine foreign investments since 1977 is clearly connected with the gradual accumulation of reserves during the last 3 years, which in 1979 amounted to US$10 billion.

Yet in recent times, most of the Latin American countries faced increasing deficits in their balance of payments, because of the rise in petroleum prices, import payments associated with fast economic growth, and world recession. As a consequence, there was a slowdown in the rate of economic growth throughout most of the region, creating adverse conditions for many industrial firms, which found themselves with an overcapacity in relation to decaying domestic demand. For certain sectors, such as the construction industry, the only alternative in view of the slowdown in public works was to search for overseas contracts. Typical of this situation is the case of Brazil, where the huge government investments in big-infrastructure projects carried out during the last decade gave rise to skilled local consulting and engineering firms. The control of public spending after the aggravation of the balance-of-payments situation and the rise of inflationary pressures led many of these companies to compete in other countries in Latin America, Africa, and the Middle East for large contracts with the support of the Brazilian government.[21]

Strategies and Motivations

Latin American corporations largely invest abroad for reasons not very different from those explaining the expansion of firms of developed countries. The Latin American evidence also seems to support the findings of Wells with regard to developing countries in Southeast Asia.[22] However, the following remarks may suggest the existence of some motivations that are not exactly similar to those of firms from either developed or other developing countries.

In a developing region like Latin America, where changing political and economic circumstances are so common, with governments shifting periodically from interventionist to conservative policies and vice versa, and critical external sectors alternating short periods of surplus and deficit, it is obvious that one of the basic motivations of local firms with regard to foreign investments is the diversification of risk by "putting the eggs in different baskets." Foreign investments by Argentine firms during the most difficult period of the last Peronist government (1973-1976), by Chilean firms during the Allende administration, and by Peruvian companies during the first years of the 1968 revolution, although generally unreported by the home governments, explain to a great extent the upsurge of LAFDI in other countries during the last decade. Such factors also explain the ephemeral life of some ventures. For instance, one middle-sized Argentine pharmaceutical firm without any international experience decided to move abroad in 1975 and took over a Mexican company. Three years later, when the business climate had improved at home, the investment was sold to another Argentine firm that had an internationally oriented strategy.

In such circumstances, most foreign investments by small firms tend to disappear or integrate within the host country. Even the firms of respectable size can find it difficult to provide the human and capital resources needed for foreign operations over a long period, especially when the original motivations involve no long-term strategies. The huge Colombian conglomerate Bavaria accepted a share in the equity of a firm in Costa Rica as payment for a sale of second-hand equipment in the late 1960s. Bavaria had no interest in such a holding and sold it to local investors after a few years.

Similarly, a Chilean state corporation involved in fishing decided to form a joint venture in Ecuador when the sudden disappearance of fish from the Chilean coast left its fleet underutilized. The expansion of the Ecuadorian project was not followed up by the Chilean company, which sold most of its majority share to the local partner.

International operations are often conceived as a device for circumventing domestic tax burdens, labor laws, and foreign-exchange restrictions. A well-known Peruvian soft drink company engineered an intricate network of companies in other Latin American countries that maintained control of patents and trademarks; the main purpose was the accumulation of foreign-exchange holdings.

. However, as the experience of the two Argentine drug firms in Mexico suggest, there are cases in which the decision to move abroad is a normal development of the firm's growth strategy. In fact, the Latin American experience offers various examples of companies that assigned a certain priority to external expansion through investments in other countries and exports of technology. Apart from the state-owned petroleum corporations, such as PETROBRAS of Brazil, which are naturally oriented to the exploration in other countries, or the big consulting and engineering firms looking for foreign contracts to compensate the cycles of domestic demand, there are cases of firms that have evolved from small ventures with a narrow domestic market into internationally oriented organizations with a regional plan and a strategy for international complementation. Carvajal, a family-owned firm of Colombia specializing in the manufacture of paper products and supplies, initiated a chain of investments in other Latin American countries after becoming one of the biggest firms in the sector. Since 1970, it established joint ventures in Costa Rica, Panama, Nicaragua, Ecuador, Chile, and Venezuela, organizing the different holdings on the basis of a combination of direct and indirect participations and under a certain division of labor between countries.

Fertica, the Central American joint venture of GUANOMEX, a Mexican public-sector company, has a regional program of production and commercialization coordinating various plants and distributors throughout the different countries. Laboratorios Bago, an Argentine pharmaceutical firm leading the domestic market, has set up its own factories and sold turnkey plants in various Latin American countries. More recently, it established a trading company to export technology and detect business opportunities abroad. PILAO Maquinas e Equipamentos, a Brazilian manufacturer of equipment for the production of paper, exporting 60 percent of its total sales, has patented its innovations in twenty-six countries, has set up subsidiaries in the United States and Mexico, and has licensed local firms in Belgium, Argentina, and Colombia.

However, business rationality is not the only motivation for investing abroad in Latin America. Political considerations and macroeconomic objectives are behind or explicit in some joint ventures involving the state enterprises, or the governments themselves, of different countries. For example, the project of YPF, the national oil company of Argentina, to build a pesticide plant in the Bolivian *altiplano* seemed to be aimed at improving the overall relations with the Andean country rather than motivated by the (apparently insufficient) rate of return of the project. Some multinational ventures, as already noted, have common-interest objectives, such as improving the bargaining power of the countries vis-à-vis the international market (as in the case of COMUNBANA, the Caribbean banana multinational) or creating an independent trading organization (as in the case of NAMUCAR, the sea fleet of the Caribbean countries, or MULTIFER, the SELA-sponsored fertilizer multinational between various Latin American countries).

It is against the background described before that the main specific motivations of firms moving abroad may be examined (obviously the following categories are not exclusive and could be simultaneously present in foreign-investment decisions).

Preservation of Export Markets

Much of the LAFDI from the larger countries of the region is a reaction to the import-substitution barriers imposed by the smaller countries to protect their late industrialization efforts. As noted earlier, for many Latin American firms, the markets of the region have gained great significance. Higher tariffs and import quotas established by less-advanced importing countries imply a direct threat to such exports. In fact, Latin American exporters began to meet circumstances very similar to those which triggered the direct investment of firms of industrialized countries in the region during the first period of import substitution in Latin America. The cases studied by INTAL revealed that most of the firms had export experience in the recipient countries before their decision to invest in them.[23]

In recent years, the growth of Latin American exports of manufactures to industrialized countries and other third-world regions also has motivated the establishment of firms in those markets which are threatened by protectionist pressures.[24] As mentioned earlier, Brazilian corporations took over some companies in the United States and spread into Africa to assemble semifinished Brazilian products. In addition, firms from Argentina have set up facilities in Europe, especially for the export-oriented agroindustry.

Defensive reasons are also behind cases of investments in other countries when the risk of losing an export market stems not from measures of host nations, but, on the contrary, from policies of the home government that tend to discourage exports through, for instance, an overvalued exchange rate or the elimination of tax or financial incentives. The anti-inflationary policies applied in recent years in countries such as Argentina have stimulated decisions to invest abroad as the only way for preserving markets that have become difficult to serve through exports.

Preservation of export markets is a typical reason for intraregional investments in assembly plants for the automotive industry, machinery, domestic appliances, and light-engineering goods as well as the formulation of drugs. For example, the Brazilian company CALOI, the main South American exporter of bicycles, decided to invest in Bolivia (where it had established an important position through previous exports) when a local firm supported by the government and stimulated by prospects of a high protection margin began to look for foreign partners for domestic production. Industrias Mecanicas del Estado, a state-owned automaker of Argentina, joined with its agents in Uruguay to assemble light trucks in view of the progressive closing of the import market for finished cars. Some local pharmaceutical firms of Argentina have set up formulation plants in less-advanced countries willing to start developing the drug industry.

Normally, the Latin American foreign investors in these cases try to minimize the number of production stages in the host country in order to continue exporting parts and components—an objective that is facilitated by the weakness of the local industrial infrastructure in the small countries of the region.

The investment package often includes a trademark owned by the Latin American parent company, enjoying prestige in the host country owing to the previous export performance of the finished products. When, some years ago, the Argentine electrical equipment manufacturer Yelmo was chosen by its Venezuelan importer over the international firm Moulinex to start assembly operations, the branded products of the former enjoyed the same reputation as the French company in the local market.

Penetration into New Markets

During the last decade, the high rates of growth of certain countries of Latin America incited the interest of many foreign firms—among them, companies of the other countries of the region. The expansion of the economies of Brazil, Venezuela, and Ecuador as well as the enlargement of domestic markets of the region through subregional integration measures, such as in the Andean Group and the Central American Common Market, explain some trends in intraregional FDI. For example, the status of Ecuador, as a less-advanced but rapidly developing country and a member of the Andean Group, was an incentive for setting up plants to serve the growing domestic demand to profit from the opportunities offered by the subregional market of five countries. The higher rates of industrial growth in Ecuador during the period 1970-1976 (with annual average increases of over 20 percent) were attained in traditional and intermediate sectors, such as food and drinks, leather, plastic products, and non-electrical machinery, in which Latin American investors of the bigger neighboring countries had sufficient experience.

Several Latin American companies had not exported before to the country in which they set up plants. Most of these firms manufacture products that, for technical or transport reasons, are not easy to export, as in the case of an Argentine investment in a factory in Venezuela to serve the local demand of road demarcation or a Venezuelan firm established in Ecuador to manufacture ceramic sanitary devices. There are also products that have to be manufactured in close proximity to the market. For example, an Argentine manufacturer of electrical cables for the automotive industry decided to set up a plant in Chile in view of the expected expansion of the local demand. The large variety of products, manufactured in short series and with different specifications than those of the Argentine market, precluded the export alternative.

The active search of investment opportunities in other countries also can be a response to recession in the home market. Overcapacity and huge fixed costs during the periods of weak local demand led Argentine, Brazilian, and Mexican engineering and construction firms to fight for big contracts throughout Latin America and other regions. The Chilean-Ecuadoran fishing joint venture referred to earlier allowed the Chilean company to get rid of some of its unused boats. In another joint venture for the manufacture of laminated steel in Ecuador, the main motivation of the Chilean steel producer was to ensure an export market for its surplus production.

In many cases, an important motivation to move abroad is the possibility of creating a stable flow of exports of parts and components for the production complex of the recipient country. The common ownership established between exporter and importer ensures the external demand and allows the enlargement of the production scale or the reduction of idle capacity in the home market. The preceding advantages, together with the challenge of import-substitution measures undertaken by importing countries, are among the reasons for LAFDI in assembly industries.

Regardless of such external constraints as domestic recession or tariff barriers in importing countries, for certain firms that have consolidated an important position in the local market, the projection abroad is a result of understanding the limited possibilities offered by narrow national boundaries. Some of the cases mentioned earlier, such as the Brazilian manufacturer of bicycles or the Argentine electrical equipment firm, belong to a category of companies that considers it necessary to carry out activities abroad in order to preserve and expand their levels of activity.

Finally, the interest in new markets is sometimes the outcome of a new trend in Latin American relations: the search for suppliers of technology within the region. Despite the historical orientation toward the market of productive resources in developed countries, there is a growing demand for the technical skills of other Latin American countries. For example, during 1978, a government mission from Ecuador visited Argentina and other countries to contact the local industries and offer them possibilities and incentives for investing in Ecuador; it returned with several projects in hand.[25]

Raw-Materials Exploitation

Several Latin American companies have moved abroad to exploit raw materials for which the home country is a net importer. In so doing they try to stabilize the supply and its prices. Such were the reasons given by the Argentine steel maker GRASSI for obtaining government approval for setting up a plant in Brazil that would ensure the supply of iron alloys threatened by the shortages of manganese reserves in Argentina.

The most relevant cases belong to the big state-owned enterprises in the oil and mineral sectors. The great dependence of Brazil on foreign oil explains the creation of a subsidiary of the state oil company PETROBRAS for undertaking exploration abroad and its projection to several Middle Eastern and African countries. In addition, the Brazilian state steel enterprise SIDERBRAS has negotiated a joint venture with the government of Colombia to exploit coal in that country as a way of gaining independence from the U.S. sources of such raw materials; and the public-sector oil company YPF of Argentina obtained an important service contract for the exploration of oil in Ecuador. Mention can be made also of the establishment in Tanzania of a subsidiary of the Mexican company CORDEMEX, specializing in the large-scale manufacture of jute, with the objective of reinforcing its influence in the international market of hard fibers.

There are, in addition, a few cases of private firms that engage in the exploitation of raw materials abroad to supply the host countries. Cia. Minera Buenaventura, a Peruvian company, has equity shares in mining projects in Venezuela, Ecuador, and other Latin American countries.

Other Motivations

Like firms from the advanced countries, some flows of foreign direct investment are motivated in part by lower labor costs in the host countries. Such was one of the most relevant reasons of an important Argentine manufacturer of agricultural machinery for setting up a plant in Brazil in the mid-1960s.

The objective of gaining access to a foreign technological innovation was present in the case of a joint venture in Venezuela among the Colombian firm Carvajal, a group of local investors, and a U.S. company owning a new process for the manufacture of cardboard packages.

Several Latin American banks have moved abroad for reasons similar to those explaining the expansion of financial institutions throughout the world. For example, Brazilian banks have established branches in Latin American countries to serve the needs of Brazilian exporters, and Colombian banks are very active in the neighbor market of Panama.

One of the most important Colombian private banks, the Banco de Bogota, has developed a strategy of international expansion based on a holding in Panama through which it controls different investments in the Caribbean and Central American countries, ranging from financial entities to trade warehouses. It has recently formed a jointly owned bank with local investors in Ecuador as a result of the growing trade links between the two countries. Trade expansion also has stimulated reciprocal investments in the banking sectors of Venezuela and Colombia.

Several Latin American banks have branches in the international financial centers, such as London, New York, and Frankfurt. Their dynamism can be explained by the new "open economy" policies of the more-advanced countries of the region and the increased possibilities of access to the world private capital markets. This projection has aided them in obtaining funds for long-term investments, large infrastructure projects, and the foreign-exchange needs of their home countries.

The most salient characteristic of the expansion of Latin American banks is the leading role played by certain policy owned entities. One of them, the Banco de Brasil, was listed seventh among the top international banks in the 1976 ranking of *The Banker*. With more than fifty dependencies abroad, its foreign assets amounted to US$10,000 million in 1976 and the profits from foreign operations accounted for 10 to 15 percent of the total.

Competitive Advantages of LAFDI

What kind of attributes and skills do those Latin American firms have that make them attractive for host countries and in fact more attractive than local alternatives and firms from industrialized nations? It appears that the main competitive advantage of these firms is related to the lower costs of their projects, derived from the adaptation of their technology to the local context and from the lower costs of the transfer of such technology. In this sense, the Latin American experience broadly coincides with that of Southeast Asia, particularly if the cases of the larger countries of the region (Argentina, Brazil, Mexico) are compared with the performance of India, Hong Kong, South Korea, and other developing countries with important industrial sectors. However, at this point it is necessary to mention certain characteristics that may be exclusive to or typical of Latin America. These will emerge from the following analysis.

Industrial activities were introduced in Latin America several decades ago on the basis of the previous experience of developed countries. European immigration, imports of equipment, foreign investments and acquisition of technology through licensing, technical assistance, or copying were the principal channels. The substance of the process of industrialization in Latin America may then be described as an imitative phenomenon.[26] Accordingly, the innovations incorporated by Latin American firms were rarely original, and if so, they were ephemeral or did not imply a major technological change. The advantages eventually enjoyed by a company from the region were normally limited to the regional context or to some of its countries.

Yet there are several cases in which the competitive advantage of a Latin American firm seems to be backed up by more or less important innovations. Mention has been made of some Mexican firms that have projected abroad on the basis of certain basic technologies of their own development: the HYLSA process for direct reduction in the steel industry, the PEMEX process for the extraction of metals while refining crude oil, and the CUSI process for manufacturing newsprint paper starting from sugar-cane waste materials.

Similarly, the international success of PILAO, the Brazilian manufacturer of equipment for the production of paper, is explained by the merits of its own system for processing the short fibers obtained from eucalyptus trees (apart from registering the patent or licensing the process in Japan, the United States, Belgium, and twenty-six other countries, PILAO has recently formed a joint venture with its main competitor, the Finnish firm Paper Machine Group Oy). Also COLTEJER, the biggest Colombian textile company, developed an outstanding system for printing fabrics on the basis of which it planned to set up a subsidiary in the United States, and Fortuny, the Argentine manufacturer of agricultural equipment with a plant in Brazil, has introduced important innovations in harvest machines.

Apart from such cases of original innovations, Latin American direct investment and transfer of technology, and their relative advantages, are based on the mastery of imported technologies that have been adapted to the Latin American conditions after years of accumulated experience by firms of the more-advanced countries of the region. The particular conditions of their local markets have impelled such firms to carry out various kinds of efforts in order to adapt the original designs to local constraints, such as the availability and cost of raw materials,[27] the relative price of production factors, the size of the market, the peculiarities of local consumers, the climatic and geographic conditions, and other aspects of the domestic context.[28] According to this view, the process of adaptation of technology gives rise to a "special asset"[29] or a "new technical package"[30] that can be transmitted later to third markets at low marginal costs. The developmental gaps existing between the more-advanced countries of the region and less-developed nations of Latin America and elsewhere make the adapted technologies appear more "appropriate" to the conditions of the latter with similar socioeconomic attributes.[31] Within this framework, it is possible to distinguish the following advantages of firms from Latin America that invest abroad.

Industrial Experience

In many cases of horizontal direct investment, the investor is a firm from a country with considerable industrial experience that has spent a long time, sometimes several decades, confined in its domestic market, where it has consolidated an important position and later exported to other countries of the region. For other countries and firms that want to start producing in the same sector, the association with entrepreneurs who have successfully experienced such production is an effective way of diminishing the risk of an unknown activity.

The case study by INTAL confirmed the importance of the experience of Latin American firms in several joint ventures in middle-sized industries in the textile, metal mechanic, fertilizer, steel, and food storage and packaging sectors. Such industries are characterized by considerable investments and a rather high capital-labor ratio, and in consequence, the success of the respective projects depends on good management of the investment and the plant operation.

In most of these cases, the machinery as well as the basic technologies originate from outside the region. However, the company typically takes care of the project planning, the purchase of the equipment and technology, and the installation of the plant. It has undergone a learning process in its home country, where a similar plant is operated. This learning process has been completed not so many years ago, so that the firm can still understand the problems of the late starters. The experienced entrepreneur knows where to buy the machinery, how to unbundle the technological package, and how to select the most appropriate type of plant; he has experienced technical specialists to build and operate the new factory in the host country. The firm's experience is still embodied in the owners, the managers, and the technicians. Examples of this situation are, among other cases, (1) the plant for steel lamination in Ecuador set up by Corporacion de Aceros del Pacifico (CAP) of Chile, one of the first steel companies in Latin America; (2) the textile plant built in Nicaragua by Fabricato, one of the oldest (1923) and larger textile firms in Colombia, with considerable knowledge of the international machinery market and of the organization needed for large-scale production of textiles; (3) the investment of a Brazilian firm in Venezuela to build and operate a large commercial cold-storage house based on modern techniques imported from a Swedish firm and applied previously in Brazil; (4) the Central American fertilizer joint venture of GUANOMEX, a Mexican state enterprise that controls almost all the production of such products in its home country; (5) the various Latin American joint ventures of CARVAJAL, the old (1910) Colombian firm with highly specialized experience in the editing and publication of telephone directories and the production of office supplies; and (6) the establishment in Chile of MOLANCA, a Colombo-Venezuelan joint venture manufacturing paper pulp packages, on the basis of technology imported from the United States and applied for several years in Venezuela.

Small-Scale, Simpler, Less-Expensive
Production Techniques

Some Latin American companies have managed to be internationally competitive in basic manufacturing sectors—characterized by high fixed investments per job and significant scale economies—to the extent of being able to set up plants abroad and provide the machinery, the production processes, and the know-how for running them. The secret of such successful experiences seems to lie in the development by these firms of appropriate techniques for small-scale production. Some examples illustrate the case. The Argentine steel company that set up a factory in Brazil for the production of iron alloys had been operating a similar plant in Argentina for several years. The technology, originating in Italy, was gradually adapted and modified over a period of 20 years in Argentina. The performance in Brazil was very successful until expansion of the Brazilian market and export possibilities made it desirable to seek a substantial increase in the scale of production, a change for which the Argentine firm had neither the experience nor the capacity. The expansion that followed, quadrupling the installed capacity, was in fact carried out with the participation of a Japanese firm. Conclusion: the Argentine technology and machinery were appropriate as long as the scale of production was small in international terms.

Another case in the steel sector is of a Brazilian firm acting as technical partner in a large integrated steel project in Paraguay. This firm defines itself as one of the few remaining specialists in a technology no longer used in the industrialized countries, characterized by its small scale, low automation, and low labor costs. Also illustrative is the previously mentioned fishing joint venture in Ecuador involving a big Chilean company with long experience in the use of land factories. This traditional system was appropriate for the conditions in Ecuador, where fish are found near the coasts. The modern methods based on factory ships and designed for long distance and large load capacities would have been unsuitable for the Chilean-Ecuadoran company.

The advantages of small-scale manufacture are also present in other sectors apart from basic industries. A Venezuelan car-repair workshop and autopart dealer decided to start producing clutches; initially, it contacted some European firms, which offered projects with a high initial cost. An Argentine firm with licenses from the main European companies was able to propose an alternative with a much lower investment in equipment and buildings, a progressive scheme of integration, and less automatic machinery adapted to several processes at the same time. Similarly, the flexibility of another Argentine firm to operate with short production runs and a wide range of products was an important factor in explaining the establishment in Chile of a small plant for manufacturing electrical cables.

In all the cases just mentioned, the advantages of Latin American firms resulted in lower costs from small-scale, less-automatic, and more labor-intensive techniques or lower investment costs.

An additional cost advantage may emerge from the lower costs of managers and engineers. The competitiveness of exports of technology through, for example, turnkey plants and infrastructure projects is to a large extent based on the low costs of Latin American engineers and technicians in comparison with the salaries paid in developed countries. This comparative advantage could be decisive for some projects in human capital-intensive industries such as the capital-goods sector, particularly when economies of scale are not very significant and the market is not concentrated. Second, Latin American firms normally do not have sufficient personnel to send abroad for long periods, so that the administrative costs of their subsidiaries and joint ventures in foreign countries tend to be relatively low.

Adaptation to Other Local Conditions and
Marketing Advantages

The international competitiveness of certain Latin American corporations is based on the adaptation of their products to climatic and geographic conditions of other developing countries. Much of the Brazilian direct investment and technology exports to African countries is being concentrated in agribusiness, an industry in which the Brazilian companies' experience in adapting goods to tropical conditions puts them in a strong position. Other products, although in many cases based on designs used in developing countries, also have been substantially modified to cope with tougher climatic and physical conditions. For example, considerable experience has been acquired by Brazil in developing vehicles able to run on unpaved roads, including the mud of Amazonia. These adaptations explain the success of automobile exports to Africa and the interest shown by some Brazilian-owned firms for starting their operations there. For instance, a company in Ghana is manufacturing bodies for bus coaches to be fixed to Brazilian-made chassis.

Although cost competitiveness appears to be the basic advantage of Latin American firms that move abroad, there are several examples in which this advantage is combined or replaced with marketing skills. An interesting case is the projection of pharmaceutical firms from Argentina to neighbor countries of Latin America.

Argentine-owned drug companies have been able to coexist with subsidiaries of transnational corporations on the basis of heavy expenses in promotion of medicines, as well as in adapting the products to the domestic consumer tastes and lower incomes. Today Argentine laboratories are operating in Brazil, Chile, Uruguay, Paraguay, Bolivia, Ecuador, and Mexico. In some cases, the Argentine firms subcontract the production to local firms in the host countries while continuing to handle the sales organization, an area in which they have excellent experience.

There are other cases of marketing-intensive strategies in the production of consumer goods. A Peruvian manufacturer of a popular light drink, Inca Kola, has managed to overcome the competition of Coca-Cola, Pepsi, and other foreign trademarks in the domestic market. It has now established plants in Ecuador, Puerto Rico, and probably other countries. An Argentine manufacturer of chocolate products, CABSHA, was persuaded by Costa Rican investors to establish a plant there and license its trademark, which has enabled the firm to compete successfully with the better-known products of Nestle and other transnational corporations. Among the cases examined before, Brazilian CALOI bicycles, Colombian FABRICATO clothing, and CARVAJAL paper manufactures have significant marketing expertise and trademark reputations.

Relations with the Transnational Corporations: Competition and Association

The preceding analysis attempts to explain the main reasons for the competitive advantages of LAFDI. Such reasons clarify the strengths of certain firms vis-à-vis other Latin American companies as well as with transnationals from outside the region. The preceeding discussion suggests that their main advantages over transnational corporations are related to the lower costs, the suitability of the projects offered by Latin American firms, in terms of the smaller-scale, simpler, more labor-intensive (less automatic), easier to absorb, and more-flexible technologies, and their lower administrative costs. In certain sectors, the firms seem to be competitive also on the basis of skills in the marketing area, which are typical of transnational corporations. Exceptionally, the success of Latin American enterprises is based on the development of their own major technological innovations.

Latin American firms have revealed significant capacity for introducing new products and processes originated in industrialized countries (including very recent technologies) and moving ahead of the decisions of transnational corporations with regard to the launching of such innovations in the region. The absence or weakness of patent protection for pharmaceutical products in Latin American countries has allowed domestic firms of experienced countries such as Argentina to anticipate the introduction of new drugs in the regional markets. This situation has arisen in other sectors as well. An Argentine firm managed to imitate a new system for road demarcation, very superior to the methods then applied in the region. Having mastered the technique, it decided to set up a plant in Venezuela. As a result, it had to overcome the resistance (legal and otherwise) of a British corporation that held a patent never exploited in Venezuela but used to maintain a monopoly for imports.

The greater mobility of Latin American firms also may arise from the ease with which they are able to imitate, adapt, and modify designs and processes in comparison with local subsidiaries of transnational corporation, which are frequently limited by the global planning and the centralized policies of their parent companies. To the extent that there are local entrepreneurs with sufficient capacity, industrial experience, and ability to quickly assimilate the technological innovations introduced in developed countries, the superior performance of Latin American firms in diffusing and commercializing such innovations is not a surprising fact. Such differential behavior could explain why, for example, TNC subsidiaries in the pharmaceutical sector are much more important as exporters than local firms, while the latter lead the regional flows of FDI and technology. The recent development of atomic energy in some Latin American countries has been immediately followed by a series of cooperation agreements for the transfer of this technology to other countries of the region.

The investment decisions of TNCs are normally based on the amount rather than the rate of the expected profits. The size of the market is an important determinant of such decisions. In this connection, some cases of

LAFDI described before may simply reflect the lack of interest of certain TNCs in investing in the small markets of the region.

Yet in other cases, when given the technological restrictions of a particular project, the market is too small for all kinds of firms (including Latin American firms), the participation of these firms could be the only solution for the scale limitations of the host country. Advantages do not arise in this case from the adaptation of the technology to the size of the market, but on the contrary, from the enlargement of the market in order to achieve the minimum demand for setting up an efficient plant. In some joint ventures between Latin American public-sector corporations, one or more of the participants open their respective domestic markets in order to ensure the minimum scale required by the project. For example, a binational project between the state oil corporations of Argentina and Bolivia to produce pesticides in the Andean country was based on the market guarantee conceded by the Argentine government for a considerable part of the output. The guaranteed market was essential for attaining the minimum demand required by the plant. A large public-sector chemical joint venture between Venezuela and Colombia, where the project is located, was established on the basis of an agreement involving the export of 20 percent of the production to Venezuela.

In these instances, the "special asset" of Latin American firms lies in their ability to integrate the host-country market with their own in the context of ad hoc intergovernmental agreements between the participating countries.[32]

Some state corporations of Latin America may offer an additional advantage to less-developed countries of the region. In fact, the public oil and mining companies such as PETROBRAS, SIDEBRAS, or YPF of Argentina, which have started to expand beyond their frontiers, can be considered as alternatives comparable to transnational corporations in the same sectors. Under certain circumstances, they could offer better conditions to recipient countries. Normally, such corporations are not members of international cartels and tend to appreciate the stability and independence of their raw-material sources rather than the level of profits.

An important differential pattern of the Latin American LAFDI lies in the area of ownership and control. It was already noted that joint ventures with local partners are the typical form of organization of Latin American ventures abroad, and that most joint ventures are controlled by a majority of local investors of the host country. Very often, this advantage (from the viewpoint of host countries, which generally face pressures from TNCs for a majority share) is a consequence of a weakness in the structure of Latin American firms. They are frequently more interested in selling their technology than in controlling their investments and have no fear of losing the control of their low, unpatented knowledge. In general, they need the participation of local investors who provide not only knowledge of the market, but also financial resources and administrative personnel. There are several cases in which the Latin American investors were not able to satisfy the needs for expansion of the joint ventures and after some time retained only a very small equity share or just sold their shares to the local partners. Besides, Latin American investors are, of course, accustomed to the pattern of local majority ownership from which they have benefited in their home countries.

Finally, the transfer of technology, with or without equity participation, by Latin American firms appears to have lower direct and indirect costs than in the cases of transnational corporations. Very often the technical knowledge is transmitted without contractual forms and against no remuneration. Lump-sum payments and fees for technical services (such as the feasibility study), the building of the plant, or the training of local personnel are more frequent than royalties. There are very few cases involving patents. Restrictive business practices such as export limitations, tie-in clauses, and other restrictions are normally absent, as should be expected in the case of firms without an internationally integrated production scheme or a high technology to protect.

Several intraregional ventures are characterized by the participation of a firm of an industrialized country as technology supplier, either through a licensing agreement or through a minority equity share. The American firm Keyes Fibre has a 5 percent share in the joint venture between Colombia and Venezuela manufacturing cardboard packages; Frigoscandia of Sweden, a world leader in the cold-storage industry participates in a Brazilian-Venezuelan joint venture; DSM, a Dutch state-owned petrochemical company, has a 10 percent share in the big Colombo-Venezuelan fertilizer project. The participation of transnational corporations as "technical partners" in Latin American joint ventures is often the result of an appeal or invitation by the Latin American partners. In the cases of Frigoscandia and Keyes, these firms were previously participating in a joint venture with one of the Latin American partners. The DSM participation derived from an international public bid for the supply of technology for the joint project.

There are also cases in which a Latin American firm has joined with a transnational corporation as a way of gaining prestige, reliability, or material support for projects in other countries. A large Argentine private oil company, for example, recently joined with Occidental Petroleum in a contract for oil exploration in Peru. Transnational corporations have also helped indirectly in the projection abroad of Latin American corporations. Some of these companies have been accepted by host countries, which took into account the credibility derived from their licensing contracts with well-known international firms.

Conclusions

The internationalization of Latin American firms should be viewed as a natural consequence of the process of industrialization in the relatively small markets of the region during the last decades. Although for the region as a whole the phenomenon is still incipient (almost nonexistent in statistical terms), there are various countries, sectors, and firms for which investments abroad and exports of technology already play a significant role. Argentina, Brazil, and Mexico have the largest, most-diversified experience as home countries and provide the most interesting cases of corporations with an international approach to their expansion strategies. In some of the smaller and less-developed countries of the region, such as Ecuador, Paraguay, and Uruguay, the activities of subsidiaries and joint ventures of firms of other Latin American countries represent a significant share of the foreign presence in the local economies. Moreover, in middle-sized countries such as Chile and Colombia, the recent adoption of legal frameworks for regulating investments abroad reflects the increasing importance of this phenomenon.

Yet the knowledge of the real scope, characteristics, and factors of the external expansion of Latin American firms is still impressionistic. Foreign investors include big public-sector corporations exploring for raw materials in other regions or undertaking binational or multinational industrial or infrastructure projects on the basis of intergovernmental agreements, large private companies with an important market share in their respective sectors and export activities threatened by protectionist measures in importing countries of the region, small firms stimulated to move abroad by the economic and institutional crises in their home countries, and in a few cases, subsidiaries of multinational corporations from developed countries exploiting opportunities that are too small for their parent companies or that require some form of rationalization between countries of the region.

Manufacturing industries are involved in the bulk of intraregional foreign investments and transfers of technology. The largest number of projects is dedicated to middle-sized or traditional industries, such as food, textiles, machine tools, and electromechanical products. There are numerous cases of export of engineering and consulting services from the most-advanced countries to the less-developed countries of the region.

The main reasons for the overwhelming concentration of flows of Latin American capital and technology within the region rely on the existence of important development gaps between the different countries. Firms in the more-advanced countries of the region have through the years accumulated industrial experience and have learned to adapt their technologies to the local conditions. Such adapted technologies and productive know-how can be later transferred to less-developed countries willing to produce the same products and facing similar restrictions in terms of market sizes, availability and costs of factors, and other local peculiarities. In most cases, there are no local competitors in the recipient countries, and the problem of finding a partner is frequently resolved by the association with a host-government development corporation.

The competitive advantages of Latin American firms vis-a-vis transnational corporations are generally related to the lower cost of their projects, stemming from their smaller scale, greater simplicity, lower automation, or less-expensive production techniques, including the lower costs of their managers and technicians. Only in a few cases is the success of the investing firms based on the development of relatively important basic innovations. There are also examples of firms with greater ability in the marketing field, as well as the capability to take faster action in introducing new products in the region. An important advantage of these firms is their higher propensity to associate with local partners and allow them to be the majority owners of the joint ventures. Similarly, the transfer of technology between Latin American firms does not seem to give rise to restrictive business practices and limitations on the recipient firms, which are usual in the case of arrangements with transnational corporations.

The participation of public enterprises as promoters and partners of Latin American joint ventures is another factor explaining the advantages over transnational corporations. There are cases in which the governments of two or more countries have decided to carry out a joint project with the purpose of avoiding or preventing excessive participation of transnationals in certain sectors or with the objective of increasing the bargaining power of the countries with regard to extraregional firms that control the technology or the markets of certain products. State participation also plays a key role when the governments agree to use their control of their own markets in order to ensure the minimum demand necessary for setting up an efficient plant when the size of only one market is not sufficient.

From the preceding analysis, some forecast can be made about the future of the international projection of Latin American firms. It seems reasonable that the increasing participation of more Latin American countries and their firms in international operations will follow the expansion of the industrialization process and the export-oriented strategies of the countries of the region, that the active presence of the privately owned and public-sector corporations in a number of industrial sectors will ensure the effectiveness of factors and motivations to expand abroad and to look for alternative sources of capital and technology in other Latin American countries, that the existing gaps of development between the different countries will not diminish substantially in the next future; and therefore that the advantages of complementation derived from the intraregional joint ventures will persist. The regional-integration efforts seem to be oriented to more flexible methods of cooperation, which will favor the creation of Latin American binational and multinational enterprises within programs of sectorial (or project by project) integration rather than through global schemes of trade liberalization.

Yet the Latin American international firms should not be viewed as *the* future alternative to transnational corporations of industrialized countries. With a few exceptions, those firms will operate in markets with a relatively low level of concentration and technological intensity. It also should be recognized that they are, to an extent, dependent on the technology of transnational corporations, which they import, imitate, or adapt. Moreover, their advantages with regard to the lower costs and greater suitability of the production techniques will depend on the pace of technological innovations and on the pattern of growth of domestic markets in the countries of the region. Latin American firms will offer better conditions to recipient countries in terms of higher local participation and less-restrictive practices as long as they remain small, less-diversified internationally and do not become dependent on patented and sophisticated technologies.

In the long run, the differences in the behaviors of Latin American joint ventures and transnational corporations will depend on the level and degree of involvement by the governments, as parties, promoters, or guides of the joint ventures. The active participation of public corporations in such projects may ensure the existence of macroeconomic and developmental objectives, but in view of the mixed, decentralized type of economic systems in Latin America, with the large private sectors, governmental action should aim at establishing the rules of the game for industrial and technological cooperation among countries of the region. It does not seem possible, nor necessary, to adopt a code of conduct for Latin American international firms. However, the Latin American countries have the opportunity, on the basis of the existing regional integration schemes, particularly at the sectorial level, to adopt programs and schemes creating a margin of preference for the capital and technologies of the region and, at the same time, a set of standards and criteria to ensure that Latin American joint ventures will serve to promote balanced and equitable development of the different countries.

Notes

1. An idea of the distortions of official statistics is given by the difference between the Brazilian Central Bank figure on foreign investments from Argentina (US$12 million in 1974) and the estimated value of the assets of 120 Brazilian firms controlled by Argentinian investors (more than US$400 million).

2. E. White, J. Campos, and G. Ondarts, *Las Empresas Conjuntas Latinoamericanas* (INTAL, 1977), p. 16.

3. *Brazilian Performance*, 1979, p. 8.

4. J. Katz and J. Ablin, "De la industria incipiente a la exportación de technología: La experiencia argentina en la venta internacional de plantas industriales y obras de ingeniería," Programa BID/CEPAL de Investigaciones en temas de Ciencia y Tecnología, Buenos Aires, 1978.

5. White, Campos, and Ondarts, *Las Empresas Conjuntas Latinoamericanas,* p. 14.

6. One of the largest business concerns of Brazil, the conglomerate Copersucar, took over in 1977 the U.S. coffee company Hills Brothers. In the same year, a group of Brazilian firms formed a joint venture with French firms to build a plant in the port of Havre to finish the manufacture of Brazilian exports (see *Jornal do Brasil*, May 24, 1977).

7. *Brazilian Business*, October 1978, p. 45.

8. Consejo Empresarial Mexicano para Asuntos Internacionales (CEMAI), "Inversiones que ha realizado Mexico en America del Sur," report delivered to INTAL, Mexico, 1976).

9. INTAL estimated that by the late 1960s 44 percent of intra-LAFTA manufactured exports was controlled by foreign-owned firms. See J.C. Casas, *Las Multinacionales y el Comercio Latinoamericano* (CEMLA, 1971).

10. A sample of twenty-nine cases in the INTAL study included none with less than 100 employees; 47 percent of the parent companies had more than 1,000 employees.

11. White, Campos, and Ondarts, *Las Empresas Conjuntas Latinoamericanas,* pp. 20-25.

12. For example, the figure for Latin American technology contracts in Venezuela was 9 percent of the total number of contracts and 8.6 percent of the total payments in 1978, in comparison with a negligible 0.8 percent of Latin American foreign investments; in Ecuador, 5 percent of the value of the technology contracts approved in 1977 was of Latin American origin.

13. By 1973, exports of manufactures accounted for 16.9 percent of total exports in Argentina, 27.2 in Brazil, and 31.8 percent in Mexico.

14. Among the largest 100 firms of Latin America, 77 were controlled by Latin Americans in 1977. *Boletín de Inversiones y Empresas Latinoamericanas* 9, (1979):6.

15. Ministerio de Economía, *Las Exportaciones Argentinas en 1973* (Buenos Aires, 1976), p. 21.

16. Juan Arango, *La Inversión Extranjera en la Industria Manufacturera Colombiana* (Universidad de los Andes, 1976), p. 307.

17. See C. Vaitsos, *La Función de las Empresas Transnacionales en los Esfuerzos de Integración Económica en América Latina* (UNCTAD, 1978).

18. See E. White, *Empresas Multinacionales Latinoamericanas* (Mexico, 1973).

19. Argentina inaugurated a subsecretary of state as head of a division charged with authorizing FDI abroad; Colombia (1968) and Chile (1979) enacted rules for governing these operations; the Central Bank of Brazil, despite the secrecy of its procedures, applies certain criteria for approving or refusing the foreign exchange requested for investments abroad; in 1977, the Foreign Investment Commission of Peru granted the first approvals to proposed investments in other countries.

20. International reserve holdings for the region increased from about US$2.5 billion in 1965 to US$13.4 billion in 1973.

21. Also in Mexico, the construction industry is trying to compensate a series of domestic bottlenecks (credit shortages, inflation) with a powerful performance in the Latin American market, where Mexican firms have carried out contracts worth US$750 million in the past 6 years. *Latin America Economic Report* (June 8, 1979):173.

22. The research work carried out by Louis Wells on the Southeast Asian experience was of considerable value as a guide to the approach used in this section.

23. White, Campos, and Ondarts, *Las Empresas Conjuntas Latinoamericanas,* p. 107.

24. In recent years, the share of manufactured exports going to industrialized countries increased from 64 to 73 percent.

25. *Boletín de Inversiones y Empresas Latinoamericanas* 8 (April 1979):7.

26. This aspect is dealt with in Jorge Katz, *Cambio Tecnológico, Desarrollo Económico y las relaciones intra y extra regionales de América Latina* (Program BID/CEPAL de Investigaciones en temas de ciencia y Technología, Buenos Aires, 1978).

27. The CUSI and PILAO innovations in the field of paper, the HYLSA process for direct reduction, and the PEMEX technology also may be appreciated as cases of adaptation to available or abundant raw materials.

28. Katz and Ablin, "De La industria incipiente," pp. 24-25.

29. Carlos Diaz Alejandro, "Foreign Direct Investment by Latin American," in T. Agmon and C.P. Kindleberger (Eds.), *Multinationals from Small Countries* (Cambridge, Mass.: M.I.T. Press, 1977), p. 171.

30. Katz and Ablin, "De la industria incipiente," p. 25.

31. At the end of a visit to Argentina in 1978, the general manager of CENDES, the development agency of Ecuador, declared: "I carry with me around thirty possibilities of specific projects. Technology here is much more effective and closer to us than that coming from highly industrialized nations which is very sophisticated and expensive, and is difficult to

adapt. . . . ." *Boletín de Inversiones y Empresas Latinoamericanas* 8 (April 1979):7.

32. In Latin America, the enlargement of domestic markets through intergovernmental arrangements is a possibility offered by regional integration and other measures for reducing tariffs and other barriers to intraregional trade. For instance, a special agreement for the "compensated exchange" of autoparts between Argentina and Uruguay is one of the factors explaining the establishment of assembly plants in Uruguay by companies located in Argentina. Some of them were subsidiaries of TNCs. In consequence, the advantages derived from regional integration measures are in principle enjoyed by Latin American firms only against TNCs without subsidiaries in Latin America. However, the Andean Group subregional integration system offers tariff reduction only to joint ventures with majority of local capital and allows easier flows of FDI between member countries only to nationally owned companies.

11 Multinationalization of Third-World Public-Sector Enterprises

Krishna Kumar

Despite the growing interest in multinational corporations from developing countries, practically no work has been done on the subject of direct foreign investment (DFI) by public-sector enterprises of these nations. There are obvious reasons for this state of affairs. Only recently have researchers started conducting meaningful studies of the public sector and its problems and prospects. Moreover, public-sector DFI by developing nations has been a recent phenomenon and the total volume of investment still remains very small. It is therefore not surprising that researchers have overlooked the subject. Whatever little has been written deals with the subject of the export of turnkey projects and consultancy services by some public-sector enterprises of developing nations.[1]

The main objective of this chapter is to examine DFI made by public-sector enterprises from third-world nations. More specifically, I propose to discuss some of the underlying factors and motivations behind the expansion of these enterprises, their competitive strengths, and their possible benefits to the home and host nations. The data base is limited. Hence my aim is not to present viable generalizations or even to put forward testable hypotheses, but to present a few ideas that can be the basis of future research. The approach is both descriptive and analytical.

Some definitional clarification is perhaps necessary to avoid any confusion. A *public enterprise* is defined as a productive entity in which public authorities own 30 percent or more of equity shares and whose output is marketed. This definition of public enterprises is indeed broader than some other conceptualizations, since it does not regard the majority ownership by a government as the defining attribute of a public enterprise. I have used an arbitrary minimum of 30 percent shares, since the ownership of 30 percent of equity shares gives public authorities a dominant voice in the management and control of a firm.

Evidence of DFI by Public-Sector Enterprises

No reliable information is available about the total number of public-sector enterprises from third-world nations that have made overseas investments of the total magnitude of their investments. However, some idea of their existence and possible role can be held from a few examples from a select number of countries.

Yacimientos Petroliferos Fiscales (YPF) is an Argentine public-sector enterprise that has been involved in several joint ventures all over Latin America. It has a joint venture with the Bolivian Oil Company for manufacturing pesticides. Besides, it is involved in oil exploration in Uruguay and Ecuador in direct competition with large multinational corporations.

Petrobras, which is ranked as the twenty-fifth largest industrial corporation outside the United States by *Fortune Magazine*, is a Brazilian state-owned firm active in petroleum and related industries. It has several subsidiaries, some of which also have overseas operations. One subsidiary, Braspetro, has a joint venture for oil exploration in Colombia and has entered into collaboration with Iran and the Philippines. Another, Interbras, serves as a channel for promoting Brazilian business abroad. It is involved in the sale of technology and supply of consultancy to developing nations and has established several overseas joint ventures.

Corporación de Aceros del Pacifico (CAP), which is based in Chile, remains one of the most important steel enterprises in Latin America. It has a joint venture with Ecuador for manufacturing iron and steel. An outside company, Adela, also has a share in the joint venture.

Balmer Lawrie is the first public-sector enterprise in India that has made direct foreign investment. The company successfully commissioned its barrel and can plant in Dubai (United Arab Emirates) in 1978.

Pernas, a Malaysian public-sector enterprise, has now 30 percent shares in Sime Darby Holdings Ltd., whose colossal empire at the time of the takeover in 1978 included 225 companies spread over 24 countries. Sime Darby is presently involved in plantations, foodgrains production, brewing and sale of beer, cigarettes, chemicals, household toilets, tin mining, assembling and manufacturing of tractors, engineering, transport and shipping, banking, and the like.

The Mexican state enterprise Guanomex acquired a fertilizer plant, Fertica, from ESSO that was based in Costa Rica and had branches in central American countries. Now this firm acts as a distributor and processor of the products manufactured by Guanomex.

The public-sector Taiwanese Fertilizer Company acquired the status of a multinational enterprise in 1979 by a deal with Saudi Arabia for building a large fertilizer plant in the Jubail Industrial Zone. This joint venture, which will have an annual production capacity of 5 million tons of urea, will cost an estimated $300 million to be shared by the two governments.

Instituto Venezolano de Petroguimica (IVP) established Monómeros Colombo-Venezolanos as early as 1968 in Colombia for manufacturing chemical fertilizers and caprolactum, a chemical used in the production of nylon. One of the reasons why IVP established this joint venture has been the limited market in Venezuela for ammonium sulfate. The company succeeded in receiving technology from DSM. IVP now has another subsidiary in the Dominican Republic.

In 1979, the ASEAN countries established a joint-venture company named P.T. ASEAN Acch Fertilizer in Sumatra (Indonesia). As the host country, Indonesia will provide 60 percent of equity capital, while the Philippines, Malaysian, and Thailand will provide 13 percent each. The remaining 1 percent will be provided by Singapore. This venture can be rightly described as ASEAN's first public-sector multinational in the sense that its ownership is vested in all the participating countries.

Cimao is a joint venture among Ghana, Togo, and Benin (formerly Dahomey) that is located in Togo for exploiting its limestone deposits. Power to this is being supplied by Ghana. It is expected that after its successful operation, this plant will be able to supply clinker to Ghana for its two cement factories and other requirements. It also will supply cement to Benin and Togo.

Under the auspices of the Latin American Economic System (SELA), which aims at the promotion of Latin American-based multinational enterprises, a navigation company has been formed. The collaborating countries are Colombia, Costa Rica, Cuba, Jamaica, Mexico, Nicaragua, Panama, and Venezuela. This company, known as Empresa Naviera Multinacional Caribe, has been conceived as an alternative to the established shipping lines in the Caribbean.

The preceding are only a few illustrations. FDI also has been made by airlines, banking institutions, and shipping companies from developing countries, which are often owned by their governments. The state-owned oil companies from several Middle East countries also have made foreign investments. Perhaps the best example in this connection is provided by National Iranian Oil Company, which during the prerevolutionary era established many subsidiaries and joint ventures involved in oil exploration, transportation, refining, and marketing.

The preceding discussion also suggests that the public-sector multinationals from developing nations can be grouped under three distinct but interrelated categories. The first category consists of those companies which are jointly owned and managed by governments of two or more developing nations for undertaking those economic activities which a single nation is not in a position to undertake or does not want to undertake. Such firms are multinational in their ownership, organizational structure, management, and operations. The examples are Cimao and P.T. ASEAN Acch Fertilizers. With the growing economic cooperation among developing nations at the regional level, the number of such undertakings is likely to grow in the future.

The second category consists of those enterprises which are originally conceived as national enterprises but expand to other nations in response to changing conditions and new opportunities. Such enterprises establish subsidiaries or joint ventures with private- or public-sector firms. They are likely to follow the route to internationalization that the private-sector firms tread. Often their strength is technological. Balmer Lawrie, the Taiwanese Fertilizer Company, and YPF provide good examples of this type of enterprise.

Finally we can mention those firms which have been operating as multinational enterprises in the private sector but which were later nationalized by their home governments for various reasons. In such cases, there is a change of ownership but not necessarily of management structure or orientation. Sime Darby is a good illustration. It was one of the largest multinationals in Southeast Asia when the Malaysian government acquired equity shares in it. One feature of the Malaysian acquisition has been that the government purchased minority shares in open market and did not introduce significant changes in the management structure.

Motivations for Overseas Expansion

It is indeed difficult to identify the various motives that underlie the foreign expansion behavior of the public-sector enterprises from developing nations. However, two points need to be kept in view in any discussion of the subject. First, the public-sector enterprises, like all governmental bureaucracies, are supposed to be the instruments of achieving national objectives. Their goal is not profit maximization or the promotion of the interests of shareholders, but to serve the wider interests of the country or a segment thereof. Second, which is related to the first, national objectives are not merely economic but social and political as well. The implication of these two points is obvious: the overseas expansion of public-sector enterprises should not be simply examined on the basis of the perceived goals and strategies of the firm, but also should be analyzed with reference to the national economic and political objectives.

Broadly speaking, five sets of motivations can be identified on the basis of the available information: (1) protecting existing markets or searching for new markets, (2) the sale of technologies, (3) access to raw materials, (4) rational utilization of productive resources at binational and regional levels, and (5) political objectives. All these motivations are indeed interrelated. Moreover, the overseas expansion behavior of a firm can be examined with reference to more than one set of motives.

Like private-sector firms, some public-sector enterprises have started overseas subsidiaries or joint ventures for protecting their existing markets

that were threatened by the import-substitution policies of the host government or the entry of new competitors. White et al., for example, mention
the case of IME, which formerly exported light freight vehicles to
Uruguay.[2] The government of Uruguay wanted to restrict the import of
these vehicles for encouraging domestic production of their components
and assembling. IME responded to the threat by establishing a joint venture
with its own representative and another local firm for assembling the light
freight vehicles. Thus the company was able to protect its export market by
its overseas investment.

Public-sector enterprises tap new markets for their products. This is
especially true of the public-sector companies from countries whose
domestic markets are limited to permit efficient production. Thus many
state-controlled enterprises from Latin America have formed foreign joint
ventures for gaining entry into new markets. Altos Hornos de Mexico, for
example, established a steel plant in Honduras with a view to gaining access
to Central American markets.[3] Earlier mention was made of Guanomex,
which acquired Fertica for processing and distributing its products.[4] It is interesting to note that the National Iranian Oil Company after 1971 tried to
expand its refinery and marketing operations in Western Europe and the
United States.[5] In fact, it signed letters of intent for establishing joint ventures with firms from Greece, Germany, Belgium, and the United States.
One of the main objectives of the proposed overseas investments was to
have assured markets for its crude oil. Practically all these planned projects
did not materialize. The reason for their nonimplementation was neither the
lack of capital nor the reluctance on the part of the foreign collaborators,
but the realization on the part of Iranians that investment in refining and
marketing were not lucrative in view of the continual rise in the prices of
petroleum. The National Iranian Oil Company still has equity shares in a
public-sector enterprise in India that manufactures chemical fertilizers.

Public-sector enterprises from developing nations also have formed
overseas joint ventures to sell manufacturing technologies. Many public
enterprises, especially those involved in the extractive sector, heavy industries, and engineering, have been able to adapt and modify technologies
which they originally secured from industrialized nations. While the process
of adaptation and innovation has been undoubtedly slow, it has made the
acquired technologies quite suitable to the needs of developing nations.
Moreover, public-sector enterprises also have been able to develop new
manufacturing technologies. Since these technologies are often suitable to
the need of developing nations, the public-sector enterprises are able to
market them. In India, state-controlled companies have been the major exporter of turnkey plants, capital goods, and consultancy services. Some of
them are now seriously considering the possibilities of establishing foreign
joint ventures in which their equity shares will be supplied in the form of

their manufacturing technologies. One of the main considerations for the Taiwanese company for forming its fertilizer joint venture in Saudi Arabia was the opportunity for selling its manufacturing technologies.[6] Similar instances also have been noted in the case of Latin America.

Another motivation for public-sector enterprises has been the search for raw materials. Many developing nations, such as Brazil, Hong Kong, South Korea, and Taiwan, have started experiencing a shortage of raw materials, especially oil and minerals, as a result of the increasing tempo of industrialization. The problem is not simply of high prices, but also of the uncertainty of materials supply. Moreover, third-world nations do not want to be perpetually dependent on large multinationals based in industrialized nations for the supply of the needed raw materials. Hence they are encouraging their firms, both in the private and the public sectors, to form foreign subsidiaries and joint ventures in extractive industries. In those countries in which the state has made investments in extractive industries, public-sector enterprises have taken a lead in establishing overseas operations for this purpose. For example, Brazil's Braspetro, the foreign trade and investment arm of Petrobras, has been quite enterprising in this respect. It has been conducting oil explorations in a half dozen Middle East countries, Madagascar, and Colombia.[7] Vale do Rio Doce of Brazil has recently acquired a coal mine in British Colombia. Siderbras of Brazil also has been participating in a joint venture with the government of Colombia for coal mines. In Asia, the Taiwanese state-run Chinese Petroleum Corporation has signed a contract with the National Petroleum Corporation of Colombia for joint exploration of the underseas oil off the Colombian coast. Oil India has worked out various kinds of collaborative arrangements with the Middle East countries, which though in theory might not fully qualify for the label of direct foreign investment, but in practice come close to it.

The overall behavior of the public-sector enterprises from developing nations in this regard has not been different from that of their counterparts from Western Europe. As we know, several European firms, such as Ente Nazionale Idocarburi (ENI), Compagnie Francaise Petroles, and ELF-Aquitaines, initiated and developed their oil-exploration activities to minimize their dependence on Anglo-American firms. British Petroleum is, of course, another state-owned firm that is multinational in its operations. Obviously, the public-sector firms from developing nations have been following a path that has been trod by their illustrious counterparts. One can only hope that they also learn from their past mistakes and experiences.

The concern for the economic utilization of national resources—human and material—also has encouraged some countries to promote public-sector joint ventures at binational and multinational levels. Such joint venture· are designed to undertake those economic activities which an individual nation is not in a position to undertake alone. Examples can be given in this connection of the several binational public-sector companies that have been formed between Paraguay and Brazil, Paraguay and Argentina, and other countries in the Plate River basin.[8] Earlier mention was made of the case of a Cimao plant in Togo to which limestone is supplied by the host nation and power by Ghana. ASEAN nations have been trying for the past few years to establish joint industrial projects in several key industries for pooling their resources and enjoying the benefits of the economy of scale. So far, only one project (for manufacturing fertilizers) has materialized. However, authorities are confident that the others will follow soon. Various international agencies such as UNCTAD and UNIDO often have stressed the need for such joint ventures among the developing nations in various sectors of the economy.

Finally, the political considerations. Two kinds of political objectives often remain implicit in the foreign expansion of public-sector enterprises: undermining the dependence of developing countries on the multinationals from industrialized nations and the promotion of political ties among third-world nations.

Political leaders in many third-world nations have been concerned about their dependence on multinational corporations based in industrialized nations and have been adopting various policies for improving their own bargaining power. Their strategies include increasing regulation of multinational firms, emphasis on equity participation, "indigenization" of management and technical personnel, restriction on the areas in which these firms are allowed to operate, and the procurement of technologies through licensing or direct purchases. The joint ventures among public-sector enterprises are often perceived as an additional weapon in the arsenal of developing nations.

It can be noted in this connection that many observers of the European public-sector enterprises have suggested that one of the unstated agenda of the continental European powers in establishing them was to challenge the supremacy of American firms by combining "state capitalism with the competitive strategies of the markets."[9] Thus Michel Drancourt wrote as early as 1969 that public-sector enterprises were engaged in a battle against the U.S. firms, and Douglas F. Lamont has recently concluded that they have lived up to their expectations. He believes that they are now posing serious challenges to the American competitive strength.[10] It is therefore not surprising that many developing nations expect the same outcome from their public-sector enterprises.

Developing countries are also likely to use overseas investments by their public enterprises for initiating and strengthening political relations with other nations. White et al. have identified many cases in Latin America where political considerations have affected overseas investments by public-sector enterprises.[11] Recently, India and Nepal signed an agreement under which joint ventures will be established in private and public sectors for manufacturing diesel water pumps and undertaking projects for lead and zinc. Indian officials do not hide the fact that even when the profitability of these joint ventures seemed doubtful for India, they were highly desirable for improving its sagging image in its neighbor country. By all accounts, Taiwan has already started using its public-sector enterprises (and private-sector firms as well) as working substitutes for political relations.

One can think of other motivations that can shed light on the overseas expansion of public-sector enterprises. Certainly it is not inconceivable that some of them might in the future establish overseas joint ventures or subsidiaries to take advantage of low labor costs, nor should we rule out the possibility that some others might prefer foreign operations to minimize risks involved in developing new technologies. The prestige associated with becoming a multinational firm may tempt still others. In short, practically all the motivations which have been discussed in the literature on multinational corporations for explaining their overseas expansion can have some explanatory value with regard to the multinationalization of public enterprises from developing nations.

Strengths and Weaknesses

The preceding discussion brings us to the subject of those strengths and weaknesses of public-sector enterprises from developing nations which can affect their entry and survival in the international arena. As mentioned earlier, public-sector enterprises have accumulated significant technological expertise and know-how. They have been able to make important adaptations and modifications in technologies which they received from industrialized nations on the basis of their operating experiences and the research-and-developmental activities undertaken by them. Thus they now possess in some industrial sectors the technologies that are not available to the firms from industrialized nations. Moreover, they also have developed new manufacturing technologies in such industries as machine tools, steel, construction, engineering, and agricultural implements. There are at least three characteristics of the technologies acquired by some of the public-sector enterprises that can be identified here. First, they can be used on a smaller scale than those supplied by the multinational firms based in the industrial world. Second, they are usually labor-intensive and do not involve huge capital outlays. Finally, they can utilize some of the raw materials that are locally available. Because of these characteristics, these technologies are very functional to the needs of third-world nations, which are characterized by surplus labor and limited domestic markets. Therefore, the public-sector enterprises often try to sell their technologies to other developing nations under various kinds of arrangements ranging from licensing to the formation of the joint ventures. One attraction for the host country for joint ventures is that the risk is shared by the partners, and the host country firm is not the sole loser in case the project fails. Thus their ability to supply technologies that are labor-intensive, use local inputs, and can operate on a small scale is one of the important assets of public-sector enterprises in their drive toward internationalization.

The second set of competitive assets of public enterprises can be attributed to the governmental assistance and cooperation they receive. Since they are supposed to serve the vital social, economic, and political interests of the country, they are the recipients of direct and indirect subsidies from their governments. For example, preferential treatment is given to them by governmental lending institutions. They also are able to receive infusions of fresh capital when needed. They get priority in the import of technologies and other inputs. Their losses are often written off by governments and they are under no great pressure to maximize their profits. Thus they are generally in a better position than a private-sector firm to compete with foreign enterprises.

More important, public-sector enterprises are usually able to use governmental bureaucracies for initiating and administering foreign projects. While the situation differs from country to country, it is not uncommon for the various foreign-policy organs of a government—embassies, consulates, trade representatives, and so forth—to scan export and investment opportunities for public-sector enterprises. Sometimes the home-government officials even help in the conduct of negotiations. When problems arise in the implementation of a project, a little governmental intervention on behalf of the public enterprise generally proves to be helpful.

Public-sector enterprises also benefit from the widespread belief that they will not be allowed to fail in the fulfillment of their foreign obligations. They are identified with national prestige and a few home governments in the third world can take their failures in the international area with equanimity. This builds up the confidence of host nations. The officials in the host country know fully well that they can exert political pressures on the home government in case a public enterprise fails to keep up its commitments.

Third, the international environment also works in favor of foreign investments by public-sector enterprises. The third-world nations are committed in theory if not in practice to the strengthening of economic and political cooperation among themselves. Public enterprises are often seen as one of the many mechanisms for fostering such a cooperation. This gives them a unique advantage over the multinationals based in industrialized nations in forming joint ventures.

The weaknesses of public-sector enterprises are too well-known to need any elaboration here. Most of them suffer from poor management. Their

management systems are generally deficient, even according to the standards of developing countries. One possible explanation is that their
managerial personnel often consist of civilian bureaucrats who do not have
the necessary professional training and expertise. In many nations, top positions are occupied by discredited bureaucrats, retired generals, and defeated
politicians who could not be accommodated in the power structure of the
country. Thus some positions in public-sector enterprises are treated as
"consolation prizes." The overall situation is definitely better in the enterprises that have been able to develop a professional cadre of middle-level
junior executives. In any case, poor management remains a severe liability
of public enterprises, and it poses an obstacle to their overseas expansion.

Besides, public enterprises are accustomed to operating in protected
markets; they enjoy monopolistic and semimonopolistic positions in their
home countries. As a result, they do not develop expertise in aggressive
marketing of their products. Nor do they have their own international
networks. This often puts them at a serious disadvantage as compared with
large multinationals. However, the problem of marketing does not arise
when they enter into collaborative arrangements with public-sector firms
that assure them a privileged position in the host-country market.

Finally, it should be recognized that the capital and technological
resources of public enterprises are limited and are likely to remain so when
compared with the multinational corporations from industrialized nations.
Even when some of them (mainly those involved in extractive industries)
have made it on the *Fortune* list of the 500 largest foreign corporations,
most of them suffer from the scarcity of capital. After all, they are based in
nations that are poor in capital resources. Thus they are not in a position to
export substantial capital to foreign countries. Besides, their technological
capabilities are confined to a limited range of industries. In no case are they
on the frontiers of technological progress in sophisticated industries, which
are monopolized by the firms from industrialized nations. The preceding
disabilities of public-sector enterprises from developing nations need to be
borne in mind when one examines their foreign expansion.

Public-Sector Enterprises and Foreign Firms

It is not out of place to mention a word about the joint ventures established
by public-sector firms and foreign private-sector companies in host developing nations. Some concern has been expressed about the desirability of such
arrangements.

The advantages of public-sector enterprises over private-sector firms in
entering into partnership with foreign companies are not difficult to con-

template.[12] First, it can be suggested that the former possess a long-range view of national objectives and priorities and are therefore in a better position to make judicious use of opportunities offered by foreign collaboration. Second, the host-country government is better able to regulate and control foreign collaborators in public- rather than private-sector enterprises. This is partly due to the fact that it has easy access to information and partly because it has a better bargaining position than the private-sector firms. Third, public-sector enterprises are in a better position to facilitate the adaptation and diffusion of imported technologies by directly linking them to the national research-and-developmental endeavor. They can more easily mobilize government-supported research institutions and universities than the private-sector firms. Finally, public-sector enterprises are in greater need than the private-sector firms in developing nations of managerial and technological expertise provide by collaborative joint ventures.

From the point of view of the private-sector foreign firm, public enterprises do not provide ideal opportunities for a functional relationship over a period of time. These firms rightly point out that there is a basic difference between their own goals and those of public-sector enterprises. The latter are involved in the achievement of a wide spectrum of socioeconomic objectives, while the former give primacy to financial and economic considerations. Private-sector enterprises can hardly afford the luxury of an attitude of "benign neglect" toward profits. This difference in attitude can contribute to policy differences in vital areas of operation of a joint venture, such as planning, finance, marketing, product mix, wages, production technologies, and even personnel policies. As a result, joint ventures between public enterprises and private foreign firms can become highly unstable arrangements.

Moreover, private-sector firms are also aware of the fact that their own bargaining strength with public-sector enterprises erodes over a period of time. As the public-sector firm gains the necessary expertise in technology and management, it finds itself in a better position to dictate its own terms.[13] This is especially true in the case of extractive industries, where the threat of nationalization hangs as a sword of Damocles. However, one major attraction that private-sector firms have in entering into a collaborative arrangement with public-sector enterprises is that the chances of the total failure of the joint ventures are minimal. They are able to get all kinds of help and assistance from the host government, which makes their survival relatively easy.

Despite these problems, collaboration between private-sector firms and public enterprises is likely to grow in developing countries. The public-sector enterprises that are seeking foreign markets for their products will find joint ventures with multinational firms with wide international networks and experience useful if not indispensable—so also for the public-sector enterprises that need modern technologies that are not available through other means.

Costs and Benefits to Home and Host Nations

Before concluding this chapter, I would like to mention some possible benefits and the costs involved to home and host nations from direct foreign investment by public-sector enterprises. The issue, it should be stressed here, is not of the advantages or disadvantages of direct foreign investment, but of those benefits and costs which are specific to public-sector enterprises.

Some possible benefits to host nations from the foreign investment by public-sector enterprises are obvious. I have already pointed out that the technologies which they transfer are more suitable to the needs of host nations than those transferred by other agencies. Moreover, the prices charged by them are usually reasonable. This is not because they do not want to make a profit, but because they are not well-established and can compete only on the basis of lower prices. In contrast to the firms from industrialized nations, they prefer joint ventures that permit more scope for local autonomy and initiative. Often the majority shares in such ventures are owned by the host country. One also expects that most of these enterprises are quite sensitive to the political and economic expectations of host governments.

The benefits to home governments are not less significant. Although the governments from developing nations are not enthusiastic about overseas investments by their public enterprises, they often reap good rewards. In the case of extractive industries, they are assured of the supply of raw materials or are able to better market their products. The home country is also able to sell its manufacturing technologies, which can have spinoff effects on its technological growth; it earns foreign exchange in the form of dividends, salaries of the expatriate personnel, and orders for raw materials and other inputs. The managerial personnel gain foreign experience, which can be useful for further expansion. In short, practically all the advantages that industrialized nations are supposed to have from their direct investments abroad must accrue to the home countries of public enterprises making direct foreign investments.

In the cases of joint ventures that are formed for the exploitation of natural resources (such as hydroelectric projects), the benefits to all the parties are widely recognized. This permits optimal utilization of capital investments. This is also true of the public-sector enterprises that are designed to complement the production of a product, such as automobiles. Besides solving the problem of scarcity of resources, the various complementary production schemes effectively deal with the production problems arising out of the smallness of national markets. It is therefore not surprising that several regional and international organizations are actively encouraging them.

We also should not minimize the political advantages for developing nations from direct foreign investment by public enterprises. Public-sector joint ventures can serve not only as countervailing forces to the transnationals from industrialized nations, but also can provide functional alternatives to them. By promoting cooperation among developing nations, they can contribute toward the evolution of a more symmetrical international economic and political system. However, in view of the relatively small volume of the overseas investments by public-sector enterprises, their contribution in this regard is at present more symbolic than substantial.

One should resist the temptation to idealize the role of public-sector enterprises. There are several disadvantages that can be associated with investments by these firms. They might not always be able to provide a continual stream of up-to-date technologies to host nations the way the private sector firms from industrialized nations do. Their undue reliance on the support of their governments can result in the survival of inefficient production techniques and processes both in home and host nations. The capital resources of the public enterprises from developing nations have not been large, and therefore, host nations cannot expect huge capital investments from them. They also may contribute to the diffusion of those management patterns by styles which put more premium on political rather than economic goals.

In conclusion, I would say that the direct foreign investment by public enterprises from developing nations should not be overlooked by serious students of the international economic and political system. These firms have been operating in various sectors of the economy, and their number is likely to grow with the increased technological and managerial sophistication of developing nations. The various motivational factors that shed light on the overseas investment behavior of private firms also explain their growth. In addition, there are political considerations, such as the assertion of national autonomy, the need for cooperation among developing nations, and the concern for building up counteracting forces to the multinationals from industrialized nations, that also deserve to be considered in this regard. Some of the competitive advantages of these enterprises lie in the innovations which they have introduced in manufacturing technologies and the direct and indirect subsidies which they receive from their governments. The prevailing international climate also works in their favor. Foreign investment by public-sector enterprises cannot be regarded as an unmixed blessing. Such investment has both costs and benefits, and these should be taken into consideration by both home and host nations.

Notes

1. The studies that can be mentioned in this regard are Katz and Ablin (1978), Lall (1979), and Rhee and Westphal (1978).

2. White et al. (1977, p. 46).

3. Ibid., p. 31. It is reported that the plant was experiencing difficulties. I am not certain about its present status.

4. Ibid., p. 116.

5. Fesharaki (1976, pp. 182-183).

6. *Hong Kong Sunday Times*, January 5, 1979.

7. Diaz-Alejandro (1977, p. 177).

8. Ibid., p. 189.

9. Lamont (1979, p. 80).

10. Ibid.

11. White et al. (1977).

12. The following advantages have been largely identified in a seminar on joint ventures and public enterprises held in Yugoslavia (December 6-12, 1979).

13. See Moran (1974) for the elaboration of this argument.

References

Diaz-Alejandro, C.F. Foreign direct investment by Latin American firms.'' In Tamir Agmon and Charles P. Kindleberger (eds.), *Multinationals from Small Countries*. Cambridge, Mass.: M.I.T. Press, 1977.

Fesharaki, F. *The Development of the Iranian Oil Industry*. New York: Praeger, 1976.

Katz, J., and E. Ablin. From infant industry of technology exports: The Argentine experience in the international sale of industrial plants and engineering works. IDS/ECLA Research Program in Science and Technology, Working Paper No. 14, Buenos Aires, 1978.

Lall, S. Developing countries as exporters of technology and capital goods: The Indian experience. Oxford University Institute of Economic and Statistics, 1979.

Lamont, D.F. *Foreign State Enterprise: A Threat to American Business*. New York: Basic Books, 1979.

Moran, T.H. *Multinational Corporations and the Politics of Dependence: Copper in Chile*. Princeton, N.J.: Princeton Univ. Press, 1974.

Report of the International Seminar on Joint Ventures and Public Enterprises in the Developing Countries. Sponsored by United Nations Division of Development Administrators and Finance and International Center for Public Enterprises in Developing Nations, 1979.

Rhee, Y., and L.E. Westphal. A note on exports of technology from the Republics of China and Korea. World Bank, 1978. Mimeographed.

White, E., J. Campos, and G. Ordartes. *Las Empresas Conjuntas Latinoamericanas*. Buenos Aires: INTAL, 1977.

Index

About the Contributors

Ram Gopal Agrawal, the deputy secretary-general and secretary of the Federation of Indian Chambers of Commerce and Industry (FICCI), received the Ph.D. in economics in 1955. He has worked with a number of delegations sponsored by the government of India and the FICCI and has had two assignments with the United Nations—one with UNDP, New York, and the other with UNCTAD, Geneva—on joint ventures among developing countries. Dr. Agrawal has published several articles and is the author of *Price Controls in India since 1947.*

D.M. Akinnusi is currently a lecturer with the Continuing Education Centre, University of Lagos, Nigeria.

Edward K.Y. Chen is the director of the Center of Asian Studies and senior lecturer at the University of Hong Kong. He received the Ph.D. in economic growth and development from Oxford University and has been a Visiting Fellow at Yale University. He has published a number of articles, monographs, and books on Asian economic development, including *Hyper-Growth in Asian Economies.*

John H. Dunning is head of the Department of Economics, University of Reading. He received the Ph.D. in economics from University College, London. He has been a visiting professor at universities in the United States and Canada as well as a consultant to the United Nations and the OECD. His publications include *American Investment in British Manufacturing Industries, Studies in International Investment, The Multinational Enterprise* (ed.), *U.S. Industry in Britian,* and *Studies in the Multinational Enterprise,* as well as several contributions to the learned and professional journals.

Olukunle Iyanda teaches marketing and economic analysis in the Department of Business Administration, University of Lagos.

Sung-Hwan Jo is a research associate at the Culture Learning Institute, East-West Center. He has been a professor of economics and director of the Research Institute for Economics and Business at Sogang University in Seoul. He received the Ph.D. in economics from Yale Univesity. Before joining the Sogang faculty, he was director in charge of international cooperation for the Federation of Korean Industries. His publications include articles and books on Korea's economic development and foreign direct investment.

Donald J. Lecraw is an assistant professor at the School of Business Administration, University of Western Ontario, London, Canada. He received the MBA from the Harvard University Graduate School of Business Administration and the Ph.D. in business economics from Harvard University. He has served as a consultant for the United Nations Centre on Transnational Corporations and the Economic Council of Canada and as chief economist for the Royal Commission on Corporate Concentration. His articles on multinational enterprises and on choice of technology have appeared in *Kyklos, Oxford Economic Papers, Journal of Development Economics,* and *Quarterly Journal of Economics.*

C.N.S. Nambudiri is currently head of the Department of Busines Administration at the University of Lagos.

Chi Schive, an assistant professor in the Department of Economics at the National Taiwan University, received the Ph.D. in economics from Case Western Reserve University. He has presented a number of papers on technology transfer and direct foreign investment and has published various articles in English and Chinese.

Kian-Wie Thee is a research associate at the National Institute of Economic and Social Research, Indonesian Institute of Sciences (LEKNAS-LIPI). He received the Ph.D. in economics from the University of Wisconsin in 1969. He is the author of *Plantation Agriculture and Export Growth: An Economic History of East Sumatra, 1863-1942,* coauthor of *Japanese Direct Investment in Indonesia—Findings of an Experimental Survey,* and coeditor of *The Regional Economic Survey of South Sumatra, 1970-1971.*

Wen-Lee Ting is a visiting professor at the Graduate School of Management of the Tatung Institute of Technology in Taiwan and a lecturer with the University of Maryland, Far East Division. He received the Ph.D. in international business from New York University. Formerly with the University of Singapore, Dr. Ting has also been a consultant to various firms and organizations in Singapore and Taiwan.

Louis T. Wells, Jr., is a professor of business administration at the Harvard University Graduate School of Business Administration, where he received the D.B.A. He has conducted fieldwork in Southeast Asia and is compiling a data bank on direct investment by firms from developing nations. In addition to his numerous articles on the subject in professional journals, he has coauthored *Managing the Multinational Enterprise* and *Manager in the International Economy.*

Eduardo White is chief of the Enterprise, Technology and Investment Division of the Institute for Latin American Integration in Buenos Aires. Most of his articles and books on regional integration, business, and investment have been published in Spanish, including *Empresas Multinacionales Latinamericanas* and *Las Empresas Conjuntas Latinamericanas* (with J. Campos and G. Ondarts).

About the Editors

Krishna Kumar is a research associate at the East-West Culture Learning Institute and coordinator of the project on transnational organizations and networks. He received the Ph.D. in sociology from Michigan State University. He has served as the assistant director of research at the Gandhi Peace Foundation and has taught at Michigan State University. He is the author of *The Social and Cultural Impacts of Transnational Enterprises,* editor of *Bonds without Bondage, Democracy and Nonviolence,* and *TNEs: Their Impact on Society and Culture,* and coeditor of *Racial Conflict, Discrimination and Power.* His other publications include various contributions to professional journals.

Maxwell G. McLeod has been associated with the East-West Culture Learning Institute project on transnational organizations as a research intern and research assistant. He received the M.B.A. from the College of Business Administration, University of Hawaii.